The mini **Rough Guide** to

London

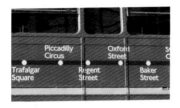

written and researched by

Rob Humphreys

with additional contributions by

Beth Chaplin, Rebecca Morrill, Sally Schafer, Helena Smith, Joe Staines and Neville Walker

ROUGH
GUIDES

NEW YORK • LONDON • DELHI

www.roughguides.com

Contents

◄◄ London bus ◄ St Paul's Cathedral

Introduction to

London

What strikes visitors more than anything else about London is the sheer size of the place. Stretching for more than thirty miles on either side of the River Thames, and with an ethnically diverse population of just under eight million, it's Europe's largest city by far. Londoners tend to cope with all this by compartmentalizing the city, identifying with the neighbourhoods in which they work or live, and just making occasional forays into the "centre of town" or "up West", to the West End, London's shopping and entertainment heartland.

London dominates the national horizon, too: this is where the country's news and money are made, it's where the central government resides and, as far as its inhabitants are concerned, provincial life begins beyond the circuit of the city's orbital motorway. In most walks of British life, if you want to get on, you've got to do it in London.

For the visitor, too, London is a thrilling place – and after winning the right to stage the Olympics in 2012, the city is also in a relatively buoyant mood. The facelift that the capital has undergone over the last decade or so has seen virtually every one of London's world-class **museums**, **galleries** and **institutions** reinvented, from the Royal Opera House to the British Museum.

In the meantime, London's traditional **sights** continue to draw in millions of tourists every year. Monuments from the capital's more glorious past are everywhere and there is also much enjoyment to be had from the city's Georgian squares, the narrow alleyways

▲ River Thames and the London Eye

of the City of London, the riverside walks, and the large expanses of green: Hyde Park, Green Park and St James's Park are all within a few minutes' walk of the West End, while, further afield, you can enjoy Hampstead Heath and Richmond Park.

You could spend days **shopping** in London, mixing with the upper classes in Harrods, or sampling the offbeat weekend markets. The **music**, **clubbing** and **gay** and **lesbian** scenes are second to none, and mainstream **arts** are no less exciting, with regular opportunities to catch outstanding theatre companies, dance troupes, exhibitions and opera. London has more Michelin star **restaurants** than Paris, as well as a vast range of low-cost, high-quality ethnic eateries. Meanwhile, the city's **pubs** have heaps of atmosphere, especially away from the centre – and an exploration of the farther-flung communities is essential to get the complete picture of this dynamic metropolis.

What to see

London has grown not through centralized planning but by a process of agglomeration, meaning that though the majority of the city's sights are situated to the north of the **River Thames**, which loops through the centre of the city from west to east, there is no single focus of interest. Visitors should make mastering the public transport system, particularly the underground (tube), a top priority.

▼ The Gherkin

If London has a centre, it's **Trafalgar Square**, home to Nelson's Column and the National Gallery. It's also as good a place as any to start exploring. South of here, **Westminster and Whitehall** was the city's royal, political and ecclesiastical power base for centuries, and you'll find some of London's most famous landmarks here: Downing Street, Big Ben, the Houses of Parliament, **Westminster Abbey** and, across St James's Park, Buckingham Palace. The grand streets and squares of **St James's**, **Mayfair** and **Marylebone**, to the north of Westminster, have been the playground of the rich since the Restoration, and now contain the city's busiest shopping zones: Piccadilly, **Bond Street**, **Regent Street** and, most frenetic of the lot, **Oxford Street**.

East of Piccadilly Circus, **Soho**, **Chinatown** and **Covent Garden** form the heart of the West End, where you'll find the largest concentration of theatres, cinemas, clubs, flashy shops, cafés and restaurants. The university quarter of **Bloomsbury** is

▲ Regent's Canal

the location of the **British Museum**, a stupendous treasure house that now boasts the largest covered public space in Europe. Welding the West End to the financial district, little-visited **Holborn** offers some of central London's most surprising treats, among them the eccentric Sir John Soane's Museum and the secluded quadrangles of the Inns of Court.

A couple of miles downstream from Westminster, **The City** – or the City of London, to give it its full title – is both the most ancient and the most modern part of London. Settled since Roman times, the area became the commercial and residential heart of medieval London, with its own Lord Mayor and its own peculiar form of local government, both of which survive (with considerable pageantry) to this day. The Great Fire of 1666 obliterated most of the City, and the resident population has dwindled to insignificance, yet this remains one of the great

Multi-ethnic London

With around three hundred languages spoken within its confines and all the major religions represented, London is Europe's most ethnically diverse city. First, second- and third-generation **immigrants** make up over thirty percent of the population, while some claim that the majority of white

▲ Chinatown

Londoners are in fact descended from French Huguenot refugees. London has, of course, always been a cosmopolitan place. The first well-documented immigrants were invaders like the Romans, Anglo-Saxons, Vikings and Normans, while over the last four centuries, the city has absorbed wave after wave of foreigners fleeing persecution at home, or simply looking for a better life. However, it is the postwar period that stands out as the age of immigration par excellence. Initially, people came here from the Caribbean and the Indian subcontinent; today's arrivals are more likely to come from the world's war zones: Somalia, Bosnia, Afghanistan, Iraq.

Though London doesn't have the sort of ghettoization that's widespread in the US, certain areas have become home-from-home for the more established communities. In general, these disparate groups live in peaceful coexistence and the traditions and customs they have brought with them have provided a vibrant contribution to London's cultural life, the most famous manifestation of which is the Notting Hill Carnival (see p.309).

financial centres of the world, dotted with the hi-tech offices of bank and insurance companies, and home to the historic Tower of London and a fine cache of Wren churches that includes the mighty **St Paul's Cathedral**.

To the east of the city, the impoverished, working-class **East End** is not conventional tourist territory, yet to ignore it is to miss out a crucial element of multi-ethnic London. With its abandoned warehouses converted into overpriced apartment blocks, **Docklands** is the converse of the down-at-heel East End, with the **Canary Wharf** tower, the country's tallest building, epitomizing the pretensions of the 1980s' developers' dream.

The **South Bank**, **Bankside** and **Southwark** together make up the small slice of central London that lies south of the Thames. The **South Bank Centre** itself, London's little-loved concrete culture bunker, is enjoying a new lease of life – thanks, in part, to the graceful London Eye, the world's largest observation wheel. Bankside, the city's low-life district from Roman times to the eighteenth century, is also enjoying a renaissance, with a new pedestrian bridge linking St Paul's with the former power station that is now home to the extraordinary **Tate Modern** art museum.

Hyde Park and **Kensington Gardens**, the largest park in central London, separates wealthy West London from the city centre. The museums of **South Kensington** – the V&A, the Science Museum and the Natural History Museum – are a must; and you may want to investigate the plush stores around Harrods, superstore to the upper echelons.

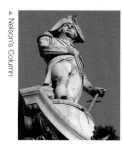
▲ Nelson's Column

Some of the most appealing parts of North London are clustered around Regent's Canal, which skirts **Regent's Park** and serves as the focus for the capital's huge weekend market at **Camden Lock**. Further out, there are unbeatable views across the city from half-wild **Hampstead Heath**. The glory of Southeast London is **Greenwich**, with its nautical associations, royal park and observatory. Finally, there are plenty of rewarding day-trips up the Thames from **Chiswick** to **Hampton Court** and, beyond, to **Windsor**, liberally peppered with stately homes.

▲ Somerset House

When to go

Considering how temperate the London **climate** is, it's amazing how much mileage the locals get out of the subject of the weather. The truth is that summers rarely get really hot and the winters aren't very cold. However, it's impossible to say with any certainty what the weather will be like in any given month. May might be wet and grey one year and gloriously sunny the next; November stands an equal chance of being crisp and clear or foggy and grim. So, whatever time of year you come, be prepared for all eventualities, and bring a pair of comfortable shoes, as, inevitably, you'll be doing a lot of walking.

Average temperatures and monthly rainfall

	Jan	Feb	Mar	Apr	May	June	July	Aug	Sept	Oct	Nov	Dec
Max. temp. (°C)	6	7	10	13	17	20	22	21	19	14	10	7
Min. temp. (°C)	2	2	3	6	8	12	14	13	11	8	5	4
Rainfall (mm)	54	40	37	37	46	45	57	59	49	57	64	48

13

things not to miss

It is not possible to see everything London has to offer in one visit and we don't suggest you try. What follows is a selective taste of the city's highlights from outstanding art collections to vibrant markets, arranged in five colour-coded categories. Each highlight has a page reference to take you into the Guide where you can find out more.

02 London Eye Page **115** • There is no better view in London – but book in advance.

01 British Museum Page **61** • The spectacular Great Court and the opening of the Round Reading Room have brought new life to the world's oldest and greatest public museum.

04 Sir John Soane's Museum
Page **81** • Part architectural set-piece, part art gallery, the Soane museum is small and perfectly formed.

03 Tower of London
Page **99** • Bloody royal history, ham Beefeaters, armour, the Crown Jewels and ravens – and a great medieval castle.

06 Tate Modern
Page **121** • One of the world's greatest modern art collections housed in a spectacularly converted riverside power station.

05 National Gallery
Page **29** • From the Renaissance to Picasso: one of the world's great art galleries.

07 Greenwich
Page **153** • Soak up the naval history at the National Maritime Museum, and climb up to the Royal Observatory to enjoy the view over the river.

08 **London pubs** Page **211** • Have a pint in one of London's many old and historic pubs.

10 **East End Sunday Markets** Page **104** • Sunday is the perfect day for a market trawl starting at Old Spitalfields and ending at Columbia Road flower market.

12 **Hampton Court Palace** Page **169** • The finest of London's royal palaces, a sprawling red-brick affair on the banks of the Thames.

09 **Highgate Cemetery** Page **150** • The city's most atmospheric Victorian necropolis, thick with trees and crowded with famous corpses.

11 **Walk along the South Bank** Page **114** • Start at the London Eye, stroll along the bank of the Thames, browse the bookstalls under Waterloo Bridge, and continue to Tower Bridge.

13 **Houses of Parliament** Page **34** • See the "mother of all parliaments" at work from the public gallery or take a climb up Big Ben.

Basics

Basics

Arrival

London's international **airports** are all less than an hour from the city centre, and the city's **train** and **bus** terminals are all pretty central, with tube stations close at hand.

By air

Heathrow (℡0870/000 0123, ⓦwww.baa.co.uk), fifteen miles west of the city centre, has four terminals, and two train/tube stations: one for terminals 1, 2 and 3, and a separate one for terminal 4. The high-speed **Heathrow Express** (ⓦwww.heathrowexpress.com) trains travel non-stop to Paddington Station (every 15min; 15–20min) for £26 return (£1 less if you book online, £2 more if you buy your ticket on board). National Express run **bus services** (℡0870/580 8080, ⓦ www.nationalexpress.com) from Heathrow direct to Victoria Coach Station (daily every 30min 6am–9.30pm; 1hr), which cost £10 single, £15 return. A much cheaper alternative is to take the Piccadilly **Underground** line into central London (every 5–9min; 50min) for £3.80 one-way. If you plan to make several sightseeing journeys on your arrival day, buy a Travelcard at the station (see p.19). From midnight, you can take **night bus** #N9 (every 30min; 1hr) from Heathrow to Trafalgar Square for a bargain fare of £1.20. Black taxis, waiting outside in designated ranks, are plentiful, whatever time you arrive, but will set you back between £40 and £70 to central London, and take around an hour (much longer in the rush hour).

Gatwick airport (℡0870/000 2468, ⓦwww.baa.co.uk), thirty miles to the south, has two terminals, North and South, connected by a monorail. The non-stop **Gatwick Express** train runs between the South Terminal and Victoria Station (every 15–30min; 30min) for £24 return. Other train options include the **Southern** services to Victoria (every 15–20min; 40min) for £9 one-way, or **Thameslink** to King's Cross (every 15–30min; 50min) for around £10 one-way.

A taxi will set you back £90 or more, and take at least an hour.

Stansted (℡0870/000 0303, ⓦwww.baa.co.uk) lies roughly 35 miles northeast of the capital, and is served by the **Stansted Express** to Walthamstow Station and Liverpool Street (every 15–30min; 45min to Liverpool Street), which costs £24 return. **Airbus #6** runs 24 hours a day to Victoria Coach Station (every 30min; 1hr 30min), and costs £10 single, £15 return. A taxi will set you back £75 or more, and take at least an hour.

Luton airport (℡01582/405100, ⓦwww.london-luton.com) is roughly thirty miles north of the city centre, and mostly handles charter flights. A **free shuttle bus** takes five minutes to transport passengers to Luton Airport Parkway station, connected by **Thameslink** trains (every 15min; 30–40min) to King's Cross and other stations in central London; tickets cost £10 for a single to Central London. Alternatively, **Green Line** bus #757 runs from Luton to Victoria Station (every 30min; 1hr 15min), costing £9 single. A taxi will cost in the region of £60 and take at least an hour to central London.

London's smallest airport, **City Airport** (℡020/7646 0000, ⓦwww.londoncityairport.com), used primarily by business folk, is situated in Docklands, ten miles east of central London. The airport's **Docklands Light Railway** (DLR) extension should be up and running by the time you read this, taking you straight to Bank in the City in around 25 minutes; tickets cost around £3.

By train or bus

Eurostar trains arrive at the central **Waterloo International**, south of the river. Arriving by train (℡08457/484950, ⓦwww.nationalrail.co.uk) from elsewhere in Britain, you'll come into one of London's numerous mainline stations, all of which have adjacent Underground stations linking into the city centre's tube network. Coming into London **by coach** (℡0870/580 8080, ⓦwww.nationalexpress.com), you're most likely to arrive at **Victoria Coach Station**, a couple of hundred yards south down Buckingham Palace Road from the train and Underground stations of the same name.

Information

London's main tourist office is the **London Visitor Centre**, near Piccadilly Circus at 1 Regent St (Mon 9.30am–6.30pm, Tues–Fri 9am–6.30pm, Sat & Sun 10am–4pm; June–Sept same times except Sat 9am–5pm; ⓦwww.visitbritain.com); there's also a tiny **tourist information** window by the side of the half-price tickets kiosk (tkts; see p.260) on Leicester Square (Mon–Fri 8am–11pm, Sat & Sun 10am–6pm; ⓦwww .visitlondon.com). Individual boroughs also run tourist offices: the most central one is on the south side of St Paul's Cathedral (May–Sept daily 9.30am–5pm; Oct–April Mon–Fri 9.30am–5pm; ⓣ020/7332 1456, ⓦwww.cityoflondon.gov .uk).

Most offices hand out a useful reference **map** of central London, plus plans of the public transport systems, but to find your way around every nook and cranny of the city you need to invest in either an *A–Z Atlas* or a *Nicholson Streetfinder*, both of which have a street index covering every street in the capital. You can get them at most bookshops and newsagents for less than £5. *London: The Rough Guide Map* is a comprehensive full-colour, waterproof and non-tearable map detailing restaurants, bars, shops and visitor attractions.

London's only comprehensive and critical weekly **listings** magazine is *Time Out*, which costs £2.50 and comes out every Tuesday afternoon. In it you'll find details of all the latest exhibitions, shows, films, music, sport, guided walks and events in and around the capital.

Websites

London Tourist Board
ⓦwww.londontouristboard .com The official LTB website is full of useful information, including an online accommodation service and news about the city's museums and galleries.

Ⓦ**www.londontown.com** Aimed at first-time visitors from abroad, with a basic rundown of the top sights, hotels and restaurants.

Smooth Hound Systems

Ⓦ**www.s-h-systems.co.uk /tourism/london** A very simply designed and basic tourist info site, which covers London in exhaustive A–Z categories.

Streetmap

Ⓦ**www.streetmap.co.uk** Type in the London address or postcode you want, and this site will locate it for you in seconds.

City transport

Transport for London (TfL) provides excellent free maps and details of bus and tube services from its **travel information** offices: the main one is at Piccadilly Circus tube station (Mon–Sat 7.15am–9pm, Sun 8.15am–8pm), and there are desks at Heathrow and various tube and train stations. They also provide a 24-hour phone line with information on all bus and tube services (☏020/7222 1234) and a website (Ⓦwww .tfl.gov.uk). One word of warning – avoid travelling during the **rush hour** (Mon–Fri 8–9.30am & 5–7pm), when tubes become unbearably crowded (and the lack of air conditioning doesn't help), and some buses get so full they literally won't let you on.

The tube

Except for very short journeys, the fastest way of moving around the city is by **Underground** or the tube (Ⓦwww.thetube.com) as it's known. Each line has its own colour and name, and the system is easy to negotiate – all you need to know is which direction you're travelling in: northbound, eastbound, southbound

Travelcards

To get the best value out of London's public transport system, buy a **Travelcard**. Available from machines and booths at all tube and train stations, and at some newsagents (look for the sign), these are valid for the bus, tube, Docklands Light Railway, Tramlink and suburban rail networks. **Day Travelcards** come in two varieties: Off-Peak – which are valid after 9.30am on weekdays and all day during the weekend – and Peak. A Day Travelcard (Off-Peak) costs £4.90 for unlimited travel in central zones 1 and 2, rising to £6.30 for zones 1–6 (including Heathrow); the Day Travelcard (Peak) starts at £6.20 for zones 1 and 2. A **3-Day Travelcard** costs £15.40 for zones 1 and 2, but is obviously only worth it if you need to travel during peak hours. If you're travelling with **kids**, you can buy them a Day Travelcard (off-peak) for zones 1–6 for just £1 each.

or westbound. Services operate from around 5am until 12.30am Monday to Saturday, and from 7.30am until 11.30pm on Sundays; you rarely have to wait more than five minutes for a train from central stations.

Tickets must be bought in advance at the station, and fed through the automatic machines; if you're caught without a valid ticket, you'll be charged an on-the-spot Penalty Fare of £20. A single journey in the central zone costs an unbelievable £3, so if you're intending to travel about a bit, a Travelcard is a much better bet (see box above).

Buses

London's red **double-decker buses** are fun to ride on, but, like all buses, tend to get stuck in traffic jams, which prevents them running to a regular timetable. In central London, and on all the extra-long "bendy buses", you must **buy your ticket before boarding** from one of the machines at the bus stop. Tickets for all bus journeys, including those on night buses, cost £1.50; you will need the exact change, and drivers can give you very short shrift if you tell them the machine is broken (which they frequently are). If this is the type of journey you'll be making once or twice a day, then it's well worth buying a block of six **Saver tickets** (£6 for adults). Another option is to buy a **One-Day Bus Pass**, which costs £3.50 for adults (Kids under 14 go free), and can be used on all buses anytime anywhere in London. Saver tickets and passes can be bought at selected newsagents.

Some buses run a 24-hour service, but most run between about 5am and midnight, with a network of **night buses** (prefixed with the letter "N") operating outside this period. Night bus routes radiate out from Trafalgar Square at approximately twenty-to thirty-minute intervals, more frequently on some routes and on Friday and Saturday nights. Travelcards (see box) are valid. At all stops you must wave to get the bus to stop, and when on the bus, press the bell in order to get off.

Suburban trains

Large areas of London's suburbs are best reached by the **suburban train** network (Travelcards valid). Wherever a sight can only be reached by overground train, we've indicated in the

The London Pass

If you're thinking of visiting a lot of fee-paying attractions in a short space of time, it's worth considering buying a **London Pass** (Ⓦ www.londonpass.com), which gives you free entry to a mixed bag of attractions including Hampton Court Palace, Kensington Palace, Kew Gardens, London Aquarium, St Paul's Cathedral, the Tower of London and Windsor Castle, plus a whole host of lesser attractions, and various discounts at selected outlets. You can choose to buy the card with or without an All-Zone Travelcard thrown in; the saving is relatively small, but it does include free travel out to Windsor. The pass costs around £27 for one day (£18 for kids), rising to £72 for six days (£48 for kids); or £32 with a Travelcard (£20 for kids) rising to £110 (£61 for kids). The London Pass can be bought online or in person from tourist offices and London's mainline train or chief underground stations.

guide the nearest train station and the central terminus from which you can depart. To find out about a particular service, phone **National Rail Enquiries** on ℡08457/484950 or check timetables on ⓦwww.nationalrail.co.uk .

Taxis

Compared to most capital cities, London's metered **black cabs** are an expensive option unless there are three or more of you – a ride from Euston to Victoria, for example, costs around £12–15 (Mon–Fri 6am–8pm). After 8pm on weekdays and all day during the weekend, a higher tariff applies, and after 10pm, a much higher one. A yellow light over the windscreen tells you if the cab is available – just stick your arm out to hail it. To order a black cab in advance, phone ℡0871/871 8710, and be prepared to pay an extra £2.

Minicabs look just like regular cars and are considerably cheaper than black cabs, but they cannot be hailed from the street. All minicabs should be licensed and able to produce a Public Carriage Office licence on demand. The best way to pick a company is to take the advice of the place you're at, unless you want to be certain of a woman driver, in which case call Lady-cabs (℡020/7254 3501), or a gay/lesbian-friendly driver, in which case call Freedom Cars (℡020/7734 1313).

Last, and definitely least, there are usually plenty of **bicycle taxis** available for hire in the West End. The oldest and biggest of the bunch are Bugbugs (℡020/7620 0500, ⓦwww.bugbugs.co.uk), who have over fifty rickshaws operating Monday to Saturday from 7pm until the early hours of the morning. The rickshaws take up to three passengers and fares are negotiable, though they should work out at around £5 per person per mile.

Boats

Boat services on the Thames are much improved, but they still do not form part of an integrated public transport system. As a result fares are quite expensive, with Travelcards currently only giving the holders a 33 percent discount on tickets.

All services are keenly affected by demand, tides and the weather, and tend to be drastically scaled down in the winter months. **Timetables** and services are complex, and there are numerous companies and small charter operators – for a full list pick up the Thames River Services booklet from a TfL information office (see p.18), or phone ☏020/7222 1234 or visit ⓦwww .tfl.gov.uk/river.

The busiest part of the river is the central section between Westminster and the Tower of London, but boats run direct as far as Greenwich, downstream, and Hampton Court upstream. Look out, too, for the MV *Balmoral* and **paddle steamer** *Waverley*, which make regular visits to Tower Pier over the summer and autumn (☏0845/130 4647, ⓦwww .waverleyexcursions.co.uk). From April to September, you can also take a boat from Westminster via Kew and Richmond **to Hampton Court** (3hr one way; £13.50 single, £19.50 return).

Sightseeing tours

Sightseeing **bus tours** are run by several rival companies, their open-top double-deckers setting off every fifteen minutes from Victoria station, Trafalgar Square, Piccadilly and other tourist spots. Tours take roughly two hours (though you can hop on and off as often as you like) and cost around £17. A money-saving option is to skip the commentary and hop on a real London double-decker – the **#11 from Victoria Station** will take you past Westminster Abbey, the Houses of Parliament, up Whitehall,

Congestion charge

The latest attempt to cut down on car usage in London is the **congestion charge**, pioneered by the Mayor of London, Ken Livingstone. All vehicles entering central London on weekdays between 7am and 6.30pm are liable to a congestion charge of £8 per vehicle. Drivers can pay for the charge online, over the phone and at garages and shops, and must do so before 10pm the same day or incur a surcharge. The congestion charging zone is bounded by Marylebone and Euston roads in the north, Commercial Street and Tower Bridge in the east, Kennington Lane and Elephant & Castle in the south, and Edgware Road and Park Lane in the west – though, beware, as there are plans to extend the zone westwards. For the latest visit ⓦ www.cclondon.com.

round Trafalgar Square, along the Strand and on to St Paul's Cathedral. Alternatively, you can climb aboard one of the bright yellow World War II amphibious vehicles used by London Duck Tours (☎020/7928 3132, ⓦwww .londonducktours.co.uk), which offers a combined **bus and boat tour** (daily 9.30am–6pm or dusk; £17.50). After departing from behind County Hall, near the London Eye, you spend forty-five minutes driving round the usual sights, before plunging into the river for a half-hour cruise. At the weekend and in the school holidays, it's as well to book ahead.

Walking tours are infinitely more appealing, mixing solid historical facts with juicy anecdotes in the company of a local specialist. Organized walks range from literary pub crawls round Bloomsbury to tours of places associated with the Beatles. They tend to cost around £5 and usually take two hours. To find out what's on offer, check the "Around Town" section of *Time Out*. The widest range of walks are offered by Original London Walks (☎020/7624 3978, ⓦwww.walks.com).

Guide

The guide

1

Westminster and Whitehall

Political, religious and regal power has emanated from **Westminster** and **Whitehall** for almost a millennium. It was Edward the Confessor (1042–66) who first established Westminster as London's royal and ecclesiastical power base, some three miles west of the City of London. The embryonic English parliament met in the abbey in the fourteenth century and eventually took over the old royal palace of Westminster. In the nineteenth century, Whitehall became the "heart of the Empire", its ministries ruling over a quarter of the world's population. Even now, though the UK's world status has diminished, the institutions that run the country inhabit roughly the same geographical area: Westminster for the politicians, Whitehall for the civil servants.

The monuments and buildings covered in this chapter also span the millennium, and include some of London's most famous landmarks – **Nelson's Column**, **Big Ben** and the **Houses of Parliament**, **Westminster Abbey** and two of the city's finest permanent art collections, the **National Gallery** and **Tate Britain**. This is a well-trodden tourist circuit since it's also one of the easiest parts of London to walk round, with all the major sights within a mere half-mile of each other and linked by one of London's most majestic streets, **Whitehall**.

Trafalgar Square

Map 4, G9. ✆ Leicester Square or Charing Cross.

Despite the pigeons and the traffic noise, **Trafalgar Square** is still one of London's grandest architectural set pieces. John Nash designed the basic layout in the 1820s, but died long before the square took its present form. The Neoclassical National Gallery filled up the northern side of the square in 1838, followed five years later by the central focal point, **Nelson's Column**, topped by the famous admiral; the very large bronze lions didn't arrive until 1868, and the fountains – a real rarity in a London square – didn't take their present shape until the late 1930s. As one of the few large public squares in London, Trafalgar Square has been both a tourist attraction and a focus for political demonstrations since the Chartists assembled here in 1848 before marching to Kennington Common. On a more festive note, the square is graced each December with a giant Christmas tree, donated by Norway in thanks for liberation from the Nazis, and on **New Year's Eve** thousands of inebriates sing in the New Year.

Stranded on a traffic island to the south of the column, and predating the entire square, is the **equestrian statue of Charles I**, erected shortly after the Restoration on the very spot where eight of those who had signed the king's death warrant were disembowelled. Charles's statue also marks the original site of the thirteenth-century **Charing Cross**, from where all distances from the capital are measured – a Victorian imitation now stands nearby, outside Charing Cross train station (Map 4, H8).

The northeastern corner of the square is occupied by James Gibbs' church of **St Martin-in-the-Fields** (ⓦwww.stmartin-in-the-fields.org), fronted by a magnificent Corinthian portico and topped by an elaborate, and distinctly

WESTMINSTER AND WHITEHALL | Trafalgar Square

unclassical, tower and steeple. Completed in 1726, the interior is purposefully simple, though the Italian plasterwork on the barrel vaulting is exceptionally rich; it's best appreciated while listening to one of the church's free lunchtime concerts (see p.253). There's a licensed café (see p.194) in the roomy **crypt**, not to mention a shop, gallery and brass-rubbing centre (Mon–Sat 10am–6pm, Sun noon–6pm).

The National Gallery

Map 4, G8. Daily 10am–6pm, Wed till 9pm; free; ⓦwww.nationalgallery.org.uk ⊖ Leicester Square or Charing Cross.

Unlike the Louvre or the Hermitage, the **National Gallery**, on the north side of Trafalgar Square, is not based on a royal collection, but was begun as late as 1824 by the British government. The gallery's subsequent canny acquisition policy has resulted in more than 2300 paintings, but the collection's virtue is not so much its size, but the range, depth and sheer quality of its contents.

To view the collection chronologically, begin with the **Sainsbury Wing**, the softly-softly, postmodern 1980s adjunct which playfully imitates elements of the original gallery's Neoclassicism. However, with more than a thousand paintings on permanent display in the main galleries, you'll need real stamina to see everything in one day, so if time is tight your best bet is to home in on your areas of special interest, having picked up a gallery plan at one of the information desks. **Audioguides**, with a brief commentary of virtually all of the paintings on display is available for a "voluntary contribution" of £4. Commentaries tend to be descriptive rather than interpretive, however, and much better are the gallery's **free guided tours** (daily 11.30am & 2.30pm, plus Wed 6 & 6.30pm, Sat also 12.30 & 3.30pm), which set off from the Sainsbury Wing foyer and take in a representative sample.

Among the National's **Italian** masterpieces are Leonardo's melancholic *Virgin of the Rocks*, Uccello's *Battle of San*

Romano, Botticelli's *Venus and Mars* (inspired by a Dante sonnet) and Piero della Francesca's beautifully composed *Baptism of Christ*, one of his earliest works. The fine collection of Venetian works includes Titian's colourful early masterpiece *Bacchus and Ariadne*, his very late, much gloomier *Death of Acteon*, and Veronese's lustrous *Family of Darius before Alexander*. Elsewhere, Bronzino's erotic *Venus, Cupid, Folly and Time* and Raphael's trenchant *Pope Julius II* keep company with Michelangelo's unfinished *Entombment*. Later Italian works to look out for include a couple by Caravaggio, a few splendid examples of Tiepolo's airy draughtsmanship, and glittering vistas of Venice by Canaletto and Guardi.

From **Spain** there are dazzling pieces by El Greco, Goya, Murillo and Velázquez, among them the provocative *Rokeby Venus*. From the **Low Countries**, standouts include van Eyck's *Arnolfini Marriage*, Memlinc's perfectly poised *Donne Triptych*, and a couple of typically serene Vermeers. There are numerous genre paintings, such as Frans Hals' *Family Group in a Landscape*, and some superlative landscapes, most notably Hobbema's *Avenue, Middleharnis*. An array of Rembrandt paintings that features some of his most searching portraits – two of them self-portraits – is followed by abundant examples of Rubens' expansive, fleshy canvases.

Holbein's masterful *Ambassadors* and several of Van Dyck's portraits were painted for the English court, and there's home-grown **British** art, too, represented by important works such as Hogarth's satirical *Marriage à la Mode*, Gainsborough's translucent *Morning Walk*, Constable's ever-popular *Hay Wain*, and Turner's *Fighting Téméraire*. Highlights of the **French** contingent include superb works by Poussin, Claude, Fragonard, Boucher, Watteau and David.

Finally, there's a particularly strong showing of **Impressionists and Post-Impressionists** in rooms 43–46 of the East Wing. Among the most famous works are Manet's unfinished *Execution of Maximilian*, Renoir's *Umbrellas*, Monet's *Thames below Westminster*, Van Gogh's *Sunflowers*,

Seurat's pointillist *Bathers at Asnières*, a Rousseau junglescape, Cézanne's proto-Cubist *Bathers* and Picasso's Blue Period *Child with a Dove*.

The National Portrait Gallery

Map 4, G8. Daily 10am–6pm, Thurs & Fri till 9pm; free; ⓦwww.npg.org .uk ⊖ Leicester Square or Charing Cross.

Around the east side of the National Gallery lurks the **National Portrait Gallery** (NPG), founded in 1856 to house uplifting depictions of the good and the great. Though it has some fine works in its collection, many of the studies are of less interest than their subjects, and the overall impression is of an overstuffed shrine to famous Brits rather than a museum offering any insight into the history of portraiture. However, it is fascinating to trace who has been deemed worthy of admiration at any moment: aristocrats and artists in previous centuries, warmongers and imperialists in the early decades of the twentieth century, writers and poets in the 1930s and 1940s, and, latterly, retired footballers, and film and pop stars. The NPG's **Sound Guide** gives useful biographical background information and is available in return for a "voluntary contribution" of £2.

Whitehall

Map 4, H10. ⊖ Charing Cross or Westminster.

Whitehall, the unusually broad avenue connecting Trafalgar Square to Parliament Square, is synonymous with the faceless, pinstriped bureaucracy charged with the day-to-day running of the country. Since the sixteenth century, nearly all the key governmental ministries and offices have migrated here, rehousing themselves on an ever-increasing scale. The statues dotted about Whitehall recall the days when this street stood at the centre of an empire on which the sun never set.

During the sixteenth and seventeenth centuries Whitehall was also synonymous with royalty, since it was the permanent residence of the kings and queens of England. The original **Whitehall Palace** was the London seat of the Archbishop of York, confiscated and greatly extended by Henry VIII after a fire at Westminster forced him to find alternative accommodation; it was here that he celebrated his marriage to Anne Boleyn in 1533, and here that he died fourteen years later.

The chief section of the old palace to survive the fire of 1698 was the **Banqueting House** (Map 4, H10; Mon–Sat 10am–5pm; £4; ⓦwww.hrp.org.uk), begun by Inigo Jones in 1619 and the first Palladian building to be built in England. The one room now open to the public has no original furnishings, but is well worth seeing for the superlative Rubens ceiling paintings glorifying the Stuart dynasty, commissioned by Charles I in the 1630s. Charles himself walked through

Changing of the Guard

The Queen is colonel-in-chief of the seven **Household Regiments**: the Life Guards (who dress in red and white) and the Blues and Royals (who dress in blue and white) are the two Household Cavalry regiments; the Grenadier, Coldstream, Scots, Irish and Welsh Guards make up the Foot Guards.

All these regiments still form part of the modern army as well as performing ceremonial functions such as the Changing of the Guard. If you're keen to find out more about the Foot Guards, pay a visit to the **Guards' Museum** (Map 4, E13; daily 10am–4pm; £2), in the Wellington Barracks on the south side of St James's Park.

The **Changing of the Guard** takes place at two separate locations in London: the two Household Cavalry regiments take it in turns to stand guard at Horse Guards on Whitehall (Mon–Sat 11am, Sun 10am, with inspection daily at 4pm), while the Foot Guards take care of Buckingham Palace (April–Aug daily 11.30am; Sept–March alternate days; no ceremony if it rains). A ceremony also takes place regularly at Windsor Castle (see p.172).

the room for the last time in 1649, when he stepped onto the executioner's scaffold from one of its windows.

Across the road, two mounted sentries of the Queen's Household Cavalry and two horseless colleagues, all in ceremonial uniform, are posted daily from 10am to 4pm. Ostensibly they are protecting the **Horse Guards** building, originally built as the old palace guard house, but now guarding nothing in particular. The mounted guards are changed hourly; those standing change every two hours. Try to coincide your visit with the Changing of the Guard (see opposite).

Further down this west side of Whitehall is London's most famous address, **Number 10 Downing Street** (Map 4, G11; ⓦwww.number-10.gov.uk), the seventeenth-century terraced house that has been the residence of the prime minister since it was presented to Robert Walpole, Britain's first PM, by George II in 1732. Just beyond the Downing Street gates, in the middle of the road, stands **Cenotaph**, designed by Edwin Lutyens to commemorate the victims of World War I. Eschewing any kind of Christian imagery, it is inscribed simply with the words "The Glorious Dead". The memorial remains the focus of the Remembrance Sunday ceremony held in early November (see p.311).

In 1938, in anticipation of Nazi air raids, the basement of the civil service buildings on the south side of King Charles Street were converted into the **Cabinet War Rooms** (Map 4, G12; daily 9.30am–6pm; £10; ⓦcwr.iwm.org.uk). It was here that Winston Churchill directed operations and held Cabinet meetings for the duration of World War II and the rooms have been left pretty much as they were when they were finally abandoned on VJ Day 1945, making for an atmospheric underground trot through wartime London. Also in the basement is the excellent **Churchill Museum**. You can hear snippets of Churchill's most famous speeches and check out his trademark bowler, spotted bow tie and half-chewed Havana, not to mention his wonderful burgundy zip-up "romper suit".

The Houses of Parliament

Map 4, H13. ⓦwww.parliament.uk ⊖ Westminster.

Clearly visible at the south end of Whitehall is one of London's best-known monuments, the Palace of Westminster, better known as the **Houses of Parliament**. The city's finest Victorian Gothic Revival building and symbol of a nation once confident of its place at the centre of the world, it is distinguished above all by the ornate, gilded clock tower popularly known as **Big Ben**, after the thirteen-ton main bell that strikes the hour (and is broadcast across the world by the BBC).

The original **Westminster Palace** was built by Edward the Confessor in the first half of the eleventh century, so that he could watch over the building of his abbey. It then served as the seat of all the English monarchs until a fire forced Henry VIII to decamp to Whitehall. The Lords have always convened at the palace, but it was only following Henry's death that the House of Commons moved from the abbey's Chapter House into the palace's St Stephen's Chapel, thus beginning the building's associations with parliament.

The medieval palace burned down in 1834, but **Westminster Hall** survived, and its huge oak hammerbeam roof makes it one of the most magnificent secular medieval halls in Europe – you get a glimpse of the hall en route to the public galleries. The **Jewel Tower** (daily: April–Oct 10am–5pm; Nov–March 10am–4pm; £2.60), across the road from parliament, is another remnant of the medieval palace, now housing an excellent exhibition on the history of parliament – worth visiting before you queue up to get into the Houses of Parliament.

To watch the proceedings in either the House of Commons or the Lords, simply join the queue for the **public galleries** outside St Stephen's Gate. Sessions run on Monday 2.30–10.30pm, from Tuesday to Thursday 11.30am–7.30pm, and on Friday 9.30am–3pm. The public is let in slowly from

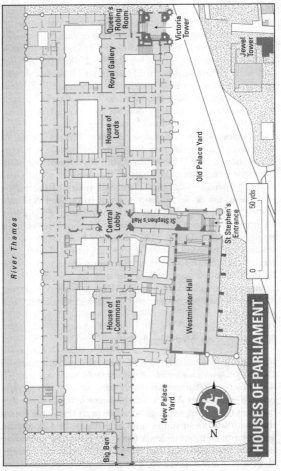

HOUSES OF PARLIAMENT

Queen's Robing Room
Royal Gallery
Victoria Tower
Jewel Tower
House of Lords
Central Lobby
St Stephen's Hall
Old Palace Yard
St Stephen's Entrance
House of Commons
Westminster Hall
River Thames
New Palace Yard
Big Ben
N

0   50 yds

about 4pm onwards on Monday, from 1pm Tuesday to Thursday, and from 10am on Friday. If you want to avoid queueing, turn up an hour or more later, when the crowds have usually thinned. **Question Time** – when the House is at its most raucous and entertaining – takes place at 2.30pm on Monday and at 11.30am Tuesday to Thursday; **Prime Minister's Question Time** is on Wednesday from noon until 12.30pm. To attend any of these you need to book a **ticket** several weeks in advance from your local MP (if you're a UK citizen) or your embassy in London (if you're not).

Recesses (holiday closures) of both Houses occur at Christmas, Easter, and from August to the middle of October; phone ☎020/7219 4272 or visit ⊛www.parliament.uk for more information. For part of the summer recess (Aug & Sept), there are also public **guided tours** of the building (Mon, Fri & Sat 9.15am–4.30pm, Tues, Wed & Thurs 1.15–4.30pm; Aug also Tues 9.15am–1.15pm; £7), lasting an hour and fifteen minutes. Visitors can book in advance by phoning ☎0870/906 3773, or simply head for the ticket office on Abingdon Green, opposite Victoria Tower. The rest of the year, it's still possible to organize a tour of the building through your MP or embassy. It's also possible to arrange a free guided tour up **Big Ben** (Mon–Fri 10.30am, 11.30am & 2.30pm; no under-11s), again through your MP or embassy.

Westminster Abbey

Map 4, G13. Mon–Fri 9.30am–4.45pm, Wed until 7pm, Sat 9.30am–1.45pm; £8; ⊛www.westminster-abbey.org ⊖ Westminster.

The Houses of Parliament dwarf their much older neighbour, **Westminster Abbey**, yet this single building embodies much of the history of England: it has been the venue for all the **coronations** since the time of William the Conqueror, and the site of more or less every royal burial for some five hundred years between the reigns of Henry III and George II. Scores of the nation's most famous citizens are honoured

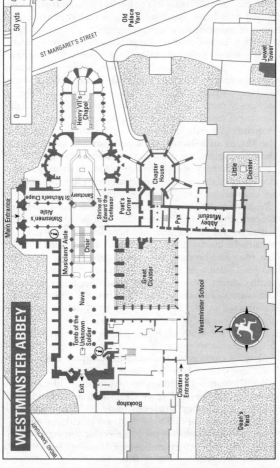

WESTMINSTER ABBEY

Henry VII's Chapel

St Michael's Chapel
Sanctuary
Shrine of the Confessor
Statesmen's Aisle
Main Entrance
Musicians Aisle
Choir
Poet's Corner
Chapter House
Little Cloister
Great Cloister
Abbey Museum
Pyx
Nave
Tomb of the Unknown Soldier
Westminster School
N
Exit
Cloisters Entrance
Bookshop
Dean's Yard
BROAD SANCTUARY
ST MARGARET'S STREET
Old Palace Yard
Jewel Tower

0   50 yds

here, too (though many of the stones commemorate people buried elsewhere), and the interior is crammed with hundreds of monuments, reliefs and statues.

Entry is via the north transept, cluttered with monuments to politicians – and traditionally known as **Statesmen's Aisle** – shortly after which you come to the abbey's most dazzling architectural set piece, the **Lady Chapel**, added by Henry VII in 1503 as his future resting place. With its intricately carved vaulting and fan-shaped gilded pendants, the chapel represents the final spectacular gasp of the English Perpendicular style. The public are no longer admitted to the **Shrine of Edward the Confessor**, the sacred heart of the building (except on a guided verger tour; £4) though you do get to inspect Edward I's **Coronation Chair**, a decrepit oak throne dating from around 1300 and still used for coronations.

Nowadays, the abbey's royal tombs are upstaged by **Poets' Corner**, in the south transept. The first occupant, Geoffrey Chaucer, was buried here not because he was a poet but because he lived nearby. By the eighteenth century, however, this zone had become an artistic pantheon, and since then has been filled with tributes to all shades of talent. From the south transept, you can view the central sanctuary, site of the coronations, and the wonderful **Cosmati floor mosaic**, constructed in the thirteenth century by Italian craftsmen, and often covered by a carpet to protect it.

Doors in the south choir aisle lead to the **Great Cloisters** (daily 8am–6pm), rebuilt after a fire in 1298. At the eastern end of the cloisters lies the octagonal **Chapter House** (daily 10.30am–4pm), where the House of Commons met from 1257. The thirteenth-century decorative paving tiles and wall-paintings have survived intact. Chapter House tickets include entry to the **Abbey Museum** (daily 10.30am–4pm), filled with generations of bald royal death masks and wax effigies.

It's only after exploring the cloisters that you get to see the **nave** itself: narrow, light and, at over a hundred feet in height, by far the tallest in the country. The most famous monument is the **Tomb of the Unknown Soldier**, set into the floor by the west door (which now serves as the main exit), with its garland of red poppies commemorating the million soldiers of the British Empire who died in World War I.

Tate Britain

Map 3, H8. Daily 10am–5.50pm; free; ⓦwww.tate.org.uk ⊖ Pimlico.

Tate Britain, the purpose-built gallery half a mile south of parliament, was founded in 1897 with money from Henry Tate – inventor of the sugar cube – and is now devoted exclusively to British art. As well as displaying British art from 1500 to the present, plus a whole wing devoted to Turner, Tate Britain also showcases contemporary British artists and continues to sponsor the Turner Prize, the country's most prestigious award for modern art.

The pictures are rehung more or less annually, but always include a fair selection of works by British artists such as Hogarth, Constable, Gainsborough, Reynolds and Blake, plus foreign artists like van Dyck who spent much of their career over here. The ever-popular **Pre-Raphaelites** are always well represented, as are established twentieth-century greats such as Stanley Spencer and Francis Bacon alongside living artists such as David Hockney and Lucien Freud. Lastly, don't miss the Tate's outstanding **Turner collection**, displayed in the Clore Gallery.

Westminster Cathedral

Map 3, G7. Mon–Fri & Sun 7am–7pm, Sat 8am–7pm; free; ⓦwww.rcdow.org.uk ⊖ Victoria.

Halfway down Victoria Street from Westminster Abbey, you'll find one of London's most surprising churches, the stripy neo-Byzantine concoction of the Roman Catholic **Westminster Cathedral**. Begun in 1895, it is one of the last and wildest monuments to the Victorian era: constructed from more than twelve million terracotta-coloured bricks and decorated with hoops of Portland stone, it culminates in a magnificent tapered **campanile** which rises to 274 feet, served by a lift (April–Nov daily 9.30am–12.30pm & 1–5pm; Dec–March Thurs–Sun 9.30am–12.30pm & 1–5pm; £2). The **interior** is only half-finished, so to get an idea of what the place will look like when it's finally completed, explore the series of **side-chapels** whose rich, multicoloured décor makes use of more than one hundred different marbles from around the world. Be sure, too, to check out the low-relief **Stations of the Cross** sculpted by the controversial Eric Gill during World War I.

St James's, Piccadilly, Mayfair and Marylebone

S t James's, **Mayfair** and **Marylebone** emerged in the late seventeenth century as London's first real suburbs, characterized by grid-plan streets feeding into grand, formal squares. This expansion set the westward trend for middle-class migration, and as London's wealthier consumers moved west, so too did the city's more upmarket shops and luxury hotels, which are still a feature of the area.

Aristocratic St James's, across St James's Park from **Buckingham Palace**, was one of the first areas to be developed, and remains the preserve of the seriously rich. **Piccadilly**, which forms the border between St James's and Mayfair, is no longer the fashionable promenade it once was, but a whiff of exclusivity still pervades **Bond Street** and its tributaries. **Regent Street** was created as a new "Royal Mile", a tangible borderline to shore up these new fashionable suburbs against the chaotic maze of Soho and the City, where the working population still lived. Now, along with **Oxford**

Street, it has become London's busiest shopping district – it's here that Londoners mean when they talk of "going shopping up the West End".

Marylebone, which lies to the north of Oxford Street, is another grid-plan Georgian development, a couple of social and property leagues below Mayfair, but a wealthy area nevertheless. It boasts a very fine art gallery, the **Wallace Collection**, and, in its northern fringes, one of London's biggest tourist attractions, **Madame Tussaud's**, the oldest and largest wax museum in the world.

St James's

Map 4, E9. ⊖ Piccadilly Circus or Green Park.

St James's, the exclusive enclave sandwiched between The Mall and Piccadilly, was laid out in the 1670s close to St James's Palace. Royal and aristocratic residences predominate along its southern border, gentlemen's clubs cluster along Pall Mall and St James's Street, while jacket-and-tie restaurants and expense-account gentlemen's outfitters line Jermyn Street. Hardly surprising, then, that most Londoners rarely stray into this area. Plenty of folk, however, frequent **St James's Park**, with large numbers heading for the Queen's chief residence, **Buckingham Palace**, and the adjacent Queen's Gallery and Royal Mews.

The Mall and St James's Park

Map 4, F10. ⊖ St James's Park.

The tree-lined sweep of **The Mall** – London's nearest equivalent to a Parisian boulevard – was laid out in the first decade of the twentieth century as a memorial to Queen Victoria, and runs from Trafalgar Square to Buckingham Palace. The bombastic **Admiralty Arch** was erected to mark the entrance at the Trafalgar Square end of The Mall, while at the other end stands the ludicrous **Victoria Memorial**, Edward VII's overblown tribute to his mother.

The best time to view The Mall is on a Sunday, when it's closed to traffic.

Flanking nearly the whole length of the Mall, **St James's Park** is the oldest of the royal parks, having been drained and enclosed for hunting purposes by Henry VIII. It was landscaped by Nash in the 1820s, and today its lake is a favourite picnic spot for the civil servants of Whitehall. Pelicans can still be seen at the eastern end of the lake, and there are ducks, swans and geese aplenty. From the bridge across the lake there's also a fine view over to Westminster and the jumble of domes and pinnacles along Whitehall.

Buckingham Palace

Map 4, C12. Aug & Sept daily 9.30am–4.15pm; £13.50; advance booking on ☏020/7321 2233, ⓦwww.royal.gov.uk ⊖ Green Park.

The graceless colossus of **Buckingham Palace**, popularly known as "Buck House", has served as the monarch's permanent London residence only since the accession of Victoria. Bought by George III in 1762, the building was overhauled by Nash in the late 1820s, and again by Aston Webb in time for George V's coronation in 1913, producing a palace that's about as bland as it's possible to be.

For two months of the year, the hallowed portals are grudgingly nudged open; timed tickets are sold from the marquee-like box office in Green Park at the western end of The Mall. The interior, however, is a bit of an anticlimax: of the palace's 660 rooms you're permitted to see around twenty, and there's little sign of life as the Queen decamps to Scotland every summer. For the other ten months of the year there's little to do here, as the palace is closed to visitors – not that this deters the crowds who mill around the railings and gather in some force to watch the **Changing of the Guard** (see p.32), in which a detachment of the Queen's Foot Guards marches to appropriate martial music from St James's Palace (unless it rains, that is).

Queen's Gallery and Royal Mews

The public can also pay through the nose to view a small portion of the Royal Collection, at the rebuilt **Queen's Gallery** (Map 4, C13; daily 10am–5.30pm; £7.50), on the south side of the palace. Exhibitions change regularly,

The Royal Family

Tourists may still flock to see London's royal palaces, but over the last decade or so the British public have become more critical of the huge tax bill that goes to support the **Royal Family** (@www.royal.gov.uk) in the style to which they are accustomed. This creeping republicanism can be traced back to 1992, which the Queen herself, in one of her few memorable Christmas Day speeches, accurately described as her *annus horribilis*. This was the year that saw the marriage break-ups of Charles and Di, and Andrew and Fergie, and the second marriage of divorcee Princess Anne.

Matters came to a head, though, over who should pay the estimated £50 million costs of repairs after a serious fire at Windsor Castle (see p.172). Misjudging the public mood, the Conservative government offered taxpayers' money to foot the entire bill. After a furore, it was agreed that some of the cost would be raised by opening up Buckingham Palace to the public for the first time (and by cranking up the admission charges on the rest of London's royal palaces). In addition, under pressure from the media, the Queen also reduced the number of royals paid out of the Civil List, and, for the first time, agreed to pay taxes on her enormous personal fortune.

Given the mounting resentment of the Royal Family, it was hardly surprising that public opinion tended to side with Princess Diana rather than Prince Charles during their various disputes. Diana's subsequent death in 1997 meant the loss of the Royal Family's most vociferous critic. Yet despite the low poll ratings, none of the political parties currently advocates abolishing the monarchy, and public appetite for stories about the antics of the princes (and their girlfriends), or the latest on whether Camilla will ever be Queen, shows little sign of abating.

drawn from a collection which is three times larger than the National Gallery, and includes masterpieces by Michelangelo, Reynolds, Gainsborough, Vermeer, van Dyck, Rubens, Rembrandt and Canaletto, as well as the odd Fabergé egg and heaps of Sèvres china.

There's more pageantry on show at the Nash-built **Royal Mews** (Map 4, C14; March–July & Oct daily except Fri 11am–4pm; Aug & Sept Mon–Sat 10am–5pm; £6), to the south along Buckingham Palace Road. The horses can be viewed in their luxury stables, along with an exhibition of equine accoutrements, but it's the royal carriages that are the main attraction. The most ornate is the Gold Carriage made for George III in 1762, smothered in 22-carat gilding and weighing four tons, its axles supporting four life-size figures. The Mews also house the Royal Family's fleet of five Rolls-Royce Phantoms and three Daimlers.

Waterloo Place to St James's Palace

Map 4, D10–F9. ⊖ Piccadilly Circus or Green Park.

St James's contains some interesting architectural set pieces, such as **Lower Regent Street** (Map 4, E8), which was the first stage in John Nash's ambitious plan to link George IV's magnificent Carlton House with Regent's Park. Like so many of Nash's grandiose schemes, it never quite came to fruition, as George IV, soon after ascending the throne, decided that Carlton House – the most expensive palace ever to have been built in London – wasn't quite luxurious enough, and had it pulled down. Instead, Lower Regent Street now opens up into **Waterloo Place** (Map 4, F9), at the centre of which stands the Guards' Crimean Memorial, fashioned from captured Russian cannons and featuring a statue of Florence Nightingale. Clearly visible, beyond, is the "Grand Old" **Duke of York's Column**, erected in 1833, ten years before Nelson's more famous one in Trafalgar Square.

As you cut across Waterloo Place, **Pall Mall** – named after the croquet-like game of *pallo a maglio* ("ball to mallet")

– leads west to **St James's Palace** (Map 4, D11), whose main red-brick gate-tower is pretty much all that remains of the Tudor palace erected here by Henry VIII. When White-hall Palace burned down in 1698, St James's became the principal royal residence and, in keeping with tradition, an ambassador to the UK is still known as "Ambassador to the Court of St James", even though the court moved down the road to Buckingham Palace when Queen Victoria ascended the throne. The rambling, crenellated complex is off limits to the public, with the exception of the **Chapel Royal** (Oct to Good Friday Sun 8.30am & 11.15am), situated within the palace, and the **Queen's Chapel** (Easter–July Sun 8.30am & 11.15am), on the other side of Marlborough Road; both are open for services only.

   Clarence House (Aug to mid-Oct daily 9.30am–6pm; £6; ⓦwww.royal.gov.uk), connected to the palace's south-west wing, was home to the Queen Mother, and now serves as the official London home of Charles and Camilla; the public are allowed to view a handful of unremarkable rooms on the ground floor by guided tour only; tours are very popular so you'll need to book ahead. An even more palatial St James's residence is Princess Diana's ancestral home, **Spencer House** (Map 4, D10; Feb–July & Sept–Dec Sun 10.30am–5.45pm; £6), a superb Palladian mansion erected in the 1750s. Inside, tour guides take you through nine of the state rooms, the most outrageous of which is Lord Spencer's Room, with its astonishing gilded palm-tree columns. Note that children under 10 are not admitted.

Piccadilly Circus

Map 4, E8. ⊖ Piccadilly Circus.

Anonymous and congested it may be, but **Piccadilly Circus**, is, for many Londoners, the nearest their city comes to having a centre. A much-altered product of Nash's grand 1812 Regent Street plan, and now a major traffic bottleneck, it's by no means a picturesque place, and is probably best seen at night, when the spread of vast illuminated signs (a feature since the Edwardian era) gives it a faint touch of Times Square dazzle.

As well as being the gateway to the West End, this is also prime tourist territory, thanks mostly to Piccadilly's celebrated aluminium statue, popularly known as **Eros**. The fountain's archer is one of the city's top attractions, a status that baffles all who live here. Despite the bow and arrow, it's not the god of love at all but the *Angel of Christian Charity*, erected to commemorate the Earl of Shaftesbury, a Bible-thumping social reformer who campaigned, among other things, against child labour.

Regent Street

Map 4, D7. ⊖ Piccadilly Circus or Oxford Circus.

Regent Street, leading north off Piccadilly Circus, is reminiscent of one of Haussmann's Parisian boulevards without the trees. Drawn up by John Nash in 1812 as both a luxury shopping street and a triumphal way between George IV's Carlton House and Regent's Park, it was the city's first attempt at dealing with traffic congestion, and also the first stab at slum clearance and planned social segregation, which would later be perfected by the Victorians.

Despite the subsequent destruction of much of Nash's work in the 1920s, it's still possible to admire the stately intentions of his original Regent Street plan. The increase in the purchasing power of the city's middle classes in the nineteenth century brought the tone of the street "down", and heavyweight stores catering for the masses now predominate. Among the oldest established stores are **Hamley's**, the world's largest toy shop, and **Liberty**, the department store that popularized Arts and Crafts designs at the beginning of the twentieth century.

Piccadilly

Map 4, E8. ⊖ Piccadilly Circus or Green Park.

Piccadilly apparently got its name from the ruffs or "pickadills" worn by the dandies who used to promenade here in the late seventeenth century. Despite its fashionable pedigree, it's no place for promenading in its current state, with traffic careering down it nose to tail most of the day and night. Infinitely more pleasant places to window-shop are the various **nineteenth-century arcades**, originally built to protect shoppers from the mud and horse dung on the streets, but now equally useful for escaping exhaust fumes.

Piccadilly may not be the shopping heaven it once was, but there are still several old firms here that proudly display their royal warrants. One of the oldest institutions is the food emporium of **Fortnum & Mason** (Map 4, D9; ⓦwww .fortnumandmason.com) at no. 181, established in the 1770s by one of George III's footmen, Charles Fortnum, and his partner Hugh Mason. In a kitsch addition dating from 1964, the figures of Fortnum and Mason bow to each other on the hour every day as the clock over the main entrance clanks out the Eton school anthem.

Further along Piccadilly, with its best rooms overlooking Green Park, stands the **Ritz Hotel** (Map 4, C9; ⓦwww .theritzhotel.co.uk), a byword for decadence since it first wowed Edwardian society in 1906. The hotel's design, with its two-storey French-style mansard roof and long arcade, was based on the buildings of Paris's Rue de Rivoli. For a prolonged look inside, you'll need to be in good appetite, dress appropriately, and book in advance for the famous afternoon tea in the hotel's Palm Court (see p.197).

The Royal Academy of Arts

Map 4, D8. Daily 10am–6pm, Fri till 10pm; £5–8; ⓦwww.royalacademy .org.uk ⊖ Green Park or Piccadilly Circus.

Across the road from Fortnum & Mason, the **Royal Academy of Arts** (RA) occupies the enormous Burlington House, one of the few survivors from the ranks of aristocratic mansions that once lined the north side of Piccadilly. The

Academy itself was the country's first-ever formal art school, founded in 1768 by a group of English painters including Thomas Gainsborough and Joshua Reynolds. Reynolds went on to become the Academy's first president, and his statue now stands in the courtyard, palette in hand.

The Academy has always had a conservative reputation for its teaching and, until recently, most of its shows. The **Summer Exhibition**, which opens in June each year, remains a stop on the social calendar of upper middle-class England. Anyone can enter paintings in any style, and the lucky winners get hung, in rather close proximity, and sold. Supposed gravitas is added by the RA "Academicians", who are allowed to display six of their own works – no matter how awful. The result is a bewildering display, which gets annually panned by highbrow critics.

As well as hosting major exhibitions, the RA has a small selection of works from its own collection on **permanent display** in the newly restored white and gold John Madejski Fine Rooms (Tues–Fri 1–4.30pm, Sat & Sun 10am–6pm; free; guided tours Tues–Fri 1pm; free). Highlights include a Rembrandtesque self-portrait by Reynolds, plus works by the likes of John Constable, Stanley Spencer and David Hockney.

Burlington Arcade

Map 4, D8. ❷ Green Park or Piccadilly Circus.

Running along the west side of the Royal Academy is the **Burlington Arcade**, built in 1819 for Lord Cavendish, then owner of Burlington House, to prevent commoners throwing rubbish into his garden. It's Piccadilly's longest and most expensive nineteenth-century arcade, lined with mahogany-fronted jewellers, gentlemen's outfitters and the like. Upholding Regency decorum, it is still illegal to whistle, sing, hum, hurry or carry large packages or open umbrellas on this small stretch, and the arcade's beadles (known as Burlington Berties), in their Edwardian frock coats and gold-braided top hats, take the prevention of such criminality very seriously.

Bond Street and around

Map 4, C7. ⊖ Green Park or Bond Street.

While Oxford Street, Regent Street and Piccadilly have all gone downmarket, **Bond Street**, which runs parallel to Regent Street, has carefully maintained its exclusivity. It is, in fact, two streets rolled into one: the southern half, laid out in the 1680s, is known as Old Bond Street; its northern extension, which followed less than fifty years later, is known as New Bond Street. They are both pretty unassuming architecturally, yet the shops that line them are among the flashiest in London, dominated by perfumeries, **jewellers** and **designer clothes** stores.

In addition to fashion, Bond Street is also renowned for its **auction houses** and for its fine-art galleries. Despite the recent price-fixing scandal that resulted in the imprisonment of one of its former chairmen and a £12 million fine, business is still booming at **Sotheby's** (Map 4, C7; ⓦwww .sothebys.com), 34–35 New Bond St, the oldest of the auction houses – its viewing galleries are open free of charge. Bond Street's **art galleries** are actually outnumbered by those on nearby Cork Street. The main difference between the two locations is that the Bond Street dealers are basically heirloom offloaders, whereas Cork Street galleries sell largely contemporary art. Both have impeccably presented and somewhat intimidating staff, but if you're interested, walk in and look around. They're only shops, after all.

Running parallel with New Bond Street and Cork Street is another classic address in sartorial matters, **Savile Row**, still the place to go for made-to-measure suits, for those with the requisite £2000 or so to spare. The number of bespoke tailors may have declined, but several venerable businesses remain. Gieves & Hawkes, at no. 1, were the first tailors to establish themselves here back in 1785, with Nelson and Wellington among their first customers, and their wares are still an exhibition of upper-class taste.

See p.276 for listings of the best shops in London.

Handel House Museum

Map 4, B6. Tues–Sat 10am–6pm, Thurs till 8pm, Sun noon–6pm; £5; ☎020/7495 1685, ⊛www.handelhouse.org ⊖ Bond Street.

The German-born composer **George Friedrich Handel** (1685–1759) spent the best part of his life in London. He produced all the work for which he is now best known at 25 Brook Street, just west of New Bond Street, and the building has since become the **Handel House Museum**. The composer used the ground floor as a sort of shop where subscribers could buy scores, while the first floor was employed as a rehearsal room. Although containing few original artefacts, the house has been painstakingly reconstructed and redecorated to show how it would have looked in Handel's day. Further atmosphere is provided by the harpsichord in the rehearsal room, which gets played by music students throughout the week, with more formal **performances** on Thursday evenings from 6pm (tickets are £7.50 and include admission to the museum). Access to the house is via the cobbled yard at the back.

Oxford Street

Map 4, C5. ⊛www.oxfordstreet.co.uk ⊖ Bond Street, Oxford Circus or Tottenham Court Road.

As wealthy Londoners began to move out of the City in the eighteenth century in favour of the newly developed West End, so **Oxford Street** – the old Roman road to Oxford – gradually became London's main shopping street. Today, despite successive recessions and sky-high rents, this two-mile hotchpotch of shops is still probably Britain's busiest street.

East of Oxford Circus, the street forms the northern border of Soho, and features two of the city's main record stores, HMV and Virgin Megastore, and the Borders mega-bookstore. West of Oxford Circus, the street is dominated by more upmarket stores, including one great landmark, **Selfridge's** (Map 3, E4; ⊛www.selfridges.co.uk), a huge Edwardian pile fronted by giant Ionic columns, with the Queen of Time riding the ship of commerce and supporting an Art Deco clock above the main entrance. The store was opened in 1909 by Chicago millionaire Gordon Selfridge, who flaunted its 130 departments under the slogan, "Why not spend a day at Selfridge's?", but was later pensioned off after running into trouble with the Inland Revenue.

The Wallace Collection

Map 3, E4. Daily 10am–5pm; free; ⊛www.wallacecollection.org
⊖ Bond Street.

Immediately north of Oxford Street, on Manchester Square, stands Hertford House, a miniature eighteenth-century French chateau which holds the splendid **Wallace Collection**, a museum-gallery best known for its eighteenth-century French paintings (especially Watteau). It also holds Frans Hals' *Laughing Cavalier*, Titian's *Perseus and Andromeda*, Velázquez's *Lady with a Fan* and Rembrandt's affectionate portrait of his teenage son, Titus. There's a modern café in the glassed-over courtyard, but at heart, the Wallace Collection remains an old-fashioned place, with exhibits piled high in glass cabinets, and paintings covering every inch of wall space. The fact that these exhibits are set amid period fittings – and a bloody great armoury – makes the place even more remarkable.

Langham Place and Portland Place

Map 4, C3. ⊖ Oxford Circus.

Regent Street stops just north of Oxford Street at **Langham Place**, site of **All Souls**, Nash's simple and ingenious little Bath-stone church, built in the 1820s. The church's unusual circular Ionic portico and conical spire, which caused outrage in its day, were designed to provide a visual full stop to Regent Street and a pivot for the awkward twist in the triumphal route to Regent's Park. Behind lies the totalitarian-looking **Broadcasting House**, BBC radio headquarters since 1931. Opposite Broadcasting House stands the **Langham Hilton**, built in heavy Italianate style in the 1860s, badly bombed in the last war, but now back to its former glory.

After the chicane around All Souls, you enter **Portland Place**, laid out by the Adam brothers in the 1770s, and incorporated by Nash in his grand route. Once the widest street in London, it's still a majestic avenue, lined exclusively with Adam-style houses boasting wonderful fanlights and iron railings.

Arguably the finest of all the buildings on Portland Place, though, is the sleek **Royal Institute of British Architects** or **RIBA** at no. 66 (Mon–Fri 8am–6pm, Tues until 9pm, Sat 8am–5pm; ⓦwww.riba.org), built in the 1930s. The highlight of the building is the interior, which you can view en route to the institute's excellent café, or during one of the frequent exhibitions and weekly lectures. The main staircase remains a wonderful period piece, with its etched glass balustrades and walnut veneer, and with two large, fluted black-marble columns rising up on either side.

Madame Tussaud's

Map 3, E3. Mon–Fri 9.30am–5.30pm, Sat & Sun 9am–6pm; £22. ⊖ Baker Street.

Madame Tussaud's, just up Marylebone Road from Baker Street tube, has been pulling in the crowds ever since the good lady arrived in London from Paris in 1802 bearing the sculpted heads of guillotined aristocrats (she herself only just managed to escape the same fate – her uncle, who started the family business, was less fortunate). The entrance fee might be extortionate, the likenesses occasionally dubious and the automated dummies inept, but you can still rely on finding London's biggest queues here. The only way to avoid joining the line is to pay extra and book a timed entry ticket in advance over the phone or on the Internet. As well as the usual parade of wax figures, the tour features live actors trained to frighten the living daylights out of visitors in the Chamber of Horrors and ends with a manic five-minute "ride" through the history of London in a miniaturized taxi.

**You can buy tickets for Madame Tussaud's in advance on
℡0870/400 3000 or ⦿www.madame-tussauds.com**

Soho and Chinatown

When **Soho** – named for the cry that resounded through the district when it was a hunting ground – was first built over in the seventeenth century, its streets were among the most sought-after addresses in the capital. By the end of the eighteenth century, the rich had moved west to Mayfair, and Soho had become, along with the East End, the city's main dumping ground for immigrants: over the years it has welcomed French Huguenots, Italians, Irish, Jews and more recently Chinese.

Nowadays Soho is very much the heart of the West End, retaining a raffish air that's unique for central London. It's been the city's premier red light district for centuries, and has long been a favourite haunt of the capital's creative bohos and literati. Jazz and skiffle venues proliferated in the 1950s, folk and rock clubs in the 1960s, and punk at the end of the 1970s. The most recent transformation has seen it become Europe's leading gay centre, with lively bars and cafés bursting out from Old Compton Street.

Soho is bounded by Regent Street to the west, Oxford Street to the north and Charing Cross Road to the east. Conventional sights are few, yet, as one of the capital's most diverse and characterful areas, it's great to wander through, with probably more streetlife than anywhere else in London. Most folk head here to visit one of the big cinemas on **Leicester Square**, to drink in the latest hip bar or to grab a bite at the innumerable cafés and restaurants, ranging from the inexpensive Chinese places that pepper the tiny enclave of **Chinatown**, to old-established Italian joints and Michelin-starred restaurants in the backstreets.

For Soho's café, pub and restaurant
listings, see chapters 16, 17 & 18.

Leicester Square

Map 4, G7. ⊖ Leicester Square.

By night, when the big cinemas and discos are doing good business, and the buskers are entertaining the crowds, **Leicester Square** is one of the most crowded places in London, particularly on a Friday or Saturday when huge numbers of tourists and half the youth of the suburbs seem to congregate here. The square began to emerge as an entertainment zone in the mid-nineteenth century, with Turkish baths, accommodation houses (for prostitutes and their clients), oyster rooms and music halls; cinema moved in during the 1930s – a golden age evoked by the sleek black lines of the Odeon on the east side – and maintains its grip on the area.

At the centre of the square, within the gardens, is a copy of the Shakespeare memorial in Westminster Abbey, looked over by a statue of Charlie Chaplin (neither of whom has any connection with the square); around the edge are busts of Isaac Newton, William Hogarth, Joshua Reynolds and a Scottish surgeon, John Hunter – all of whom lived hereabouts in the eighteenth century when the place was still fashionable. If you find yourself near the monumentally ugly **Swiss Centre**, in the northwest corner, you may be assaulted by a five-minute medley played by the wall-mounted **campanile** (Mon–Fri noon & on the hour 6–8pm, Sat & Sun noon & on the hour 2–8pm) to a surreal procession of cows and peasants.

Chinatown

Map 4, F7. ⊖ Leicester Square.

Chinatown, hemmed in between Leicester Square and Shaftesbury Avenue, is a self-contained jumble of shops, cafés and restaurants that makes up one of London's most distinct and popular ethnic enclaves. **Gerrard Street**, Chinatown's main drag, has been endowed with ersatz touches – telephone kiosks rigged out as pagodas and fake oriental gates or *paifang* – though few of London's 60,000 Chinese actually live in the three small blocks of Chinatown. Nonetheless, it remains a focus for the community, a place to do business or the weekly shopping, celebrate a wedding, or just meet up for meals, particularly on Sundays, when the restaurants overflow with Chinese families tucking into *dim sum*.

The **Chinese New Year** celebrations, instigated here in 1973, are a community-based affair, drawing in thousands of Londoners for the Sunday nearest to New Year's Day (late Jan or early Feb). To a cacophony of fireworks, huge papier-mâché lions dance through the streets devouring cabbages hung from the upper floors by strings pinned with money. The noise is deafening and, if you want to see anything other than the backs of people's heads, you'll need to position yourself close to one of the cabbages around noon and stand your ground.

For Chinatown restaurant listings, see p.204.

For the rest of the year, most Londoners come to Chinatown simply to eat – easy and inexpensive enough to do, though the choice of **restaurants** is somewhat overwhelming, especially on Gerrard Street itself. Cantonese cuisine predominates, though there's a smattering of Shanghai and Szechuan outlets. You're unlikely to be disappointed wherever you go.

Charing Cross Road and Shaftesbury Avenue

Map 4, G6. ⊖ Leicester Square or Tottenham Court Road.

Charing Cross Road, Soho's eastern border and a thoroughfare from Trafalgar Square to Oxford Street, boasts the highest concentration of **bookshops** anywhere in London. One of the first to open here was Foyles at no. 119, which now struggles to compete with the nearby heavyweight chain bookshops such as Borders and Blackwell's. The street retains more of its original character south of Cambridge Circus, where you'll find Alhoda, the Islamic bookshop, along with a cluster of ramshackle secondhand bookshops, such as Quinto.

One of the nicest places for secondhand book browsing is **Cecil Court** (Map 4, G7), the southernmost alleyway between Charing Cross Road and St Martin's Lane. This short, pedestrianized street boasts specialist bookshops devoted to theatre, Italy, new age philosophies and the like, plus various antiquarian dealers. Another place you shouldn't miss, just off Charing Cross Road, is the **Photographers' Gallery** (Map 4, G7; Mon–Sat 11am–6pm, Sun noon–6pm; free; ⓦwww.photonet.org.uk) at 5 and 8 Great Newport St, which hosts temporary exhibitions that are invariably worth a look, and has a lovely, peaceful café.

Sweeping northeast towards Bloomsbury from Piccadilly Circus, and separating Soho proper from Chinatown, the gentle curve of **Shaftesbury Avenue** is the heart of mainstream theatreland, with numerous theatres and cinemas along its length. Like Charing Cross Road, it was conceived in the late 1870s, ostensibly to relieve traffic congestion but with the dual purpose of destroying the slums that lay in its path. Ironically, it was then named after Lord Shaftesbury, whose life had been spent trying to help the likes of those dispossessed by the road scheme.

Old Compton Street and central Soho

Map 4, F6. ⊖ Leicester Square or Piccadilly Circus.

If Soho has a main drag, it has to be **Old Compton Street**, which runs parallel with Shaftesbury Avenue. The peep shows, boutiques and trendy cafés here are typical of the area and a good barometer of the latest fads. Soho has been a permanent fixture on the **gay scene** for the better part of a century, and today gay bars, clubs and cafés jostle for position on Old Compton Street and around the corner in Wardour Street.

For gay and lesbian listings, see p.238.

The streets round here are lined with Soho institutions past and present. One of the best known is London's longest-running **jazz** club, *Ronnie Scott's*, on Frith Street, founded in 1958 and still capable of pulling in the big names. Opposite is *Bar Italia*, a venerable Italian café with late-night hours popular with Soho's clubbers. It was in this building, appropriately enough for an area in which many TV, film and media companies make their home, that John Logie Baird made the world's first public television transmission in 1926.

Wardour Street and beyond

Map 4, E6. ⊖ Leicester Square or Tottenham Court Road.

At the western end of Old Compton Street runs **Wardour Street**, a kind of dividing line between the trendier, eastern half of Soho and the slightly more porn-prolific western zone. The street is largely given over to the film and TV industry – Warner Bros is based here, along with numerous smaller production companies.

Immediately west of Wardour Street, the vice and prostitution rackets still have the area well staked out. Paul Raymond's long-established Folies Bergères-style *Revue Bar* on Brewer Street has finally closed, no doubt in part due to pressures from the slick lapdancing clubs leading the new boom in the West End sex industry, though there are still plenty of dodgy video shops and short con outfits operating all over Soho.

In among the video shops and triple-X-rated cinemas is the unlikely sight of **Berwick Street Market**, one of the capital's finest (and cheapest) fruit and vegetable markets (Mon–Sat). The street itself is no beauty spot, but the market's barrow displays are works of art in themselves, while, on either side of the marketholders, are some of London's best specialist record shops.

Carnaby Street

Map 4, D6. ⊖ Oxford Circus.

Until the 1950s, **Carnaby Street** (ⓦwww.carnaby.co.uk) was a backstreet on Soho's western fringe, occupied, for the most part, by sweatshop tailors who used to make up the suits for nearby Savile Row. Then, sometime in the mid-1950s, several trendy boutiques opened catering for the new market in flamboyant men's clothing. In the mid-1960s Mods, West Indian Rude Boys and other "switched-on people", as the *Daily Telegraph* noted, began to hang out here. The area quickly became the epicentre of Swinging Sixties London, and its street sign London's most popular postcard. A victim of its own hype, Carnaby Street quickly declined into an avenue of overpriced tack, and so it remained for the next twenty-odd years. More recently, things have started to pick up again as contemporary London fashion and hip record stores have now moved in, though it's never going to recapture the excitement of the 1960s.

Bloomsbury and the British Museum

Bloomsbury was built in grid-plan style from the 1660s onwards, and the formal bourgeois squares laid out then remain the area's main distinguishing feature. In the twentieth century, Bloomsbury acquired a reputation as the city's most learned quarter, dominated by the dual institutions of the **British Museum** and **London University**, and was home to many of London's chief book publishers, as well as literary luminaries like T.S. Eliot and Virginia Woolf. Today, the British Museum is clearly the star attraction, but there are some smaller, quirkier sights, including **Dickens' House** and the **Foundling Museum**. Only in its northern fringes does the character of the area change dramatically, becoming steadily seedier as you near the main line train stations of **Euston**, **St Pancras** and **King's Cross**.

The British Museum

Map 4, G3. Daily 10am–5.30pm, Thurs & Fri until 8.30pm; free; ⓦwww .british-museum.ac.uk ⊖ Tottenham Court Road or Russell Square.

The **British Museum** is one of the great museums of the world. With seventy thousand exhibits ranged over two and

4

The Bloomsbury Group

The **Bloomsbury Group** were essentially a bevy of upper middle-class friends who lived in and around Bloomsbury. The Group revolved around Virginia, Vanessa, Thoby and Adrian Stephen, who moved into 46 Gordon Square in 1904. Thoby's Thursday evening gatherings and Vanessa's Friday Club for painters attracted a whole host of Cambridge-educated snobs who subscribed to Oscar Wilde's theory that "aesthetics are higher than ethics". Their diet of "human intercourse and the enjoyment of beautiful things" was hardly revolutionary, but their behaviour, particularly that of the two sisters (unmarried, unchaperoned, intellectual and artistic), succeeded in shocking London society, especially through their louche sexual practices (most of the group swung both ways).

All this, though interesting, would be forgotten were it not for their individual work. In 1922 Virginia declared, without too much exaggeration, that "Everyone in Gordon Square has become famous". Lytton Strachey had been the first to make his name with *Eminent Victorians*, a series of unprecedentedly frank biographies; Vanessa, now married to the art critic Clive Bell, had become involved in Roger Fry's prolific design firm, Omega Workshop; and the economist John Maynard Keynes had become an adviser to the Treasury (he later went on to become the leading economic theorist of his day). The Group's most celebrated figure, Virginia, now married to Leonard Woolf and living in Tavistock Square, had become an established novelist; she and Leonard had also founded the Hogarth Press, which published T.S. Eliot's *The Waste Land* in 1922. Whatever their limitations, the Bloomsbury Group were Britain's most influential intellectual coterie of the interwar years, and their appeal shows little sign of waning.

a half miles of galleries, the museum boasts one of the largest and most comprehensive collections of antiquities, prints and drawings to be housed under one roof – seven million at the last count (a number increasing daily with the stream of new acquisitions, discoveries and bequests). Its assortment of Roman and Greek art is unparalleled, its Egyptian collection is the most significant outside Egypt and, in addition, there are fabulous treasures from Anglo-Saxon and Roman Britain, from China, Japan, India and Mesopotamia – not to mention an enormous collection of prints and drawings, only a fraction of which can be displayed at any one time.

The building itself, begun in 1823, is the grandest of London's Greek Revival edifices, dominated by the giant Ionian colonnade and portico that forms the main entrance. At the heart of the museum is the **Great Court** (Mon–Wed, Sat & Sun 9am–6pm, Thurs & Fri 9am–11pm), with its remarkable, curving glass-and-steel roof, designed by Norman Foster. At the centre stands the copper-domed former **Round Reading Room**, built in the 1850s to house the British Library. It was here, reputedly at desk O7, beneath one of the largest domes in the world, that Karl Marx penned *Das Kapital*. The building is now a public study area, and features a multimedia guide to the museum's displays.

You'll never manage to see everything in one visit, so the best advice is to concentrate on one or two areas of interest, or else sign up with one of the museum's **guided tours**. One place you could start is the BM's collection of **Roman and Greek antiquities**, perhaps most famous for the Parthenon sculptures, better known as the **Elgin Marbles**, after the British aristocrat who walked off with the reliefs in 1801.

The Great Court also houses the museum shop, with its excellent selection of books and periodicals, as well as a café and restaurant.

The museum's **Egyptian collection** is easily the most significant outside Egypt, and ranges from monumental sculptures, such as the colossal granite head of Amenophis III, to the ever-popular mummies and their ornate outer caskets. Also on display is the **Rosetta Stone**, which finally unlocked the secret of Egyptian hieroglyphs. Close by the Egyptian Hall, you'll find a splendid series of **Assyrian reliefs** from Nineveh, depicting events such as the royal lion hunts of Ashurbanipal, in which the king slaughters one of the cats with his bare hands. Among the most extraordinary artefacts from **Mesopotamia** are the enigmatic Ram in the Thicket (a lapis lazuli and shell statuette of a goat), an equally mysterious box known as the Standard of Ur, and the remarkable hoard of goldwork known as the Oxus Treasure.

The leathery half-corpse of the 2000-year-old **Lindow Man**, discovered in a Cheshire bog, and the Anglo-Saxon treasure from the **Sutton Hoo** ship burial, are among the highlights of the prehistoric and Romano-British collection. The medieval and modern collections, meanwhile, range from the twelfth-century Lewis chessmen, carved from walrus ivory, to twentieth-century exhibits such as a copper vase by Frank Lloyd Wright.

The dramatically lit Mexican and North American galleries, plus the African galleries in the basement, represent just a small fraction of the museum's **ethnographic collection**, while select works from the BM's enormous collection of **prints and drawings** can be seen in special exhibitions. In addition, there are fabulous **Oriental treasures** in the north wing, closest to the back entrance on Montague Place. The displays include ancient Chinese porcelain, ornate snuff-boxes, miniature landscapes, a bewildering array of Buddhist and Hindu deities.

Foundling Museum

Map 3, I2. Tues–Sat 10am–6pm, Sun noon–6pm; £5; ☏020/7841 3600, ⓦwww.foundlingmuseum.org.uk ❸ Russell Square.

The **Foundling Museum** tells the fascinating story of the Foundling Hospital, London's first home for abandoned children, founded in 1756 by retired sea captain Thomas Coram. As soon as it was opened, it was besieged, and soon forced to reduce its admissions drastically and introduce a ballot system. After 1801 only illegitimate children were admitted, and even then only after the mother had filled in a questionnaire and given a verbal statement confirming that "her good faith had been betrayed, that she had given way to carnal passion only after a promise of marriage or against her will; that she therefore had no other children; and that her conduct had always been irreproachable in every other respect".

One of the hospital's founding governors – he even fostered two of the children – was the artist **William Hogarth**, who decided to set up an art gallery at the hospital to give his fellow artists somewhere to display their works and to attract useful potential benefactors. As a result the museum boasts an impressive art collection including works by artists such as Gainsborough and Reynolds, now hung in the eighteenth-century interiors carefully preserved in their entirety from the original hospital. To the south of the museum, the hospital's original whitewashed loggia now forms the border with **Coram's Fields**, a wonderful inner-city park for children, with a whole host of hens, horses, sheep, pigs and rabbits. Adults are not allowed into the grounds unless accompanied by a child.

Dickens' House

Map 3, J3. Mon–Sat 10am–5pm, Sun 11am–5pm; £4; ⓦ www
.dickensmuseum.com ⊖ Russell Square.

Despite the plethora of blue plaques marking the residences of local luminaries, **Dickens' House**, at 48 Doughty St, in Bloomsbury's eastern fringes, is the area's only literary museum. Dickens moved here in 1837 shortly after his marriage to Catherine Hogarth, and they lived here for two years, during which time he wrote *Nicholas Nickleby* and *Oliver Twist*. Although the author painted a gloomy Victorian world in his books, the drawing room here, in which he entertained his literary friends, was decorated in a rather upbeat Regency style. Letters, manuscripts and first editions, the earliest known portrait (a miniature painted by his aunt in 1830) and the reading copies he used during extensive lecture tours in Britain and the States are the rewards for those with more than a passing interest in the novelist. You can also watch a film about his life (30min).

The University

Map 4, G2. Ⓦ www.lon.ac.uk ↔ Russell Square or Goodge Street.

London has more students than any other city in the world (over half a million at the last count), which isn't bad going for a city that only organized its own **University** in 1826, more than six hundred years after the likes of Oxford and Cambridge. The university started life in Bloomsbury, but it wasn't until after World War I that the institution really began to take over the area.

The university's piecemeal development means that its departments are spread over a wide area, though the main focus is between the 1930s **Senate House** skyscraper, behind the British Museum, and the Neoclassical **University College** (UCL; Ⓦ www.ucl.ac.uk), near the top of Gower Street. UCL is home to London's most famous art school, the **Slade**, which puts on temporary exhibitions from its collection in the **Strang Print Room**, in the south cloister of the main quadrangle (term-time Wed–Fri 1–5pm; free). Also on display in the south cloisters is the fully clothed skeleton of philosopher **Jeremy Bentham** (1748–1832), one of the university's founders, topped by a wax head and wide-brimmed hat.

The university also runs a couple of specialist museums. On the first floor of the D.M.S. Watson building on Malet Place, off Torrington Place, the **Petrie Museum of Egyptian Archeology** (Map 4, F1; Tues–Fri 1–5pm, Sat 10am–1pm; free; Ⓦ www.petrie.ucl.ac.uk) has a couple of rooms jam-packed with antiquities, including the world's oldest dress.

Further east down Torrington Place, tucked away in the southeast corner of Gordon Square, at no. 53, the **Percival David Foundation of Chinese Art** (Map 3, H3; Mon–Fri 10.30am–5pm; free; ⓦwww.pdfmuseum.org.uk) houses two floors of top-notch Chinese ceramics. Lastly, the temporary exhibitions of photography and art at the **Brunei Gallery** (Map 4, G1; Mon–Fri 10.30am–5pm; free), which is part of the School of Oriental and African Studies, east of Malet Street, are usually well worth visiting.

The British Library

Map 3, H2. Mon & Wed–Fri 9.30am–6pm, Tues 9.30am–8pm, Sat 9.30am–5pm, Sun 11am–5pm; free; ⓦwww.bl.uk ⊖ King's Cross or Euston.

The **British Library**, located on the busy Euston Road on the northern fringes of Bloomsbury, opened to the public in 1998. As the country's most expensive public building it was hardly surprising that the place drew fierce criticism from all sides. Yet while it's true that the building's red-brick brutalism is horribly out of fashion, and compares unfavourably with its cathedralesque Victorian neighbour, the former *Midland Grand Hotel*, the interior of the library has met with general approval, and the high-tech exhibition galleries are superb.

With the exception of the reading rooms, the library is open to the general public. The three exhibition galleries are to the left as you enter; straight ahead is the spiritual heart of the BL, a multistorey glass-walled tower housing the vast **King's Library**, collected by George III and donated to the museum by George IV in 1823; to the side of the King's Library are the pull-out drawers of the **philatelic collection**. If you want to explore the parts of the building not normally open to the public, you must sign up for a **guided tour** (Mon, Wed & Fri 3pm, Sat 10.30am & 3pm; £6; Sun 11.30am & 3pm if you want to see the reading rooms; £7).

The first of the three exhibition galleries to head for is the dimly lit **John Ritblat Gallery**, where a superlative selection of the BL's ancient manuscripts, maps, documents and precious books, including the richly illustrated Lindisfarne Gospels, is displayed. One of the most appealing innovations is **"Turning the Pages"**, a small room off the main gallery, where you can turn the pages of selected texts "virtually" on a computer terminal. The **Workshop of Words, Sounds and Images** is a hands-on exhibition of more universal appeal, where you can design your own literary publication, while the **Pearson Gallery of Living Words** puts on excellent temporary exhibitions, for which there is sometimes an admission charge.

Covent Garden and the Strand

Covent Garden's transformation from a fruit and vegetable market into a fashion-conscious *quartier* was one of the most miraculous and enduring developments of the 1980s. More sanitized and brazenly commercial than neighbouring Soho, it's a far cry from the district's heyday when the **piazza** was the great playground (and red-light district) of eighteenth-century London. The buskers in front of St Paul's Church, the nearby theatres and the **Royal Opera House** on Bow Street are survivors in this tradition, and on a balmy summer evening **Covent Garden Piazza** is still an undeniably lively place to be. Another positive side effect of the market development has been the renovation of the run-down warehouses to the north of the piazza, especially around the Neal Street area, which now boasts some of the most fashionable shops in the West End, selling everything from shoes to skateboards.

As its name suggests, the **Strand**, just to the south of Covent Garden, once lay along the riverbank: it achieved its present-day form when the Victorians shored up the banks of the Thames to create the Embankment. The Strand's most intriguing sight is **Somerset House,** the sole survivor of the street's grandiose river palaces, which now houses several museums and galleries as well as a lovely fountain courtyard.

Covent Garden Piazza

Map 4, I6. ⊖ Covent Garden.

London's oldest planned square, laid out in the 1630s by Inigo Jones, **Covent Garden Piazza** was initially a great success, its novelty value alone attracting a rich and aristocratic clientele. Over the next century, though, the tone of the place fell as the fruit and vegetable market expanded, and theatres and coffee houses began to take over the peripheral buildings. When the flower market closed in 1974, the piazza narrowly survived being turned into an office development. Instead, the elegant Victorian market hall and its environs were restored to house shops, restaurants and arts-and-crafts stalls.

St Paul's Church

Map 4, H7.

Of Jones's original piazza, the only remaining parts are the two rebuilt sections of north-side arcading, and **St Paul's Church**, facing the west side of the market building. The proximity of so many theatres has earned it the nickname of the "Actors' Church", and it's filled with memorials to international thespians from Boris Karloff to Gracie Fields. The space in front of the church's Tuscan portico – where Eliza Doolittle was discovered selling violets by Henry Higgins in George Bernard Shaw's *Pygmalion* – is now a legalized venue for buskers and street performers, who must audition for a slot months in advance.

The piazza's history of entertainment goes back to May 1662, when the first recorded performance of Punch and Judy in England was staged by Italian puppeteer Pietro Gimonde, and witnessed by Samuel Pepys. This historic event is commemorated every second Sunday in May by a **Punch and Judy Festival**, held in the gardens behind the church; for the rest of the year, the churchyard provides a tranquil respite from the activity outside (access is from King Street, Henrietta Street or Bedford Street).

London Transport Museum

Map 4, I6. Daily 10am–6pm, Fri opens 11am; £5.95; ⓦwww .ltmuseum.co.uk

A former flower-market shed on the piazza's east side is now home to the **London Transport Museum**, which is undergoing a thorough refurbishment and won't be open again until 2007. It's impossible to say how the museum will be set out, but you can be sure that there'll still be a great collection of old buses, trains and trams to clamber over and a whole lot of interactive fun to keep children amused.

Theatre Museum

Map 4, I6. Tues–Sun 10am–6pm; free; ⓦwww.theatremuseum.org

The rest of the old flower market now houses the **Theatre Museum**, an outpost of the V&A (see p.133) displaying three centuries of memorabilia from every conceivable area of the performing arts in the western world. The museum's temporary exhibitions are consistently engaging, as are the workshops, make-up demonstrations and occasional live performances.

The Royal Opera House

Map 4, I6. ☏020/7304 4000, ⓦwww.royaloperahouse.org

The arcading in the northeast side of the piazza was rebuilt as part of the redevelopment of the **Royal Opera House** (ⓦwww.royaloperahouse.org), whose main Neoclassical facade dates from 1811 and opens onto Bow Street. Now, however, you can reach the opera house from a passageway in the corner of the arcading. The spectacular wrought-iron

Floral Hall (daily 10am–3pm), on the first floor, serves as the opera house's main foyer, and is open to the public, as is the *Amphitheatre* bar/restaurant (open from 1hr 30min before the performance to the end of the last interval), which has a glorious terrace overlooking the piazza. For **backstage tours**, it's best to book in advance (Mon–Fri 10.30am, 12.30 & 2.30pm, Sat also 11.30am; £9; ☎020/7304 4000).

North of the piazza

Map 4, H6. ⊖ Covent Garden.

The area to the north of Covent Garden Piazza is, on the whole, more interesting in terms of its shops, pubs and eating places than the piazza itself. Floral Street, Long Acre, Shelton Street and especially Neal Street are all good shopping locales, with a mixture of chains, trendy designer shops and small, offbeat independent stores.

Looking east down the gentle curve of Long Acre, it's difficult to miss the austere, Pharaonic mass of the **Freemasons' Hall** (Map 4, I5; Mon–Fri 10am–5pm; free; ⊛freemasonry .london.museum), built as a memorial to all the masons who died in World War I. Whatever you may think of this reactionary, male-only, secretive organization, the interior is worth a peek for the Grand Temple alone, whose pompous, bombastic décor is laden with heavy symbolism. To see the Grand Temple, turn up for one of the free hourly **guided tours** (Mon–Fri usually 11am, noon, 2, 3 & 4pm; free; ☎020/7395 9258).

North from Long Acre runs **Neal Street**, one of the most-sought-after commercial addresses in Covent Garden, which features some fine Victorian warehouses, complete with stair towers for loading and shifting goods between floors. Today, Neal Street is dominated by big fashion stores like Mango and Diesel. A decade or so ago, though, the feel of the street was a lot less moneyed and more alternative – an ambience that partially survives in the area around **Neal's Yard**, a tiny little courtyard off Shorts Gardens, prettily festooned with flower boxes and ivy.

West of Neal Street is **Seven Dials** (Map 4, G6), the meeting point of seven streets which make up a little circus centred on a slender column topped by six tiny, blue sundials (the seventh dial is formed by the column itself and the surrounding road). **Earlham Street**, which runs west from Seven Dials, harbours an ironmonger's and a local butcher's alongside clubbers' shops. It was once a flourishing market street, and of the handful of stalls that remain is one of London's very best flower stalls – a visual treat at any time of year.

Strand

Map 4, H8. ⊖ Charing Cross or (Mon–Sat only) Temple.

Once famous for its riverside mansions, and later its music halls, the **Strand** – the main road connecting Westminster to the City – is a shadow of its former self. There's a vestige of the street's former glory at no. 440, home to what was once London's largest private bank, **Coutts & Co** (ⓦwww.coutts .com), whose customers include the Queen herself. It was founded in 1692 by the Scottish goldsmith, John Campbell, a mock-up of whose original premises stands behind a screen in the bank's concrete and marble atrium. Today's male employees still sport anachronistic tail-coated suits.

Some way further east on the opposite side of the Strand, the blind side street of Savoy Court – the only street in the country where the traffic drives on the right – leads to **The Savoy**, London's grandest hotel, built in 1889 on the site of the medieval Savoy Palace. César Ritz was the original manager, Guccio Gucci started out as a dishwasher here, and the list of illustrious guests is endless: Monet painted the Thames from one of the south-facing rooms, Sarah Bernhardt nearly died here, and Strauss the Younger arrived with his own orchestra.

Victoria Embankment

Map 4, I9. ⊖ Embankment.

The **Victoria Embankment**, built between 1868 and 1874, was the inspiration of French engineer Joseph Bazalgette, whose project simultaneously relieved congestion along the Strand, provided an extension to the underground railway and sewage systems, and created a new stretch of parkland with a riverside walk – no longer much fun due to the volume of traffic. The 1626 **York Watergate**, in the Victoria Embankment Gardens to the east of Villiers Street, gives you an idea of where the banks of the Thames used to be; the steps through the gateway once led down to the river.

London's oldest monument, **Cleopatra's Needle**, languishes little-noticed on the Thames side of the busy Victoria Embankment, guarded by two Victorian sphinxes. The 60-foot-high, 180-ton stick of granite in fact has nothing to do with Cleopatra – it's one of a pair erected in Heliopolis in 1475 BC (the other one is in New York's Central Park) and taken to Alexandria by the emperor Augustus fifteen years after Cleopatra's suicide. This obelisk was presented to Britain in 1819 by the Turkish viceroy of Egypt, but nearly sixty years passed before it finally made its way to London.

Aldwych

Map 5, A5. ⊖ Holborn or (Mon–Sat only) Temple.

The wide crescent of **Aldwych**, forming a neat "D" with the eastern part of the Strand, was driven through the slums of this zone in the last throes of the Victorian era. A confident ensemble occupies the centre, with the enormous **Australia House** and **India House** sandwiching **Bush House**, home of the BBC's World Service (ⓦwww.bbc.co.uk/worldservice) since 1940. Despite its thoroughly British associations, Bush House was actually built by the American speculator Irving T. Bush, whose planned trade-centre flopped in the 1930s. The giant figures on the north facade and the inscription,

"To the Eternal Friendship of English-speaking Nations", thus refer to the friendship between the US and Britain, and are not, as many people assume, the declaratory manifesto of the current occupants.

The eastern stretch of the Strand, beyond Aldwych, is covered in chapter 7.

Somerset House

Map 5, A6. Courtyard and terrace: daily 10am–11pm; free. Public rooms: daily 10am–6pm; free; ⓦwww.somerset-house.org.uk
⊖ Temple (Mon–Sat only) or Covent Garden.

Opposite the south side of Bush House stands **Somerset House**, sole survivor of the grand edifices which once lined this stretch of the riverfront, its four wings enclosing a large **courtyard**. From March to October, the courtyard features a wonderful 55-jet fountain that spouts straight from the cobbles; in winter, an ice rink is set up in its place. The present building was begun in 1776 by William Chambers as a purpose-built governmental office development, but now also houses a series of museums and galleries.

The south wing, overlooking the Thames, is home to the **Hermitage Rooms** (daily 10am–6pm; £6; ⓦwww.hermitage rooms.com), featuring changing displays drawn from St Petersburg's Hermitage Museum, and the **Gilbert Collection** (daily 10am–6pm; £5; ⓦwww.gilbert-collection.org .uk), a museum of decorative arts displaying gaudy European silver and gold nick-nacks, micro-mosaics, clocks, portrait miniatures and snuffboxes. Alternatively, save yourself some money and go and admire the Royal Naval Commissioners' gilded eighteenth-century barge in the **King's Barge House**, at ground level in the south wing.

In the north wing are the **Courtauld Institute galleries** (daily 10am–6pm; £5; free Mon 10am–2pm; ⓦwww.courtauld .ac.uk), chiefly known for their dazzling collection of

Impressionist and Post-Impressionist paintings. Among the most celebrated works are a small-scale version of Manet's *Déjeuner sur l'herbe*, Renoir's *La Loge*, and Degas's *Two Dancers*, plus a whole heap of Cézanne's canvases, including one of his series of *Card Players*. The Courtauld also boasts a fine selection of works by the likes of Rubens, Van Dyck, Tiepolo and Cranach the Elder. The collection has recently been augmented by the long-term loan of a hundred top-notch twentieth-century paintings and sculptures by, among others, Kandinksy, Matisse, Dufy, Derain, Rodin and Henry Moore.

St Mary-le-Strand and St Clement Danes

Map 5, B5. ⊖ Temple (Mon–Sat only) or Covent Garden.

Two historic churches survived the Aldwych development, and are now stranded amid the traffic of the Strand. The first is James Gibbs' **St Mary-le-Strand** (Mon–Fri 11am–4pm, Sun 10am–3pm), his first commission, completed in 1724 in Baroque style and topped by a delicately tiered tower. Even in the eighteenth century, parishioners complained of the noise from the roads, and it's incredible that recitals are still given here (Wed 1pm). The entrance is flanked by two lovely magnolia trees, and the interior has a particularly rich plastered ceiling in white and gold.

In allusion to his own St Mary's, Gibbs placed a 115-foot-tower on top of Christopher Wren's nearby **St Clement Danes** (daily 8.30am–4.30pm; ⓦwww.raf.mod.uk), whose bells play out the tune of the nursery rhyme "Oranges and Lemons" each day at 9am, noon, 3pm and 6pm. Reduced to a smouldering shell during the Blitz, St Clement Danes was handed over to the RAF in the 1950s and is now a very well-kept memorial to those killed in the air battles of the last war, the nave and aisles studded with more than 800 squadron and unit badges.

In front of the church are statues of the two wartime air chiefs: to the right, **Lord Dowding**, the man who oversaw the Battle of Britain; to the left, **Sir Arthur Harris** (better known as "Bomber Harris"), architect of the saturation bombing of Germany that resulted in the slaughter of thousands of civilians. Although Churchill was ultimately responsible, most of the opprobrium was left to fall on Harris, who was denied the peerage all the other service chiefs received, while his forces were refused a campaign medal.

6

Holborn, Clerkenwell and Hoxton

Holborn, **Clerkenwell** and **Hoxton** lie on the periphery of the financial district of the City. Holborn (pronounced "Ho-burn") has long been associated with the law, and its **Inns of Court** make for an interesting stroll, their archaic, cobbled precincts exuding the rarefied atmosphere of an Oxbridge college, and sheltering one of the city's oldest churches, the twelfth-century **Temple Church**. Close by the Inns, in Lincoln's Inn Fields, is the **Sir John Soane's Museum**, one of the most memorable and enjoyable of London's small museums, packed with architectural illusions and an eclectic array of curios.

Clerkenwell, further to the northeast, is definitely off the conventional tourist trail with just a few minor sights, including vestiges of two pre-Fire of London priories, and the **Marx Memorial Library**, where the exiled Lenin plotted revolution. Since the 1990s, however, parts of the area have been transformed and, to a certain extent, gentrified, by an influx of young, loft-living designers and media types, whose arrival has had a marked effect on the choice and style of bars and restaurants on offer.

Neighbouring Hoxton (aka Shoreditch), to the east, has also acquired a certain cachet due to the high density of artists and architects who currently live and/or work here. Visually, Hoxton, a slum area badly damaged in the Blitz, remains harsher on the eye than Clerkenwell, though it, too, has its fair share of trendy bars and restaurants. Several of London's contemporary art dealers now have Hoxton outlets, and there's the excellent **Geffrye Museum** of furniture design to aim for too.

- -

For details of restaurants and bars in
Clerkenwell and Hoxton, see p.206 and p.218.

- -

Temple and the Law Courts

Map 5, D5. ⊖ Temple (Mon–Sat only) or Covent Garden.

Temple is the largest and most complex of the Inns of Court, where every barrister in England must study before being called to the Bar. Temple itself is comprised of two Inns – **Middle Temple** (ⓦwww.middletemple.org.uk) and **Inner Temple** (ⓦwww.innertemple.org.uk) – both of which lie to the south of the Strand and, strictly speaking, just within the boundaries of the City of London. A few very old buildings survive here, but the overall scene is dominated by neo-Georgian reconstructions that followed the devastation of the Blitz. Still, the maze of courtyards and passageways is fun to explore – especially after dark, when Temple is gas-lit.

There are several points of access, simplest of which is Devereux Court. Medieval students ate, attended lectures and slept in the **Middle Temple Hall** (Mon–Fri 10am–noon & 3–4pm), across the courtyard, still the Inn's main dining room. The present building was constructed in the 1560s and provided the setting for many great Elizabethan masques and plays – Shakespeare's *Twelfth Night* is believed to have been premiered here in 1602. The hall is worth a visit for its fine hammer-beam roof, wooden panelling and decorative Elizabethan screen.

The two Temple Inns share use of the complex's oldest building, **Temple Church** (Wed–Sun 11am–4pm; ⊛www .templechurch.com), built in 1185 by the Knights Templar. An oblong chancel was added in the thirteenth century, and the whole building was damaged in the Blitz, but the original round church – modelled on the Church of the Holy Sepulchre in Jerusalem – still stands, with its striking Purbeck-marble piers, recumbent marble effigies of knights and tortured grotesques grimacing in the spandrels of the blind arcading.

Temple Bar and the Royal Courts of Justice

Map 5, C4. ⊖ Temple (Mon–Sat only).

If you walk to the top of Middle Temple Lane, you'll hit the Strand right at **Temple Bar**, a plinth topped by a winged dragon, the latest in a long line of structures marking the boundary between Westminster and the City of London.

Occupying the north side of the Strand before it hits Temple Bar are the **Royal Courts of Justice** (Mon–Fri 9am–4.30pm; ⊛www.hmcourts-service.gov.uk), home to the Court of Appeal and the High Court, where the most important civil cases are tried. Appeals and libel suits are heard here – it was from here that the Guildford Four and Birmingham Six walked to freedom, and it is here that countless pop and soap stars have battled it out with the tabloids. The fifty-odd courtrooms are open to the public, though you have to go through stringent security checks first (strictly no cameras allowed).

Lincoln's Inn Fields

Map 5, B2. ⊖ Holborn.

North of the Law Courts lies **Lincoln's Inn Fields**, London's largest square, laid out in the early 1640s with **Lincoln's Inn** (Mon–Fri 9am–6pm; ⊛www.lincolnsinn.org .uk), the first – and in many ways the prettiest – of the

Inns of Court on its east side. The Inn's fifteenth-century **Old Hall** is open by appointment only (☎020/7405 1393), but you can view the early seventeenth-century **chapel** (Mon–Fri noon–2pm), with its unusual fan-vaulted open undercroft and, on the first floor, its late Gothic nave, hit by a zeppelin in World War I and much restored since.

Hunterian Museum

Map 5, A2. Tues–Sat 10am–5pm; free; ⓦwww. rcseng.ac.uk
⊖ Holborn.

First opened in 1813 and beautifully refurbished in 2005, the **Hunterian Museum** (Tues–Sat 10am–5pm; free; ☎020/7869 6560, ⓦwww.rcseng.ac.uk), on the first floor of the Royal College of Surgeons building, contains the unique specimen collection of the surgeon-scientist, John Hunter (1728–93). Most of the exhibits are comprised of jars of pickled skeletons and body pieces – from a pig's tibia to a human tongue – prepared by Hunter himself and displayed as he wished in a "Crystal Gallery". The museum has even older exhibits, too, such as diarist John Evelyn's anatomical tables from the 1640s, in which arteries and nerves are displayed on wooden boards. Among the prize exhibits are the skeleton of the "Irish giant", Charles Byrne (1761–83), who was seven feet ten inches tall, and, in the adjacent McCrae Gallery, of the Sicilian midget Caroline Crachami (1815–24), who stood at only one foot ten and a half inches when she died at the age of nine.

Sir John Soane's Museum

Map 5, A2. Tues–Sat 10am–5pm; first Tues of the month also 6–9pm; free; ⓦwww.soane.org ⊖ Holborn.

A group of buildings on the north side of Lincoln's Inn Fields house the delightful **Sir John Soane's Museum**, one of London's best-kept secrets. The chief architect of the Bank of England, Soane (1753–1837) was an avid collector who designed this house not only as a home and office, but also as a place to stash his large collection of art and antiquities. Arranged much as it was in his lifetime, the ingeniously planned house has an informal, treasure-hunt atmosphere, with surprises in every alcove; the museum has also begun to exhibit contemporary art. At 2.30pm every Saturday, a fascinating, hour-long **guided tour** (£3) takes you round the museum and the enormous research library, next door, containing architectural drawings, books and exquisitely detailed cork and wood models.

Chancery Lane and Gray's Inn

Map 5, C2. ⊖ Holborn or Chancery Lane (Mon–Sat only).
Running along the eastern edge of Lincoln's Inn is legal London's main thoroughfare, **Chancery Lane**, home of the Law Society (the solicitors' regulatory body) and lined with shops where barristers, solicitors and clerks can buy their wigs, gowns, legal tomes, stationery and champagne. Halfway up the street are the **London Silver Vaults** (Map 5, C1; Mon–Fri 9am–5.30pm, Sat 9am–1pm; free; ⓦwww.thesilvervaults.com), which began life as the Chancery Lane Safe Deposit for London's wealthy elite, but now house a strange, claustrophobic lair of subterranean shops selling every kind of silverware – mostly antique, mostly English and often quite tasteless.

The last of the four Inns of Court, **Gray's Inn** (Map 3, J3; Mon–Fri 10am–4pm; ⓦwww.graysinn.org.uk), lies hidden to the north of High Holborn, at the top of Chancery Lane; the entrance is through an anonymous cream-coloured building next door to the venerable *Cittie of Yorke* pub. Established in the fourteenth century, most of what you see today was rebuilt after the Blitz, with the exception of the hall (by appointment only; ☏020/7458 7800), with its fabulous Tudor screen and stained glass, where Shakespeare's *Comedy of Errors* is thought to have premiered in 1594.

Heading east along High Holborn, it's worth pausing to admire **Staple Inn** (Map 5, D1) on the right, not one of the Inns of Court, but one of the now defunct Inns of Chancery, which used to provide a sort of foundation course for those aspiring to the Bar. Its overhanging half-timbered facade and gables date from the sixteenth century and are the most extensive in the whole of London. They survived the Great Fire, which stopped just short of Holborn Circus, but had to be extensively rebuilt after the Blitz.

Clerkenwell

Map 3, K3. ⊖ Farringdon.
Poverty and overcrowding were the main features of nineteenth-century Clerkenwell, and **Clerkenwell Green** became known in the press as "the headquarters of republicanism, revolution and ultra-non-conformity". The Green's connections with **radical politics** have continued and its oldest building, built as a Welsh Charity School in 1737, is now home to the **Marx Memorial Library** (Mon–Thurs 1–2pm or by appointment; closed Aug; free; ⓦwww.marxlibrary.net), at no. 37a. One-time headquarters of the Social Democratic Federation press, this is where **Lenin** edited seventeen editions of the Bolshevik paper *Iskra* in 1902–3. The poky little back room where he worked is maintained as it was then, as a kind of shrine – you can view it along with the workerist Hastings Mural from 1935.

St John's Gate

Map 3, K3. Mon–Fri 10am–5pm, Sat 10am–4pm; free; ⓦwww.sja.org .uk ⊖ Farringdon.
Of Clerkenwell's three medieval religious establishments, remnants of two survive, hidden away to the southeast of Clerkenwell Green. The oldest is the priory of the Order

of St John of Jerusalem; the sixteenth-century **St John's Gate**, on the south side of Clerkenwell Road, is the most visible survivor of the foundation. Today, the gatehouse forms part of a **museum**, which traces the development of the order before its dissolution in this country by Henry VIII, and its reestablishment in the nineteenth century. In 1877, the St John's Ambulance was founded to provide a voluntary first-aid service to the public. It's in this field that the order is now best known in Britain – a splendid interactive gallery is devoted to the history of the service.

To get to see the rest of the gatehouse, and to visit the Norman crypt of the Grand Priory Church over the road, you must take a **guided tour** (Tues, Fri & Sat 11am & 2.30pm; £5 donation requested).

Charterhouse

Map 3, L3. Guided tours only April–Aug Wed 2.15pm; £5 ⊖ Barbican.
A little to the southeast of St John's, on the edge of Smithfield, lies **Charterhouse**, founded in 1371 as a Carthusian monastery. The public school, with which the foundation is now most closely associated, moved out to Surrey in 1872, but forty-odd pensioners – known, in the monastic tradition, as "brothers" – continue to be cared for here. The only way to visit the site is to join one of the exhaustive two-hour **guided tours**, which start at the gatehouse on Charterhouse Square. Very little remains of the original monastic buildings, but there's plenty of Tudor architecture to admire, dating from after the Dissolution, when Charterhouse was rebuilt as a private residence.

Hoxton

Map 3, N2. ⊖ Old Street.
Until recently **Hoxton** was an unprepossessing amalgam of wholesale clothes and shoe shops, striptease pubs and roaring

traffic. Over the last decade, however, it has been colonized by artists, designers and architects and transformed itself into the city's most vibrant enclaves. The geographical focus of the area's current transformation is **Hoxton Square (**Map 3, N1), situated northeast of Old Street tube, a strange and not altogether happy mixture of light industrial units and artists' studios arranged around a leafy, formal square. Despite the lack of aesthetic charm, the area has become an increasingly fashionable place to live and work and several leading West End **art galleries** have opened up premises here, among them Jay Jopling's White Cube at the south end of the square itself. Otherwise, there are no real sights as such.

Wesley's Chapel

Map 3, M2. Mon–Sat 10am–4pm, Sun noon–1.45pm; free; ⓦwww .wesleyschapel.org.uk ⊖ Old Street.

Set back from City Road stands the Georgian ensemble of **Wesley's Chapel and House** (Mon–Sat 10am–4pm; free). A place of pilgrimage for Methodists, the uncharacteristically ornate chapel, built in 1777, heralded the coming of age of Wesley's sect. Predictably, the **Museum of Methodism** in the basement makes only a passing reference to the insanely jealous 40-year-old widow Wesley married, and who eventually left him. Wesley himself spent his last two years in the delightful Georgian house to the right of the main gates, and inside you can see his deathbed, plus an early shock-therapy machine of which he was particularly fond.

Geffrye Museum

Map 3, N1. Tues–Sat 10am–5pm, Sun noon–5pm; free; ⓦwww.geffrye-museum.org.uk ⊖ Liverpool Street then bus #149 or #242.

Hoxton's one conventional tourist sight is the **Geffrye Museum**, a museum of furniture design, set back from Kingsland Road in a peaceful little enclave of eighteenth-century ironmongers' almshouses. A series of period living rooms, ranging from the oak-panelled seventeenth century through refined Georgian and cluttered Victorian, leads to the state-of-the-art New Gallery Extension, housing the excellent twentieth-century section and a pleasant café/restaurant.

7

The City

T he City is where London began. Long established as
the financial district, it stretches from Temple Bar in
the west to the Tower of London in the east – administrative boundaries that are only slightly larger than
those marked by the old Roman walls and their medieval
successors. However, in this Square Mile (as the City is sometimes called), you'll find few leftovers of London's early days,
since four-fifths of the area burned down in the Great Fire of
1666. Rebuilt in brick and stone, the City gradually lost its
centrality as London swelled westwards, though it has maintained its position as Britain's financial heartland. What you
see now is mostly the product of three fairly recent phases:
the Victorian construction boom of the late nineteenth
century; the postwar reconstruction following the Blitz; and
the building frenzy that began in the 1980s, which has seen
nearly fifty percent of the City's office space rebuilt.

When you consider what has happened here, it's amazing that so much has survived to pay witness to the City's
two-thousand-year history. Wren's spires still punctuate
the skyline here and there, and his masterpiece, **St Paul's
Cathedral**, remains one of London's geographical pivots.
At the eastern edge of the City, the **Tower of London** still
stands protected by some of the best-preserved medieval-
fortifications in Europe. Other relics, such as the City's few
surviving medieval alleyways, Wren's **Monument** to the

The Corporation of London

The one unchanging aspect of the City is its special status, conferred on it by William the Conqueror and extended and reaffirmed by successive monarchs and governments ever since. Nowadays, with its Lord Mayor, its Beadles, Sheriffs and Aldermen, its separate police force and its select electorate of freemen and liverymen, the City is an anachronism of the worst kind and pretty much a law unto itself. **The Corporation** (ⓦ www .corpoflondon.gov.uk), which runs the City like a one-party mini-state, is an unreconstructed old boys' network whose medievalist pageantry camouflages the very real power and wealth which it holds – the Corporation owns nearly a third of the Square Mile (and several tracts of land elsewhere in and around London). Its anomalous status is all the more baffling when you consider that the City was once the cradle of British democracy: it was the City that traditionally stood up to bullying sovereigns.

Great Fire, and London's oldest synagogue and church, are less conspicuous, and even locals have problems finding the more modern attractions such as the **Museum of London** and the **Barbican** arts complex.

Perhaps the biggest change of all, though, has been in the City's population. Up until the eighteenth century the majority of Londoners lived and worked in or around the City; nowadays over a million commuters spend the best part of Monday to Friday here, but only five thousand people remain at night and at weekends. The result of this demographic shift is that the City is fully alive only during office hours. This means that by far the **best time to visit** is during the week, since many pubs, restaurants and even some tube stations and tourist sights close down at the weekend.

Fleet Street

Map 5, E4. ⊖ Temple (Mon–Sat only) or Blackfriars.

In 1500 a certain Wynkyn de Worde, a pupil of William

Caxton, moved the Caxton presses from Westminster to **Fleet Street**, in order to be close to the lawyers of the Inns of Court and to the clergy of St Paul's. However, the street really boomed two hundred years later, when in 1702, the now defunct *Daily Courant*, Britain's first daily newspaper, was published from here. By the nineteenth century, all the major national and provincial dailies had their offices and printing presses in the Fleet Street district, a situation that prevailed until the 1980s, when the press barons relocated their operations elsewhere.

The best source of information about the old-style Fleet Street is the so-called "journalists' and printers' cathedral", the church of **St Bride's** (Map 5, F4; Mon–Fri 9am–5pm, Sat 11am–3pm; @www.stbrides.com), which boasts Wren's tallest and most exquisite spire (said to be the inspiration for the tiered wedding cake). The crypt contains a little museum of Fleet Street history, with information on the *Daily Courant* and the *Universal Daily Register*, which later became *The Times*, claiming to be "the faithful recorder of every species of intelligence ... circulated for a particular set of readers only".

The western section of Fleet Street was spared the Great Fire, which stopped just short of **Prince Henry's Room** (Map 5, D4; Mon–Sat 11am–2pm; free; @www.cityoflondon .gov.uk/phr), a fine Jacobean house with timber-framed bay windows. The first-floor room now contains material relating to the diarist **Samuel Pepys**, who was born nearby in Salisbury Court in 1633 and baptized in St Bride's. Even if you've no interest in Pepys, the wooden-panelled room is worth a look – it contains one of the finest Jacobean plasterwork ceilings in London, and a lot of original stained glass.

Numerous narrow alleyways lead off the north side of Fleet Street, two of which – Bolt Court and Hind Court – eventually open out into Gough Square, on which stands **Dr Johnson's House** (Map 5, E3; May–Sept Mon–Sat 11am–5.30pm; Oct–April Mon–Sat 11am–5pm; £4.50; @www.drjh.dircon.co.uk). The great savant, writer and lexicographer lived here from 1747 to 1759 whilst compiling the 41,000 entries for the first dictionary of the English language, two first editions of which can be seen in the grey-panelled rooms of the house. You can also view the open-plan attic, in which Johnson and his six helpers put together the dictionary.

St Paul's Cathedral

Map 5, I4. Mon–Sat 8.30am–4pm; £8; Ⓦwww.stpauls.co.uk ⊖ St Paul's.
Designed by Christopher Wren and completed in 1711, **St Paul's Cathedral** remains a dominating presence in

The Blitz

The **Blitz** bombing of London in World War II began on September 7, 1940, and continued for 57 consecutive nights, then intermittently until the final and most devastating attack on the night of May 10, 1941, when 550 Luftwaffe planes dropped more than 100,000 incendiaries and hundreds of explosive bombs in a matter of hours. The death toll that night topped 1400, bringing the total killed during the Blitz to between 20,000 and 30,000, with some 230,000 homes wrecked. Along with the East End, the City was particularly badly hit: in a single raid on December 29 (dubbed the "Second Fire of London"), 1400 fires broke out across the Square Mile.

The authorities were ready to build mass graves, but unable to provide adequate air-raid shelters. Around 180,000 Londoners made use of the tube, despite initial government reluctance, by simply buying a ticket and staying below ground. The cheery photos of singing and dancing in the Underground which the censors allowed to be published tell nothing of the stale air, rats and lice that people had to contend with. And even the tube stations couldn't withstand a direct hit, as occurred at Bank, when more than 100 died. In the end, the vast majority of Londoners – some sixty percent – simply stayed at home in their back-garden shelters or hid under the sheets and prayed.

the City, despite the encroaching tower blocks. Topped by an enormous lead-covered dome that's second in size only to St Peter's in Rome, its showpiece west facade is particularly magnificent. Westminster Abbey has the edge, however, when it comes to celebrity corpses, pre-Reformation sculpture, royal connections and sheer atmosphere. St Paul's, by contrast, is a soulless but perfectly calculated architectural set piece, a burial place for captains rather than kings – though it does contain more artists than Westminster Abbey.

The best place from which to appreciate the glory of St Paul's is beneath the **dome**, decorated (against Wren's wishes) by Thornhill's trompe l'oeil frescoes. The most richly decorated section of the cathedral, however, is the Quire or **chancel**, where the mosaics of birds, fish, animals and greenery, dating from the 1890s, are particularly spectacular. The intricately carved oak and limewood **choir stalls**, and the imposing organ case, are the work of Wren's master carver, Grinling Gibbons. Meanwhile, in the south-choir aisle you'll find the only complete effigy to have survived from Old St Paul's, the upstanding shroud of **John Donne**, poet, preacher and one-time dean of St Paul's.

The cathedral's services, featuring the renowned St Paul's choir, are held Mon–Sat 5pm, Sun 10am, 11.30am & 3.15pm.

A series of stairs, beginning in the south aisle, leads to the dome's three **galleries**, the first of which is the internal **Whispering Gallery**, so called because of its acoustic properties – words whispered to the wall on one side are distinctly audible over 100ft away on the other, though the place is often so busy you can't hear much above the hubbub. The other two galleries are exterior: the wide **Stone Gallery**, around the balustrade at the base of the dome; and ultimately the tiny **Golden Gallery**, below the golden ball and cross which top the cathedral.

The City of London tourist office, to the south of
St Paul's, is open May–Sept daily 9.30am–5pm; Oct–April
Mon–Fri 9.30am–5pm; ☎020/7332 1456, ⓦwww
.cityoflondon.gov.uk

Although the nave is crammed full of overblown monuments to military types, burials in St Paul's are confined to
the **crypt**, reputedly the largest in Europe. The whitewashed
walls and bright lighting, however, make this one of the
least atmospheric mausoleums you could imagine. Immediately to your right you'll find Artists' Corner, which boasts
as many painters and architects as Westminster Abbey has
poets, including Christopher Wren himself, who was commissioned to build the cathedral after its Gothic predecessor,
Old St Paul's, was destroyed in the Great Fire. The crypt's
two other star tombs are those of **Nelson** and **Wellington**,
both occupying centre stage and both with more fanciful
monuments upstairs.

Paternoster Square to Smithfield

Map 5, H3. ⊖ St Paul's.

The Blitz destroyed the area immediately to the north of
St Paul's. In its place, the City authorities built the brazenly
modernist **Paternoster Square**, a grim pedestrianized
piazza that has now been demolished to make way for a new,
more restrained master plan courtesy of William Whitfield,
who is seen as a compromise choice in the modernism-
versus-classicism debate. One happy consequence of the
square's redevelopment is that **Temple Bar**, the last surviving City gate, found its way back to London after over a
hundred years of exile, languishing in a park in Hertfordshire.
Designed by Wren himself, the triumphal arch used to stand
at the top of Fleet Street, and was used to display the heads
of traitors (see p.80). Looking weathered but clean, it now
forms the entrance to Paternoster Square from St Paul's,

with the Stuart monarchs James I and Charles II and their consorts occupying the niches.

To the west along Newgate Street, you'll find the Central Criminal Court, more popularly known as the **Old Bailey** (Mon–Fri 10.30am–1pm & 2–4pm; ☏020/7248 3277, ⓦwww.cjsonline.org). Built on the site of the notoriously harsh Newgate Prison, where folk used to come to watch public hangings, the Old Bailey is now the venue for all the country's most serious criminal court cases; you can watch the proceedings from the visitors' gallery, but note that bags, cameras, mobiles, personal stereos and food and drink are not allowed in, and there is no cloakroom.

St Bartholomew's Hospital and church

Map 5, H1. ⊖ St Paul's or Farringdon.
North of the Old Bailey lies **St Bartholomew's Hospital**, affectionately known to Londoners as Bart's. It's the oldest hospital in London, founded in 1123 by Rahere, court jester to Henry I, on the orders of St Bartholomew, who appeared to him in a vision while he was in malarial delirium on a pilgrimage to Rome. You can visit the hospital's church, and the nearby **museum** (Tues–Fri 10am–4pm; free), which has a short video on the history of Bart's. This also gives you a chance to glimpse the mid-eighteenth-century interior, which features murals by Hogarth. To see and learn more, you need to go on a **guided tour** (Fri 2pm; £4; ☏020/7601 8152), which also takes in Smithfield and the surrounding area.

St Bartholomew-the-Great (Map 7, A1; Tues–Fri 8.30am–5pm, Sat 10.30am–1.30pm, Sun 8.30am–1pm & 2.30–8pm; mid-Nov to mid-Feb closes 4pm Tues–Fri; ⓦwww.greatstbarts.com), hidden away to the north of the hospital, is London's oldest and most exquisite parish church. Begun in 1123, it was partly demolished in the Reformation, and afterwards fell into ruins. Restoration didn't begin until 1887, though by no means the whole church was rebuilt.

To get an idea of the scale of the original, approach through the half-timbered Tudor **gatehouse** on Little Britain Street, which incorporates the thirteenth-century arch that once formed the entrance to the nave. One side of the medieval cloisters survives to the south, as does the **chancel**, where stout Norman pillars separate the main body of the church from the ambulatory. There are various pre-Fire monuments to admire, the most prominent being the tomb of Rahere itself, which shelters under a fifteenth-century canopy north of the main altar.

Smithfield

Map 5, F1. ⊖ Farringdon.

Smithfield, to the north of Bart's, was for a long time a popular venue for **public executions** – in particular burnings, which reached a peak during the reign of "Bloody" Mary, when hundreds of Protestants were burned at the stake for their beliefs. These days, Smithfield is synonymous with its **meat market**, and if you want to see it in action, you'll need to get here early – the activity starts around 4am and is all over by 9am or 10am. The compensation for getting up at this ungodly hour are the early licensing laws, which mean you can get a hearty breakfast and an early-morning pint from the local pubs.

Museum of London

Map 7, B1. Mon–Sat 10am–5.50pm, Sun noon–5.50pm; free; Ⓦwww .museumoflondon.org.uk ⊖ St Paul's or Barbican.

Despite London's long pedigree, very few of its ancient structures are now standing. However, numerous Roman, Saxon and Elizabethan remains have been discovered during the City's various rebuildings, and many of these finds are now displayed at the **Museum of London**, hidden above the western end of London Wall, in the southwestern corner of the Barbican complex. The museum's permanent exhibition is basically an educational trot through London's past from prehistory to the present day; hence the large number of school groups who pass through. The displays are imaginatively set out, if a little dated, with only the new prehistory gallery having much in the way of hands-on stuff. Specific exhibits to look out for include the Bucklersbury Roman mosaic; a pair of Wellington's boots; and the Lord Mayor's heavily gilded coach (still used for state occasions). The real strength of the museum, though, lies in the excellent temporary exhibitions, lectures, walks and videos it organizes throughout the year.

The Barbican

Map 7, D1. ⊖ Barbican or Moorgate.
The City's only large residential complex is the **Barbican**, a phenomenally ugly and expensive concrete ghetto built on the heavily bombed Cripplegate area. The zone's solitary prewar building is the heavily restored sixteenth-century church of **St Giles Cripplegate** (Map 7, C1; Mon–Fri 11am–4pm), situated across from the infamously user-repellent **Barbican Arts Centre** (ⓦwww.barbican.org.uk), London's supposed answer to Paris's Pompidou Centre, which was formally opened in 1982. The complex, which is at least traffic-free, serves as home to the London Symphony Orchestra and holds free gigs in the foyer area.

Guildhall

Map 7, D2. May–Sept daily 10am–5pm; Oct–April Mon–Sat 10am–5pm; free; ⓦwww.cityoflondon.gov.uk ⊖ St Paul's or Bank.
Situated at the geographical centre of the City, **Guildhall** has been the ancient seat of the City administration for over eight hundred years. It remains the headquarters of the Corporation of London (see p.88), and is still used for many of the City's formal civic occasions. Architecturally, however, it is not quite the beauty it once was, having been badly

damaged in both the Great Fire and the Blitz, and scarred by the addition of a 1970s concrete cloister and wing.

Nonetheless, the **Great Hall**, basically a postwar reconstruction of the fifteenth-century original, is worth a brief look, as is the **Clockmakers' Museum** (Mon–Fri 9.30am–4.30pm; free; ⊕www.clockmakers.org), a collection of more than six hundred timepieces, including one of the clocks that won John Harrison the Longitude prize (see p.159). Also worth a visit is the purpose-built **Guildhall Art Gallery** (Mon–Sat 10am–5pm, Sun noon–4pm; £2.50, free Fri and daily after 3.30pm), which contains one or two exceptional works, such as Rossetti's *La Ghirlandata* and Holman Hunt's *The Eve of St Agnes*, plus a massive painting depicting the 1782 Siege of Gibraltar, commissioned by the Corporation, and a marble statue of Margaret Thatcher. In the basement, you can view the remains of a **Roman amphitheatre**, dating from around 120 AD, which was discovered during the gallery's construction.

Bank and around

Map 7, F4. ⊖ Bank.

Bank is the finest architectural arena in the City. The heart of the finance sector and the busy meeting point of eight streets, it's overlooked by a handsome collection of Neoclassical buildings – among them the Bank of England, the Royal Exchange and Mansion House (the Lord Mayor's official residence) – each one faced in Portland stone.

Sadly, only the **Bank of England** (Map 7, F3; ⊕www .bankofengland.co.uk), which stores the nation's vast gold reserves in its vaults, actually encourages visitors. Established in 1694 by William III to raise funds for the war against France, the so-called "Grand Old Lady of Threadneedle Street" wasn't erected on its present site until 1734. All that remains of the building on which architect John Soane spent the best part of his career from 1788 onwards is the windowless, outer curtain wall, which wraps itself round the

3.5-acre island site. However, you can view a reconstruction of Soane's Bank Stock Office, with its characteristic domed skylight, in the **museum** (Mon–Fri 10am–5pm; free), which has its entrance on Bartholomew Lane.

Three churches worth exploring are situated to the south of Bank. On Walbrook, behind Mansion House, stands the church of **St Stephen Walbrook** (Map 7, E4; Mon–Thurs 10am–4pm, Fri 10am–3pm), Wren's most spectacular after St Paul's, with dark-wood furnishings by Grinling Gibbons. Hidden a short distance down King William Street is **St Mary Woolnoth** (Map 7, F4; Mon–Fri 7.45am–5pm), a typically idiosyncratic creation of Nicholas Hawksmoor, one of Wren's pupils, featuring a striking altar canopy held up by barley-sugar columns. A complete contrast to Hawksmoor's church is provided by Wren's **St Mary Abchurch** (Map 7, F5; Mon–Thurs 10am–2pm), on Abchurch Lane, off King William Street. The interior is dominated by a vast dome fresco painted by a local parishioner and lit by oval lunettes, while the lime-wood reredos is again by Gibbons.

The Gherkin and Lloyd's

Map 7, H4. ⊖ Bank or Monument.

To the south of St Helen is the giant, bland Commercial Union skyscraper, now thoroughly upstaged by Norman Foster's glass diamond-clad **Gherkin**, officially known as 30 St Mary Axe (ⓦwww.30stmaryaxe.com) and currently headquarters of the reinsurers Swiss Re. Completed in 2003, it occupies the site of the old Baltic Exchange, destroyed by the 1990s IRA bombing campaign. It's obscenely large – at 590ft it's only just surpassed by the NatWest Tower (now known as Tower 42) – but most Londoners seem to quite like it for its cheeky shape.

To the south, on Leadenhall Street, stands Richard Rogers' glitzy **Lloyd's Building**, completed in 1984. "A living, breathing machine" of a building, it's a vertical version of Rogers' own Pompidou Centre, a jumble of blue-steel pipes with glass lifts zipping up and down the exterior. Despite the building's modernity, it's still guarded by porters in antiquated waiters' livery, in recognition of the company's modest origins in a seventeenth-century coffee house.

⑦ Bevis Marks Synagogue

Map 7, J3. Guided tours Wed & Fri noon, Sun 11.15am; £2; Ⓦwww .sandp.org ⊖ Aldgate or Liverpool Street.

Hidden away behind a modern red-brick office block in a little courtyard off Bevis Marks, north up St Mary Axe from the Lloyd's Building, the **Bevis Marks Synagogue** was built in 1701 by Sephardic Jews who had fled the Inquisition in Spain and Portugal. This is the country's oldest surviving synagogue, and its roomy, rich interior gives an idea of just how wealthy the congregation was at the time. Nowadays, the Sephardic community has dispersed across London and the congregation has dwindled, though the magnificent array of chandeliers makes it popular for candle-lit Jewish weddings.

London Bridge and the Monument

Map 7, F7. ⊖ Monument.

Until 1750, **London Bridge** was the only bridge across the Thames. The Romans were the first to build a permanent crossing here, but it was the medieval bridge that achieved world fame: built of stone and crowded with timber-framed houses, it became one of the great attractions of London (there's a model in the nearby church of St Magnus the Martyr, Map 7, G6; Tues–Fri 10am–4pm, Sun 10am–1pm). The houses were finally removed in the mid-eighteenth century, and a new stone bridge erected in 1831; that one now stands in the middle of the Arizona desert, having been bought for $2.4 million in the late 1960s by a gentleman who, so the story goes, was under the impression he had purchased Tower Bridge. The present concrete structure, without doubt the ugliest yet, dates from 1972.

The Great Fire of London

In the early hours of September 2, 1666, the **Great Fire** broke out at Farriner's, the king's bakery in Pudding Lane. The Lord Mayor refused to lose any sleep over it, dismissing it with the line, "Pish! A woman might piss it out." Four days and four nights later, the Lord Mayor was found crying "like a fainting woman": the Fire had destroyed some four-fifths of London, including 87 churches, 44 livery halls and 13,200 houses. The medieval city was no more.

Miraculously, there were only nine recorded fatalities, but 100,000 people were made homeless. "The hand of God upon us, a great wind and a season so very dry" was the verdict of the parliamentary report on the Fire; Londoners preferred to blame Catholics and foreigners. The poor baker eventually "confessed" to being an agent of the pope and was executed, after which the following words, "but Popish frenzy, which wrought such horrors, is not yet quenched", were added to the Latin inscription on the Monument. (The lines were erased in 1831.)

The only reason to go anywhere near London Bridge is to see the **Monument** (Map 7, G6; daily 9am–5.30pm; £2), which was designed by Wren to commemorate the Great Fire of 1666. Crowned with spiky gilded flames, this plain Doric column stands 202ft high, making it the tallest isolated stone column in the world; if it were laid out flat it would touch the bakery where the Fire started, east of Monument. The bas-relief on the base, now in very bad shape, depicts Charles II and the Duke of York in Roman garb conducting the emergency relief operation. The 311 steps to the viewing gallery once guaranteed an incredible view; nowadays it is somewhat dwarfed by the buildings around it.

The Tower of London

Map 7, K7. March–Oct Mon & Sun 10am–6pm, Tues–Sat 9am–6pm; Nov–Feb closes 5pm; £14.50; ⓦ www.hrp.org.uk ⊖ Tower Hill.

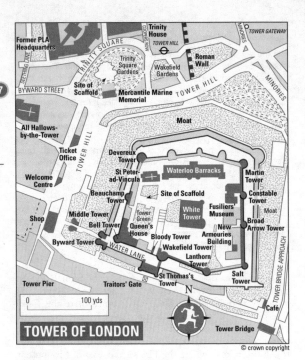

Former PLA Headquarters
Trinity House
TOWER HILL
TOWER GATEWAY
COPPER ROW
SEETHING LANE
BYWARD STREET
Trinity Square Gardens
Wakefield Gardens
Roman Wall
MINORIES
MINORIES
Site of Scaffold
Mercantile Marine Memorial
TOWER HILL
All Hallows-by-the-Tower
Ticket Office
Moat
TOWER HILL
Devereux Tower
Welcome Centre
St Peter-ad-Vincula
Waterloo Barracks
Martin Tower
Beauchamp Tower
Site of Scaffold
Constable Tower
White Tower
Fusiliers' Museum
Moat
Shop
Middle Tower
Tower Green
Broad Arrow Tower
Bell Tower
Queen's House
New Armouries Building
Byward Tower
Bloody Tower
WATER LANE
Wakefield Tower
Lanthorn Tower
Salt Tower
TOWER BRIDGE APPROACH
Tower Pier
Traitors' Gate
St Thomas's Tower
N
0   100 yds
Café
TOWER OF LONDON
Tower Bridge
© crown copyright

One of Britain's main tourist attractions, the **Tower of London** overlooks the river at the eastern boundary of the old city walls. Despite all the hype and heritage claptrap, it remains one of London's most remarkable buildings, site of some of the goriest events in the nation's history and somewhere all visitors and Londoners should explore at least once. Chiefly famous as a place of imprisonment and death, it has variously been used as a royal residence, armoury, mint, menagerie, observatory and – a function it still serves – a safe-deposit box for the Crown Jewels.

Before you set off to explore the Tower complex, it's a good idea to get your bearings by taking one of the free **guided tours**, given every thirty minutes or so by one of the Tower's **Beefeaters** (officially known as Yeoman Warders). Visitors today enter the Tower along Water Lane, but in times gone by most prisoners were delivered through **Traitors' Gate**, on the waterfront. The nearby **Bloody Tower**, which forms the main entrance to the Inner Ward, is where the 12-year-old Edward V and his 10-year-old brother were accommodated "for their own safety" in 1483 by their uncle, the future Richard III, and later murdered. It's also where **Walter Ralegh** was imprisoned on three separate occasions, including a thirteen-year stretch.

The **White Tower**, at the centre of the Inner Ward, is the original "Tower", begun in 1076, and now home to displays from the **Royal Armouries**. Even if you've no interest in military paraphernalia, you should at least pay a visit to the **Chapel of St John**, a beautiful Norman structure on the second floor that was completed in 1080 – making it the oldest intact church building in London. To the west of the White Tower is the execution spot on **Tower Green** where seven highly placed but unlucky individuals were beheaded, among them Anne Boleyn and her cousin Catherine Howard (Henry VIII's second and fifth wives).

The Waterloo Barracks, to the north of the White Tower, hold the **Crown Jewels**, perhaps the major reason so many people flock to the Tower; however, the moving walkways are disappointingly swift, allowing you just 28 seconds' viewing during peak periods. The oldest piece of regalia is the twelfth-century **Anointing Spoon**, but the vast majority of exhibits postdate the Commonwealth (1649–60), when many of the royal riches were melted down for coinage or sold off. Among the jewels are the three largest cut diamonds in the world, including the legendary **Koh-i-Noor**, set into the Queen Mother's Crown in 1937.

Tower Bridge

Map 7, K8. Daily 9.30am–6pm; £5.50; ⓦwww.towerbridge.org.uk
⊖ Tower Hill.

Tower Bridge ranks with Big Ben as the most famous of all London landmarks. Completed in 1894, its neo-Gothic towers are clad in Cornish granite and Portland stone, but conceal a steel frame, which, at the time, represented a considerable engineering achievement, allowing a road crossing that could be raised to give tall ships access to the upper reaches of the Thames. The raising of the bascules (from the French for "see-saw") remains an impressive sight – phone ahead to find out when the bridge is opening (ⓣ020/7940 3984). For a fee, you get to take the lift to the elevated walkways linking the summits of the towers – closed from 1909 to 1982 due to their popularity with prostitutes and the suicidal – and visit the Engine Room, on the south side of the bridge, where you can see the now-defunct giant coal-fired boilers which drove the hydraulic system until 1976 and play some interactive engineering games.

8

The East End and Docklands

Few places in London have engendered as many myths as the **East End**, a catch-all title which covers just about everywhere east of the City, but has its heart closest to the latter. Its name is synonymous with slums, sweatshops and crime, as epitomized by antiheroes such as Jack the Ripper and the Kray Twins, but also with the rags-to-riches careers of the likes of Harold Pinter and Vidal Sassoon, and whole generations of Jews who were born in the most notorious of London's cholera-ridden quarters and have now moved to wealthier pastures. Old East Enders will tell you that the area's not what it was – and it's true, as it always has been. The East End is constantly changing as newly arrived immigrants assimilate and move out.

The East End's first immigrants were French Protestant **Huguenots**, fleeing religious persecution in the late seventeenth century. Within three generations the Huguenots were entirely assimilated, and the **Irish** became the new immigrant population, but it was the influx of **Jews** escaping pogroms in eastern Europe and Russia that defined the character of the East End in the second half of the nineteenth century. The area's Jewish population has now dispersed throughout London, though the East End remains at the bottom of the pile; even the millions poured into the **Docklands** development have failed to make much impression on local unemployment and housing problems. Racism is still a problem, and is directed, for the most part, against the large **Bengali** community, who came here from the poor rural area of Sylhet in Bangladesh in the 1960s and 1970s.

As the area is not an obvious place for sightseeing, and certainly no beauty spot – Victorian slum clearances, Hitler's bombs and postwar tower blocks have all left their

Sunday markets

Most visitors to the East End come here for the **Sunday markets**. Approaching from Liverpool Street, the first one you come to, on the east side of Bishopsgate, is **Petticoat Lane** (Map 7, J2; Sun 9am–2pm; Liverpool Street or Aldgate East), not one of London's prettiest streets, but one of its longest-running Sunday markets, specializing in cheap (and often pretty tacky) clothing. The authorities renamed the street Middlesex Street in 1830 to avoid the mention of ladies' underwear, but the original name has stuck.

Two blocks north of Middlesex Street, down Brushfield Street, lies **Old Spitalfields Market** (organic market Fri & Sun 10am–5pm, general market Mon–Fri 11am–3pm & Sun 10am–5pm; ⊖ Liverpool Street), once the capital's premier wholesale fruit and vegetable market, now specializing in organic food, plus clothes, crafts and jewellery. Further east lies **Brick Lane** (Map 7, M1; Sun 8am–1pm; ⊖ Aldgate East, Shoreditch or Liverpool Street), heart of the Bengali community, famous for its bric-a-brac Sunday market, wonderful curry houses and non-stop bagel bakery, and now also something of a magnet for young designers. From Brick Lane's northernmost end, it's a short walk to **Columbia Road** (Sun 8am–1pm; ⊖ Aldwych or Liverpool Street then bus #26), the city's best market for flowers and plants; you'll need to ask the way or head in the direction of the folk bearing plants.

mark – most visitors to the East End come for its famous **Sunday markets** (ⓦwww.eastlondonmarkets.com). However, there's plenty more to get out of a visit, including a trio of **Hawksmoor churches**, and the vast **Canary Wharf** redevelopment, which can be gawped at from the area's overhead light railway. One part of the East End that is set to be totally transformed is the lower Lea valley, a rundown industrial area between Bow and Stratford, where the **Olympic Games** are due to be held in 2012 (see p.110).

Whitechapel and Spitalfields

Map 2, J4. ⊖ Liverpool Street or Aldgate East.

The districts of **Whitechapel**, and in particular **Spitalfields**, within sight of the sleek tower blocks of the financial sector, represent the old heart of the East End, where the French Huguenots settled in the seventeenth century, where the Jewish community was at its strongest in the late nineteenth century, and where today's Bengali community eats, sleeps, works and prays. If you visit just one area in the East End, it should be this zone, which preserves mementos from each wave of immigration.

Spitalfields Market and around

Map 7, I1–K1. ⊖ Liverpool Street.

A short stroll east of Liverpool Street station lies **Spitalfields Market**, the red-brick and green-gabled market hall built in 1893, half of which was recently demolished in order to make way for yet more City offices. Facing the hall is **Christ Church** (Map 7, K1; Tues 11am–4pm, Sun 1–4pm; ⓦwww.christchurchspitalfields.org.uk), built between 1714 and 1729 to a characteristically bold design by Nicholas Hawksmoor. Best viewed from Brushfield Street, the church's main features are its huge 225-foot-high spire and a giant Tuscan portico, raised on steps and shaped like a Venetian window (a central arched opening flanked by two smaller rectangles), a motif repeated in the tower and doors.

You can, on occasion, visit the extraordinary **18 Folgate Street** (℡020/7247 4013, ⊛www.dennissevershouse.co.uk), to the north of the market, home of the American **Dennis Severs** until his death in 1999. In this old house Severs created a theatrical experience which he described as "passing through a frame into a painting". The house is entirely candle-lit and log-fired, and decked out as it would have been two hundred years ago. Visitors are free to explore the ten rooms (in silence), and are left with the distinct impression that its original inhabitants have literally just left the room. The house cat prowls, food aromas waft through the kitchen, and you can hear horses' hooves on cobbles. "The Experience" takes place on the first and third Sunday of the month (2–5pm; £8), and on the Mondays (noon–2pm; £5) following those Sundays; plus every Monday, you can book ahead for "Silent Night" (April–Sept 8–11pm; Oct–March 6–9pm; £12).

Whitechapel Road

Map 7, N2. ⊖ Aldgate or Aldgate East.

Whitechapel Road – as Whitechapel High Street and the Mile End Road are collectively known – is still the East End's main street, shared by all the many races who live in the borough of Tower Hamlets. The East End institution that draws in more outsiders than any other here is the **Whitechapel Art Gallery** (Map 7, M2; Tues–Sun 11am–6pm, Thurs until 9pm; ⊛www.whitechapel.org), housed in a beautiful crenellated 1899 Arts and Crafts building by Charles Harrison Townsend, architect of the similarly audacious Horniman Museum (p.153). The gallery stages some of London's most innovative exhibitions of contemporary art, as well as hosting the biennial East End Academy, a chance for local artists to get their work shown to a wider audience.

The most visible symbol of the new Muslim presence in the East End is the Saudi-financed **East London Mosque**, (Map 2, J4) an enormous red-brick building that's a short walk up Whitechapel Road from the art gallery; it stands in marked contrast to the tiny **Great Synagogue** (Map 2, J4), dating from 1899, behind the mosque in Fieldgate Street. Neither of these buildings is open to the public, but you can pay a visit to the small exhibition in the nearby **Whitechapel Bell Foundry** (Map 2, J4; Mon–Fri 9am–4.15pm; guided tours occasionally Sat 10am & 2pm; £8; no under-14s; book in advance on ☏020/7247 2599, ⓦwww.whitechapelbellfoundry.co.uk), on the corner of Fieldgate Street. Big Ben, the Liberty Bell, the Bow Bells and numerous English church bells (including those of Westminster Abbey) all hail from the foundry, established here in 1738.

It was on the Mile End Road – the extension of Whitechapel Road – that Joseph Merrick, better known as the **"Elephant Man"**, was discovered in a freak show by Dr Treves, and subsequently admitted as a patient to the **Royal London Hospital** (Map 2, J4) on Whitechapel Road. He remained there, on show as a medical freak, until his death in 1890 at the age of just 27. There's a small section, and an interesting twenty-minute documentary, on Merrick in the **Hospital Museum** (Mon–Fri 10am–4.30pm; free), housed beside the red-brick church (now the medical college library) on Newark Street.

Just before the point where Whitechapel Road turns into Mile End Road stands the gabled entrance to the former Albion Brewery, where the first bottled brown ale was produced in 1899. Next door lies the **Blind Beggar** (Map 2, J4), the East End's most famous pub since March 8, 1966, when Ronnie Kray walked into the crowded bar and shot gangland rival George Cornell for calling him a "fat poof". This murder spelled the end of the infamous Kray Twins, Ronnie and Reggie, both of whom were sentenced to life

Jack the Ripper

In the space of just eight weeks between August and November 1888, five prostitutes were stabbed to death in and around Whitechapel; all were found with their innards removed. Few of the letters received by the press and police, which purported to come from the murderer, are thought to have been genuine, including the one which coined the nickname **Jack the Ripper**, and to this day the murderer's identity remains a mystery. At the time, it was assumed by many that he was a Jew, probably a *shochet* (a ritual slaughterman), since the mutilations were obviously carried out with some skill. The theory gained ground when the fourth victim was discovered outside the predominantly Jewish Working Men's Club in Berner Street (now Henriques Street), and for a while it was dangerous for Jews to walk the streets at night for fear of reprisals.

Ripperologists have trawled through the little evidence there is to produce numerous other suspects, none of whom can be positively proven guilty. The crime writer Patricia Cornwell has recently spent millions in an attempt to prove that the artist Walter Sickert was the Ripper, but the man who usually tops the lists is a cricket-playing barrister named Druitt, whose body was found floating in the Thames some weeks after the last murder, though there is no firm evidence linking him with any of the killings.

The one positive outcome of the murders at the time was that they focused the attention of the rest of London on the squalor of the East End. Philanthropist Samuel Barnett, for one, used the media attention to press for improved housing, street lighting and policing to combat crime and poverty in the area. Today, the murders continue to be exploited in gory, misogynistic detail by the likes of Madame Tussaud's and the London Dungeon, while guided walks retracing the Ripper's steps set off every week throughout the year (see p.22).

imprisonment, though their well-publicized gifts to local charities created a Robin Hood image that still persists in these parts of town.

Bethnal Green Museum of Childhood

Map 2, J4. Daily except Fri 10am–5.50pm; free; ⓦwww
.museumofchildhood.org.uk ⊖ Bethnal Green.

North of the Whitechapel Road, the **Bethnal Green
Museum of Childhood**, is conveniently situated opposite
Bethnal Green tube station. The open-plan, wrought-iron
hall, originally part of (and still a branch of) the V&A (see
p.133), was transported here in the 1860s to bring art to the
East End. The museum is due to re-open in Novemeber
2006 after a major refurbishment so it's impossible to say
exactly how the exhibits will be arranged. However, pride
of place will, no doubt, still be reserved for its unique collection of antique dolls' houses dating back to 1673. Among
the other curiosities are model trains, cars and rocking
horses, dolls made from found objects and a handful of
automata – Wallace the Lion gobbling up Albert is always a
firm favourite.

Docklands

The architectural embodiment of Thatcherism, a symbol of
1980s smash-and-grab culture according to its critics, or a
blueprint for inner-city regeneration to its free-market sup-
porters – the **Docklands** redevelopment provokes extreme
reactions. Despite its catch-all name, however, Docklands is far
from homogeneous. Canary Wharf, with its Manhattan-style
skyscrapers, is only its most visible landmark; industrial-estate
sheds and riverside flats of dubious architectural merit are
more indicative of the area. **Wapping**, the westernmost district, has retained much of its old Victorian warehouse architecture, while the **Royal Docks**, further east, are only just
beginning to be transformed from an industrial wasteland.

The docks were originally built from 1802 onwards to
relieve congestion on the Thames quays, and eventually

Against all the odds, London won the right to stage the **Olympic Games** in 2012. Even more surprisingly, the focus of the games, the Olympic Park, is going to be in the East End, in an unpromising, rundown industrial estate by the River Lea, between Hackney Wick and Stratford. The main 80,000-seat Olympic Stadium will become a 25,000-sear athletics stadium after the games, while close by, there'll be a 20,000-seat aquatic centre, a velodrome and BMX track, a hockey complex and, on the site of the former Hackney greyhound stadium, a multi-sports complex for basketball, handball and volleyball. The Olympic village, housing nearly 18,000 athletes, will also be here, and will be converted to public housing after the games.

The rest of the events will take place in and around London, mostly in existing venues: Wimbledon will obviously host the tennis and the new Wembley stadium the football, while ExCel, in Docklands, will be used for boxing, judo, taekwondo, weightlifting and wrestling, and Eton's new rowing centre will serve for some canoeing and kayaking events as well as for skulling. The Dome will finally serve a useful purpose by hosting the artistic gymnastics, trampolining and basketball finals, along with a smaller temporary venue for rhythmic gymnastics, table tennis and badminton. Equestrian events are scheduled for Greenwich Park, while Hyde Park will host the triathlon and road cycling and Regent's Park the baseball and softball. Archery will take place at Lord's cricket ground, shooting at the Royal Artillery Barracks in Woolwich and – the one piece of planning that's really grabbed the headlines – beach volleyball will be staged on Horse Guards Parade.

The games will certainly generate employment, and provide some badly needed housing for a deprived area, though it's difficult to judge how great the long-term benefits will really be. Despite protestations to the contrary, the environmental costs will undoubtedly be high, and council taxes in London – already among the highest in the country – are set to rise to pay for the privilege.

Docklands transport

Although Canary Wharf is now on the Jubilee tube line, the best way to view Docklands is either from one of the boats that course up and down the Thames (see p.21), or from the driverless, overhead **Docklands Light Railway** or DLR (ⓦwww.tfl.gov.uk /dlr), which sets off from Bank, or from Tower Gateway, close to Tower Hill tube. Travelcards are valid on the DLR, or you can buy a variety of DLR-only day passes giving you unlimited travel on certain sections of the network. Tour guides give a free running commentary on DLR trains that set off on the hour from Tower Gateway (daily 10am–2pm) and Bank (Mon–Fri 11am–2pm, Sat & Sun 10am–2pm) as far as Cutty Sark station. If you're heading for Greenwich, and fancy taking a boat back into town, it might be worth considering a Rail River Rover ticket (£9.50), which gives you unlimited travel on the DLR and City Cruises services between Greenwich and Westminster.

became the largest enclosed cargo-dock system in the world. However, competition from the railways and, later, the development of container ships, signalled the closure of the docks in the 1960s. Then, at the height of the recession in the 1980s, regeneration began in earnest. No one thought the old docks could ever be rejuvenated and, twenty-five years on, more has been achieved than many thought possible, but less than was originally promised. Travelling through on the overhead railway, Docklands comes over as an intriguing open-air design museum, not a place one would choose to live or work – most people stationed here see it as artificially removed from the rest of London – but a spectacular sight nevertheless.

Wapping to Limehouse

Map 2, K4.

From the DLR overhead railway, you get a good view of two of Hawksmoor's landmark East End churches. The first one is **St George-in-the-East**, built in 1726 and visible to the south just before you reach Shadwell station. It's easy to spot thanks to its four domed corner towers and distinctive west-end tower topped by an octagonal lantern. You're missing nothing by staying on the train, though, as the interior was devastated in the Blitz. As the DLR leaves Limehouse station and skirts Limehouse Basin marina, Hawksmoor's **St Anne's Church** is visible to the north. Begun in 1714 and dominated again by a gargantuan west tower, the church is topped by an octagonal lantern and adorned with the highest church clock in London. Again, the interior isn't worth the effort as it was badly damaged by fire in 1850.

An alternative to the DLR is to walk from Wapping to Limehouse, along the Thames Path, which sticks to, or close to, the riverbank. You begin at **St Katharine Dock** (Map 7, M7; Ⓦwww.stkaths.co.uk), immediately east of the Tower of London, and the first of the old docks to be renovated way back in the 1970s. St Katharine's redeeming qualities are the old swing bridges and the boats themselves, many of which are beautiful old sailing ships. Continue along **Wapping High Street**, lined with tall brick-built warehouses, most now tastefully converted into yuppie flats, and you will eventually find yourself in Limehouse, beyond which lies the Isle of Dogs. The fairly well-signposted walk is about two miles in length, and will bring you eventually to Westferry Circus – for details of riverside pubs along the way, see p.220.

The Isle of Dogs

Map 2, L5.

The Thames begins a dramatic horseshoe bend at Limehouse, thus creating the **Isle of Dogs**, the geographical and ideological heart of the new Docklands. The area reaches its apotheosis in **Canary Wharf** (Ⓦwww.canarywharf.com), the strip of land in the middle of the former West India Docks, previously a destination for rum and mahogany, later tomatoes and bananas (from the Canary Islands – hence the name).

The only really busy bit of the new Docklands, Canary Wharf, is best known as the home of Britain's tallest building, Cesar Pelli's landmark tower, officially known as **One Canada Square**. The world's first skyscraper to be clad in stainless steel, it's an undeniably impressive sight, both from a distance (its flashing pinnacle is a feature of the horizon at numerous points in London) and close up. It no longer stands alone, having been joined recently by several other skyscrapers that stop just short of Pelli's stumpy pinnacle.

One of the few original warehouses left to the north of Canary Wharf has been converted into the **Museum in Docklands** (daily 10am–6pm; £5; ⓦwww.museumin docklands.org.uk), an excellent stab at charting the history of the area from Roman times to the present day. Highlights include a great model of old London Bridge, an eight-foot-long watercolour and a soft play area for kids.

The DLR cuts right through the middle of the Canary Wharf office buildings under a parabolic steel-and-glass canopy and heads south through the rest of the Isle of Dogs, a surreally lifeless, uneasy mix of drab high-rises, council estates, and expensive apartments. If you're heading for Greenwich (see p.153), you have a choice: either get off at **Island Gardens**, Christopher Wren's favourite spot from which to contemplate his masterpieces across the river (the Royal Naval College and Royal Observatory), and walk through the 1902 foot tunnel to Greenwich; alternatively, you can stay on the DLR, which now tunnels underneath the Thames, and alight at Cutty Sark station.

The South Bank

The **South Bank** (🌐www.southbanklondon.com) – the area immediately opposite Victoria Embankment – is best known for the **London Eye**, the world's largest observation wheel and one of the capital's most popular millennium projects. The arrival of the Eye helped kick-start the renovation of the **South Bank Centre**, London's much unloved concrete culture bunker of theatres and galleries, built, for the most part, in the 1960s. After decades in the doldrums, the centre is currently under inspired artistic direction and the whole area is enjoying something of a renaissance.

The wheel's success has rubbed off on the rest of the area too, prompting a major refurbishment programme beginning with the transformation of **Hungerford Bridge**, connecting the South Bank to Embankment, into a gleaming double suspension footbridge. What's more, you can now happily explore the whole area on foot, free from the traffic noise and fumes that blight so much of central London, thanks to the well-marked **Thames Path** which runs along the riverside.

It's also worth visiting the **Imperial War Museum**, a short walk inland from the river, which contains the most detailed exhibition on the Holocaust in Britain.

South Bank Centre

Map 6, B3. ⊖ Waterloo.

The modern development of the South Bank dates back to the 1951 **Festival of Britain**, when the South Bank Exhibition was held on derelict land south of the Thames. The festival was an attempt to revive postwar morale by celebrating the centenary of the Great Exhibition (when Britain really did rule more than half the world). The most striking features of the site were the Royal Festival Hall (which still stands), the ferris wheel (inspiration for the current London Eye), the saucer-shaped Dome of Discovery (disastrously revisited in the guise of the Millennium Dome), and the cigar-shaped Skylon tower.

The Festival of Britain's success provided the impetus for the eventual creation of the **South Bank Centre** (⊕www.sbc.org.uk), now home to artistic institutions such as the Royal Festival Hall (⊕www.rfh.org.uk), the Hayward Gallery (⊕www.hayward.org.uk), the National Film Theatre (NFT), the high-tech BFI London IMAX Cinema, and lastly, looking like a multistorey car park, Denys Lasdun's National Theatre (⊕www.nt-online.org). Luckily, the SBC's unprepossessing appearance is softened by its riverside location, its avenue of trees, its fluttering banners, its occasional buskers and skateboarders and the secondhand bookstalls outside the National Film Theatre. The crop of newish eating places linked to the Royal Festival Hall join the NFT café to offer a number of pleasant riverside dining experiences.

**For details of the venues in the
South Bank Centre, see chapters 21 & 22.**

London Eye

Map 6, A5. Daily: April–Sept 9.30am–10pm; Oct–March 9am–8pm;

£12.50; ☎0800/500 0600; ⓦwww.ba-londoneye.com ⊕ Waterloo or Westminster.

South of the South Bank Centre is the **London Eye**, the magnificently graceful millennium wheel which spins slowly and silently over the Thames. Standing 443ft high, the wheel is the largest ever built, and it's constantly in slow motion – a full-circle "flight" in one of its 32 pods takes around thirty minutes, and lifts you high above the city. It's one of the few places (apart from a plane window) from which London looks a manageable size, as you can see right out to where the suburbs slip into the countryside. Ticket prices are outrageously high, and queues can be very bad at the weekend, so book in advance over the phone or online.

County Hall

Map 6, A6. ⊕ Westminster or Waterloo.

Next to the London Eye is the only truly monumental building on the South Bank, **County Hall**, with its distinctive colonnaded crescent. Designed to house the LCC (London County Council), it was completed in 1933 and enjoyed its greatest moment of fame as the headquarters of the GLC (Greater London Council), abolished by Margaret Thatcher in 1986, leaving London as the only European city without an elected authority. In 2000, the former GLC leader Ken Livingstone was elected as Mayor of London, and moved into the new GLA (Greater London Authority) building near Tower Bridge (see p.127). County Hall, meanwhile, is in the hands of a Japanese property company, and currently houses two hotels, several restaurants, a giant aquarium, a glorified amusement arcade called Namco Station, and a couple of art galleries.

The London Aquarium

Daily 10am–6pm or later; £9.75; ⓦwww.londonaquarium.co.uk

So far, the most popular attraction in County Hall is the **London Aquarium**, laid out on two subterranean levels.

With some super-large tanks, and everything from dog-face puffers to piranhas, this is an attraction that's pretty much guaranteed to please younger kids. The Touching Pool, where children can actually stroke the (non-sting) rays, is particularly popular. Impressive in scale, the aquarium is fairly conservative in design, though, with no walk-through tanks. Ask at the main desk for the times of the daily presentations.

Saatchi Gallery

Mon–Thurs & Sun 10am–6pm, Fri & Sat 10am–10pm; £8.50; Ⓦwww .saatchi-gallery.co.uk

County Hall is also home (until 2007) to the **Saatchi Gallery** of contemporary art, which now occupies the imposing former council chamber on the first floor – it's badly signposted so you may have to ask the way. Charles Saatchi, the Jewish Iraqi-born art collector behind the gallery, was, in fact, the man whose advertising for the Tory government helped topple County Hall's original incumbents, the GLC. Saatchi is perhaps best known as the main promoter of the Young British Artists of the 1990s, who snapped up seminal Turner Prize-nominated works by the likes of Damien Hirst and Tracey Emin. The gallery has no permanent collection, but puts on changing exhibitions drawn from Saatchi's vast collection in this slightly incongruous setting.

Dalí Universe

Daily 10am–6pm (later in the summer); £9.75; Ⓦwww.daliuniverse .com

Three giant Surrealist sculptures on the river-facing side of County Hall advertise **Dalí Universe**. There's no denying Dalí was an accomplished and prolific artist, but you'll be disappointed if you're expecting to see his "greatest hits" – those are scattered across the globe. Most of the works here are little-known bronze and glass sculptures, and various drawings from the many illustrated books which he published, ranging from Ovid to the Marquis de Sade. Aside from these, there's one of Dalí's numerous lobster telephones, which Edward James commissioned for his London home, a copy of his famous Mae West lips sofa, and the oil painting from the dream sequence in Hitchcock's movie *Spellbound*.

Lambeth

South of Westminster Bridge, you leave the South Bank proper, and enter what used to be the village of **Lambeth** (now the name of the entire borough stretching as far south as Brixton). This stretch of the riverbank affords the best views of the Houses of Parliament, and there are a few sights worth considering, such as the **Florence Nightingale Museum**. Inland lies London's most even-handed military museum, the **Imperial War Museum**, housed in a former lunatic asylum.

Florence Nightingale Museum

Map 3, I6. Mon–Fri 10am–5pm, Sat & Sun 10am–4.30pm; £5.80; ⓦwww.florence-nightingale.co.uk ⊖ Westminster.

On the south side of Westminster Bridge, on Lambeth Palace Road and in the midst of St Thomas's Hospital, the **Florence Nightingale Museum** celebrates the devout woman who revolutionized the nursing profession by establishing the first school of nursing at St Thomas' in 1860 and publishing her *Notes on Nursing*, emphasising the importance of hygiene, decorum and discipline. The exhibition gives a strictly orthodox and uncritical account, but hits just the right note by putting the two years she spent in the Crimea in the context of a lifetime of tireless social campaigning. Exhibits include the white lantern that earned her the nickname "The Lady with the Lamp", a reconstruction of a Crimean military hospital ward and a slightly disappointing twenty-minute slide show.

Museum of Garden History

Map 3, I7. March to mid-Dec daily 10.30am–5pm; free, £3 donation suggested; ⓦwww.cix.co.uk/~museumgh ⊖ Westminster.

A short walk south of St Thomas's is the Kentish ragstone church of St Mary-at-Lambeth, which now contains a café and an unpretentious little **Museum of Garden History**. The graveyard has been transformed into a small seventeenth–century garden, where two interesting sarcophagi lurk among the foliage: one belongs to Captain Bligh, the commander of the *Bounty* in 1787; the other is a memorial to John Tradescant, gardener to James I and Charles I.

The Imperial War Museum

Map 3, K7. Daily 10am–6pm; free; ⓦwww.iwm.org.uk ⊖ Lambeth North or Elephant & Castle.

The domed building at the east end of Lambeth Road, formerly the infamous lunatic asylum "Bedlam", is now the **Imperial War Museum**, by far the best military museum in the capital. The treatment of the subject is impressively wide-ranging and fairly sober, with the main hall's militaristic display offset by the lower-ground-floor array of documents and images attesting to the human damage of war. The museum also has a harrowing **Holocaust Exhibition** (not recommended for children under 14), which you enter from the third floor. The exhibition pulls few punches, and has made a valiant attempt to avoid depicting the victims of the Holocaust as nameless masses by focusing on individual cases, and interspersing the archive footage with eyewitness accounts from contemporary survivors.

10

Southwark

Until well into the seventeenth century, the only reason for north-bank residents to cross the Thames, to what is now **Southwark**, was to visit the infamous Bankside entertainment district around the south end of London Bridge, which lay outside the jurisdiction of the City. What started out as a red-light district under the Romans reached its peak as the pleasure quarter of Tudor and Stuart London, where disreputable institutions banned in the City – most notably theatres – continued to flourish until the Puritan purges of the 1640s.

Thanks to wholesale regeneration in the last few years, Southwark's riverfront is once more somewhere to head for. A whole cluster of sights vie for attention, most notably the **Tate Modern** art gallery, housed in a converted power station, and next to it a reconstruction of Shakespeare's **Globe Theatre**. The **Thames Path** connects the district with the South Bank to the west, and allows you to walk east along Clink Street and Tooley Street, home to a further rash of popular sights such as the **London Dungeon**. Further east still, **Butler's Wharf** is a thriving little warehouse development centred on the excellent **Design Museum**.

Bankside: the Tate and the Globe

⊖ Southwark or Blackfriars.

Bankside, which lies between Blackfriars and Southwark Bridge, was the most nefarious area in London in Elizabethan times, thanks to its brothels, bearpits and theatres. Four hundred years on, and Bankside is once more a magnet for visitors and Londoners alike, thanks to the reconstructed **Globe Theatre** (where most of Shakespeare's plays had their first performances), and the **Tate Modern** housed in the old Bankside power station. In addition, the area is linked to St Paul's and the City by the fabulous Norman Foster-designed **Millennium Bridge**, the first to cross the Thames for over a century, and London's first pedestrian-only bridge.

Tate Modern

Map 7, A7. Daily 10am–6pm; Fri & Sat until 10pm; free; ⓦwww.tate.org.uk ⊖ Southwark or Blackfriars.

Bankside is dominated by the austere power station of the same name, transformed by the Swiss duo Herzog & de Meuron into the **Tate Modern**. The masterful conversion has left plenty of the original, industrial feel, while providing wonderfully light and spacious galleries in which to show off the Tate's vast international twentieth-century art collection. The best way to enter is down the ramp from the west, so you get the full effect of the stupendously large turbine hall. It's easy enough to find your way around the galleries, with levels 3 and 5 displaying the permanent collection, level 4 used for fee-paying temporary exhibitions, and level 7 home to a café with a great view over the Thames.

Given that Tate Modern is the largest modern art gallery in the world, you need to spend the best part of a day here to do justice to the place, or be very selective. Pick up a plan (and, for an extra £1, an audioguide), and take the escalator to level 3. The curators have eschewed the usual chronological approach through the "isms", preferring to group works together thematically: Landscape/Matter/Environment, Still Life/Object/Real Life, History/Memory/Society, and Nude/Action/Body. On the whole this works very well, though the early twentieth-century canvases in their gilded frames do struggle when made to compete with contemporary installations.

Although the displays change every six months or so, you're still pretty much guaranteed to see at least some works by **Monet** and Bonnard, Cubist pioneers **Picasso** and Braque, Surrealists such as **Dalí**, abstract artists like **Mondrian**, Bridget Riley and Pollock, and Pop supremos **Warhol** and Lichtenstein. There are seminal works such as a replica of **Duchamp**'s urinal, entitled *Fountain* and signed "R. Mutt" and Yves Klein's totally blue paintings. And such is the space here that several artists get whole rooms to themselves, among them Joseph Beuys and his shamanistic wax and furs, and **Mark Rothko**, whose abstract "Seagram Murals", originally destined for a posh restaurant in New York, have their own shrine-like room in the heart of the collection.

Shakespeare's Globe Theatre

Map 7, B7. Box office ☎020/7401 9919, ⓦwww.shakespeares-globe .org ⊖ Southwark or Blackfriars.

Seriously dwarfed by the Tate Modern is the equally spectacular **Shakespeare's Globe Theatre**, a reconstruction of the polygonal playhouse where most of the Bard's later works were first performed, and which was originally erected on nearby Park Street in 1598.

**For more on attending performances
at the Globe, see p.263.**

To find out more about Shakespeare and the history of Bankside, the Globe's stylish **exhibition** (daily: May–Sept 9am–noon & 12.30–5pm; Oct–April 10am–5pm; £9) is well worth a visit. It begins by detailing the long campaign by American actor Sam Wanamaker to have the Globe rebuilt, but it's the imaginative hands-on exhibits that really hit the spot. You can have a virtual play on medieval instruments such as the crumhorn or sackbut, prepare your own edition of Shakespeare, and feel the thatch, hazelnut shell and daub used to build the theatre. Visitors also get taken on an informative **guided tour** round the theatre itself, except in the afternoons during the summer season, when you can only visit the exhibition (for a reduced entrance fee).

You can view the archeological remains of another
Elizabethan playhouse, the **Rose Theatre**, nearby at
56 Park St, by arrangement with the Globe ☎020/7902 1500
(May–Sept daily 12.30–5pm; £9).

Clink Street, Southwark Cathedral and around

➾ London Bridge.

East of Bankside, beyond Southwark Bridge, lies **Vinopolis** (Map 7, D8; Mon, Fri & Sat noon–9pm, Tues–Thurs & Sun noon–6pm; £11.50; ⊛www.vinopolis.co.uk), discreetly housed in former wine vaults under the railway arches on Clink Street. It's a strange fish: part wine bar-restaurant, part wine retailers, part museum. The focus of the complex is the "Wine Odyssey", a rather disjointed trot through the world's wine regions, for which it's pretty much essential to pay the extra £2 for an audioguide. Tickets are pricey, even if they do include five wine tastings.

Further down the suitably gloomy confines of dark and narrow Clink Street is the **Clink Prison Museum** (Map 7, D8; daily 10am–6pm; until 9pm in summer; £4; ⊛www .clink.co.uk), built on the site of the former Clink Prison, origin of the expression "in the clink". The prison began as a dungeon for disobedient clerics, built under the Bishop of Winchester's Palace, and later became a dumping ground for heretics, prostitutes and a motley assortment of Bankside lowlife. Today's exhibition features a handful of prison life tableaux, and dwells on the torture and grim conditions within, but, given the rich history of the place, it's a disappointingly lacklustre display.

An exact replica of the **Golden Hinde** (Map 7, E8; phone for times ☎0870/011 8700; £2.75; ⓦwww.goldenhinde.co.uk), the galleon in which Francis Drake sailed around the world from 1577 to 1580, nestles in St Mary Overie Dock, at the eastern end of Clink Street. The ship is surprisingly small, and its original crew of eighty-plus must have been cramped to say the least. There's a lack of interpretive panels, so it's worth paying the little bit extra and getting a guided tour from one of the folk in period garb – ring ahead to check a group hasn't booked the place up.

Southwark Cathedral

Map 7, E8. Mon–Fri 7.30am–6pm, Sat & Sun 8.30am–6pm; ⓦwww.dswark.org/cathedral ⊖ London Bridge.

Close by the *Golden Hinde* stands **Southwark Cathedral**, built as the medieval Augustinian priory church of St Mary Overie, and given cathedral status only in 1905. Of the original thirteenth-century church, only the choir and retrochoir now remain, separated by a tall and beautiful stone Tudor screen, making them probably the oldest Gothic structures left in London. The nave was entirely rebuilt in the nineteenth century, but the cathedral contains numerous interesting monuments, from a thirteenth-century oak effigy of a knight to an early twentieth-century memorial to Shakespeare.

Bramah Tea and Coffee Museum

Map 7, D9. Daily 10am–6pm; £4; ⓦwww.bramahmuseum.co.uk ⊖ London Bridge.

The **Bramah Tea and Coffee Museum**, at 40 Southwark St, a couple of blocks southwest of the cathedral, is endearingly ramshackle and well worth a visit. Founded in 1992 by Edward Bramah, who began his career on an African tea garden in 1950, the museum's emphasis is firmly on tea, though the café also serves a seriously good cup of coffee. There's an impressive array of teapots from Meissen to the world's largest, plus plenty of novelty ones, and coffee machines spanning the twentieth century, from huge percolator siphons to espresso machines.

The Old Operating Theatre

Map 7, F9. Daily 10.30am–5pm; £4; ⓦwww.thegarret.org.uk
⊖ London Bridge.

The most educational and strangest of Southwark's museums, the **Old Operating Theatre**, **Museum** and **Herb Garret** is located to the east of the cathedral on St Thomas Street, on the other side of Borough High Street. Built in 1821 at the top of a church tower, where the hospital apothecary's herbs were stored, this women's operating theatre dates from the pre-anaesthetic era. Despite being entirely gore-free, the museum is as stomach-churning as the London Dungeon (see overleaf). The surgeons who used this room would have concentrated on speed and accuracy (most amputations took less than a minute), but there was still a thirty percent mortality rate, with many patients simply dying of shock, and many more from bacterial infection, about which very little was known.

Tooley Street and around

Map 7, G8. ⊖ London Bridge.

The vaults beneath the railway arches of London Bridge train station, on the south side of **Tooley Street**, are now occupied by two museums. Young teenagers and the credulous probably get the most out of the ever-popular

London Dungeon (daily: March to mid-July, Sept & Oct 10am–5.30pm; mid-July to Aug 9.30am–7.30pm; Nov–Feb 10.30am–5pm; £10.95; ⊛www.thedungeons.com) – to avoid the inevitable queue, buy your ticket online. The life-sized waxwork tableaux inside include a man being hung, drawn and quartered, and one being boiled alive, the general hysteria being boosted by actors, dressed as top-hatted Victorian vampires, pouncing out of the darkness. Visitors are then herded into a courtroom, condemned to the "River of Death" boat ride, and forced to endure the "Jack the Ripper Experience", an exploitative trawl through postmortem photos and wax mock-ups of the victims, followed by the "Great Fire of London", in which you experience the heat and the smell of the plague-ridden city, before walking through a revolving tunnel of "flames".

A little further east along Tooley Street is **Winston Churchill's Britain at War** (Map 7, H9; daily: April–Sept 10am–5.30pm; Oct–March 10am–4.30pm; £6.50; ⊛www.britain atwar.co.uk), an illuminating insight into the stiff-upper-lip London mentality during the Blitz. The museum contains hundreds of wartime artefacts, including an Anderson shelter, where you can hear the chilling sound of the V-1 "doodle-bugs" and tune in to contemporary radio broadcasts. The final set piece is a walk through the chaos of a just-bombed street.

On the other side of Tooley Street is **Hay's Galleria** (Map 7, H8), a shopping precinct built over what used to be Hay's Dock. The idea of filling in the curvaceous dock and covering it with glass and steel barrel-vaulting, while retaining the old Victorian warehouses on three sides, is an effective one. The pastiche effect of phoney market barrows, gravel underfoot and red phone boxes, along with the gimmicky kinetic sculpture at the centre, however, are disappointing.

HMS Belfast

Map 7, I8. Daily: March–Oct 10am–6pm; Nov–Feb 10am–5pm; £8; ⊛www.iwm.org.uk ⊖ London Bridge.

Permanently moored just along the riverfront from Hay's Galleria is the **HMS Belfast**, a World War II cruiser. Armed with six torpedoes, and six-inch guns with a range of over fourteen miles, the Belfast spent more than two years of the war in the Royal Naval shipyards after being hit by a mine in the Firth of Forth at the beginning of hostilities. It later saw action in the Barents Sea during World War II, and during the Korean War, before being decommissioned. The maze of cabins is fun to explore but if you want to find out more about the Belfast, head for the exhibition rooms in zone 5.

City Hall

Map 7, J9. Mon–Fri 8am–8pm; ⓦ www.london.gov.uk
⊖ London Bridge.

A short stroll east of the Belfast is Norman Foster's startling glass-encased **City Hall**, which looks like a giant car head-light or fencing mask. Headquarters for the Greater London Authority and the Mayor of London, it's a "green" building that uses a quarter of the energy a high-specification office would normally use. Visitors are welcome to stroll around the building and watch the London Assembly proceedings from the second floor. On certain weekends, access is also possible to "London's Living Room" on the ninth floor, from which there's a great view over the Thames.

Butler's Wharf:
the Design Museum

Map 7, L9. ⊖ Tower Hill, London Bridge or Bermondsey.

In contrast to the brash offices on Tooley Street, **Butler's Wharf**, east of Tower Bridge, has retained its historical character. **Shad Thames**, the narrow street at the back of Butler's Wharf, has kept the wrought-iron overhead gang-ways by which the porters used to transport goods from the wharves to the warehouses further back from the river, and is one of the area's most atmospheric alleyways. The eight-storey Butler's Wharf warehouse itself, with its shops and restaurants, forms part of Terence Conran's commercial empire and caters for a moneyed clientele, but the wide promenade on the riverfront is open to the public.

The chief attraction of Butler's Wharf is Conran's superb riverside **Design Museum** (daily 10am–5.45pm, Fri until 9pm; £6; ⊛www.designmuseum.org), a stylish, Bauhaus-like conversion of a 1950s warehouse at the eastern end of Shad Thames. The museum has no permanent display, but instead hosts a series of temporary exhibitions (up to four at any one time) on important designers, movements or single products. The small coffee bar in the foyer is a great place to relax, and there's a pricier restaurant on the top floor.

11

Hyde Park, Kensington, Chelsea and Notting Hill

Hyde Park, together with its westerly extension, Kensington Gardens, covers a distance of two miles from Oxford Street in the northeast to Kensington Palace in the southwest. At the end of your journey, you've made it to one of London's most exclusive districts, the Royal Borough of **Kensington** and **Chelsea**, which makes up the bulk of this chapter. Other districts go in and out of fashion, but this area has been in vogue ever since royalty moved into **Kensington Palace** in the late seventeenth century.

Aside from the shops around Harrods in Knightsbridge, however, the popular tourist attractions lie in **South Kensington**, where three of London's top (and currently free) **museums** – the Victoria and Albert, Natural History and Science museums – stand on land bought with the proceeds of the Great Exhibition of 1851. Chelsea, to the south, has a slightly more bohemian pedigree. In the 1960s, the **King's Road** carved out its reputation as London's catwalk, while in the late 1970s it was the epicentre of the punk explosion. Nothing so rebellious goes on in Chelsea now, though its residents like to think of themselves as rather more artistic and intellectual than the purely moneyed types of Kensington.

Once slummy, now swanky, **Bayswater** and **Notting Hill**, to the north of Hyde Park, were the bad boys of the borough for many years, dens of vice and crime comparable to Soho. Despite gentrification over the last 25 years, they remain the borough's most cosmopolitan districts, with a strong Arab presence and vestiges of the African–Caribbean community who initiated and still run the city's (and Europe's) largest street **carnival**, which takes place every August Bank Holiday.

Hyde Park and Kensington Gardens

Map 3, D5. ⊖ Marble Arch, Hyde Park Corner or Lancaster Gate.

Seized from the Church by Henry VIII to satisfy his desire for yet more hunting grounds, **Hyde Park** (ⓦwww.royalparks.gov.uk) was first opened to the public by James I, and soon became a fashionable gathering place for the beau monde, who rode round the circular drive known as the Ring, pausing to gossip and admire each other's *équipage*. Hangings, muggings and duels, the Great Exhibition of 1851 and numerous public events have all taken place in Hyde Park – and it's still a popular gathering point or destination for political demonstrations. For most of the time, however, the park is simply a leisure ground – a wonderful open space which allows you to lose all sight of the city beyond a few persistent tower blocks.

Located at the treeless northeastern corner of the park, **Marble Arch** (Map 3, D4) was originally erected in 1828 as a triumphal entry to Buckingham Palace, but is now stranded on a ferociously busy traffic island at the west end of Oxford Street. This is the most historically charged spot in Hyde Park, as it marks the site of **Tyburn gallows**, the city's main public execution spot until 1783. It's also the location of **Speakers' Corner**, a peculiarly English Sunday morning tradition, featuring an assembly of ranters and hecklers.

A better place to enter the park is at **Hyde Park Corner** (Map 3, F6), the southeast corner, where the **Wellington Arch** (Wed–Sun: April–Sept 10am–6pm; Oct 10am–5pm; Nov–March 10am–4pm; £3) stands in the midst of another of London's busiest traffic interchanges. Erected in 1828 to commemorate Wellington's victories in the Napoleonic Wars, the arch was originally topped by an equestrian statue of the Duke himself, later replaced by Peace driving a four-horse chariot. Inside, you can view an exhibition on London's outdoor sculpture and take a lift to the top of the monument, where the exterior balconies offer a bird's-eye view of the swirling traffic.

Close by stands **Apsley House** (Map 3, F6; Tues–Sun: April–Oct 10am–5pm; Nov–March 10am–4pm; £4.95), Wellington's London residence and now a museum to the "Iron Duke". Unless you're a keen fan of the Duke (or the architect, Benjamin Wyatt), the highlight of the museum is the **art collection**, much of which used to belong to the King of Spain. Among the best pieces, displayed in the Waterloo Gallery on the first floor, are works by de Hooch, Van Dyck, Velázquez, Goya, Rubens and Murillo. The famous, more than twice life-size, nude statue of Napoleon by Antonio Canova stands at the foot of the main staircase.

Hyde Park is divided in two by the **Serpentine Lake**, which has a popular **Lido** (mid-June to mid-Sept daily 10am–6pm; £3.50) on its south bank. By far the prettiest section of the lake, though, is the upper section known as the **Long Water**, which narrows until it reaches a group of four fountains, laid out symmetrically in front of an Italianate summerhouse designed by Wren.

The western half of the park is officially known as **Kensington Gardens**, and its two most popular attractions are the **Serpentine Gallery** (Map 3, C6; daily 10am–6pm; free; ⓦwww.serpentinegallery.org), which has a reputation for lively, and often controversial, contemporary art exhibitions, and the richly decorated, high-Gothic **Albert Memorial** (Map 3, B6), clearly visible to the west. Erected in 1876, the monument is as much a hymn to the glorious achievements of Britain as to its subject, Queen Victoria's husband (who died of typhoid in 1861). Recently restored to his former gilded glory, Albert occupies the central canopy, clutching a catalogue for the 1851 Great Exhibition that he helped to organize.

The Exhibition's most famous feature, the gargantuan glasshouse of the Crystal Palace, no longer exists, but the profits were used to buy a large tract of land south of the park, now home to South Kensington's remarkable cluster of museums and colleges, plus the vast **Royal Albert Hall** (Map 3, C6; ⓦwww.royalalberthall.com), a splendid iron-and-glass-domed concert hall, with an exterior of red brick, terracotta and marble that became the hallmark of South Ken architecture. The hall is the venue for Europe's most democratic music festival, the Henry Wood Promenade Concerts, better known as the **Proms**, which take place from July to September, with standing-room tickets for as little as £4.

For more on the Proms, see p.252.

Kensington Palace

Map 3, A6. Daily: March–Oct 10am–6pm; Nov–Feb 10am–5pm; £11; ⓦwww.hrp.org.uk ⊖ High Street Kensington or Queensway.

On the western edge of Kensington Gardens stands **Kensington Palace**, a modestly proportioned Jacobean brick mansion bought by William and Mary in 1689, and the

⑪

chief royal residence for the next fifty years. KP, as it's fondly known in royal circles, is best known today as the place where **Princess Diana** lived until her death in 1997.

Visitors don't get to see Diana's apartments, which were on the west side of the palace, where various minor royals still live. Instead, they get to view some of the frocks worn by Diana, and also several worn by the Queen, and then the sparsely furnished state apartments. The highlights are the trompe l'oeil ceiling paintings by William Kent, in particular the Cupola Room, and the oil paintings in the King's Gallery. En route, you also get to see the tastelessly decorated rooms in which the future Queen Victoria spent her unhappy childhood. To recover from the above, take tea in the exquisite **Orangery** (times as for palace), to the north of the palace.

Victoria and Albert Museum

Map 8, E7. Daily 10am–5.45pm; Wed & last Fri of month until 10pm; free; ⊛www.vam.ac.uk ⊖ South Kensington.

In terms of sheer variety and scale, the **Victoria and Albert Museum** (popularly known as the V&A), on Cromwell Road, is the greatest museum of applied arts in the world. The range of exhibits on display here means that, whatever your taste, there is almost bound to be something to grab your attention. Beautifully but haphazardly displayed across a seven-mile, four-storey maze of halls and corridors, the V&A's treasures are impossible to survey in a single visit. Floor plans from the information desks can help you decide which areas to concentrate on. If you're flagging, there's an edifying, snacky café in the museum's period-piece **Poynter, Morris and Gamble** refreshment rooms.

The most celebrated of the V&A's numerous exhibits are the **Raphael Cartoons**, seven vast biblical paintings that served as designs for a set of tapestries destined for the Sistine Chapel. Close by, you can view highlights from the country's largest costume collection, and the world's largest collection of Indian art outside India. In addition, there are galleries devoted to British, Chinese, Islamic, Japanese and Korean art, as well as costume jewellery, glassware, metalwork and photography. Wading through the huge collection of European sculpture, you come to the surreal **Plaster Casts** gallery, filled with copies of European art's greatest hits, from Michelangelo's *David* to Trajan's Column (sawn in half to make it fit). There's even a gallery of twentieth-century *objets d'art* – everything from Bauhaus furniture to Swatch watches – to rival that of the Design Museum (see p.128).

Science Museum

Map 8, D6. Daily 10am–6pm; free; ⓦ www.sciencemuseum.org.uk ⊖ South Kensington.

Established as a technological counterpart to the V&A, the **Science Museum**, on Exhibition Road, is undeniably impressive, filling seven floors with items drawn from every conceivable area of science, including space travel, digital technology, steam engines and carbon emissions. Keen to dispel the enduring image of museums devoted to its subject as boring and full of dusty glass cabinets, the Science Museum has updated its galleries with interactive displays, and puts on daily demonstrations to show that not all science teaching has to be deathly dry.

First stop inside should be the **information desk**, where you can pick up a museum plan and find out what events and demonstrations are taking place; you can also sign up for a free **guided tour** on a specific subject. Most people will want to head for the **Wellcome Wing**, full of state-of-the-art interactive computers and an IMAX cinema, and geared to appeal to even the most museum-phobic teenager. To get there, you must first pass by the world's first steam engines, through the Space gallery, to the far side of the Making of the Modern World, a display of iconic inventions from Robert Stephenson's *Rocket* train of 1829 to the Ford Model T, the world's first mass-produced car.

The **Launch Pad**, one of the first hands-on displays aimed at kids, remains as popular and enjoyable as ever, as do the **Garden** and **Things** galleries all of which are in the basement. The **Materials** gallery, on the first floor, is aimed more at adults, and is an extremely stylish exhibition covering the use of materials ranging from aluminium to zerodur (used for making laser gyroscopes), while **Energy**, on the second floor, has a great "do not touch" electric shock machine that absolutely fascinates kids.

Natural History Museum

Map 8, C7. Mon–Sat 10am–5.50pm, Sun 11am–5.50pm; free; ⓦwww.nhm.ac.uk ⊖ South Kensington.

Alfred Waterhouse's purpose-built mock-Romanesque colossus ensures the **Natural History Museum**'s status as London's most handsome museum. The museum has been massively redeveloped over the last decade or so, and is now, by and large, imaginatively designed, though there are still one or two sections that remain little changed since the place opened in 1881. The museum's dinosaur collection is a real hit with the kids, but its collections are also an important resource for serious zoologists.

The **main entrance**, in the middle of the museum's 675-foot terracotta facade, leads to what are now known as the **Life Galleries**. Just off the vast Central Hall, dominated by an 85ft-long plaster cast of a diplodocus skeleton, you'll find the Dinosaur gallery, with its grisly life-sized animatronic tableau of two oviraptors roosting while carnivorous velociraptors get ready to attack. Other popular sections include the Creepy-Crawlies Room, the Mammals gallery with its life-size model of a blue whale, and the excellent **Investigate** gallery (Mon–Sat 10.30am–5pm, Sun 11.30am–5pm; term time Mon–Fri 2.30–5pm, Sat 10.30am–5pm, Sun 11.30am–5pm), where children aged 7 to 14 get to play at being scientists (you need to obtain a timed ticket).

Visitors can view more of the museum's millions of zoological specimens in the collections store of the **Darwin Centre**. To see the rest of the building, however, you need to sign up for a **guided tour** (book ahead either online or by phone ☎020/7942 6128; free). These set off roughly every thirty minutes and last about half an hour, allowing visitors to get a closer look at the specimens. You also get to see behind the scenes at the labs, and even talk to one of the museum's 350 scientists about their work.

If the queues for the museum are long (as they can be at weekends and during school holidays), you might be better off heading for the side entrance on Exhibition Road, which leads into the former Geology Museum, now known as the **Earth Galleries**, an expensively revamped and visually exciting romp through the earth's evolution. The most popular sections are the slightly tasteless Kobe earthquake simulator, and the spectacular display of gems and crystals in the Earth's Treasury.

Kensington High Street and around

Map 3, A7. ⊖ High Street Kensington.

Shopper-thronged **Kensington High Street** is dominated architecturally by the twin presences of George Gilbert Scott's neo-Gothic church of St Mary Abbots, whose 250-foot spire makes it London's tallest parish church, and the Art Deco colossus of Barkers department store, remodelled in the 1930s.

Hidden away in the backstreets to the north of High Street Kensington is the densely wooded **Holland Park**, a spot popular with the neighbourhood's army of nannies and au pairs, who take their charges to the excellent adventure playground. To get there, take one of the paths along the east side of the former Commonwealth Institute, a bold 1960s building that's now a conference centre with a startling tent-shaped Zambian copper roof. The park is laid out in the former grounds of **Holland House** – only the east wing of the Jacobean mansion could be salvaged after World War II, but it gives a fairly good idea of what the place used to look like. A youth hostel is linked to the east wing (see p.179), while a concert tent to the west stages theatrical and musical performances throughout the summer (@www.operahollandpark.com). Several **formal gardens** surround the house, most notably the Japanese-style Kyoto Gardens, while the rest of the park is dotted with a series of abstract sculptures.

A number of wealthy Victorian artists rather self-consciously founded an artists' colony in the streets that lie between the High Street and Holland Park. It's now possible to visit one of the most remarkable of these pads, **Leighton House** (daily except Tues 11am–5.30pm; guided tours Wed & Thurs 2.30pm; £3; @www.rbkc.gov.uk/leightonhousemuseum), at 12 Holland Park Road. "It will be opulence, it will be sincerity," Lord Leighton opined before starting work on the house in the 1860s – he later became President of the Royal Academy and was ennobled on his deathbed. The big attraction is the domed Arab Hall, decorated with Saracen tiles, gilded mosaics and woodwork drawn from all over the Islamic world. The other rooms are less spectacular but, in compensation, are hung with paintings by Lord Leighton and his Pre-Raphaelite chums.

Knightsbridge

Map 3, D7. ⊖ Knightsbridge.

Knightsbridge is irredeemably snobbish, revelling in its reputation as the swankiest shopping area in London, a status epitomized by **Harrods** (Mon–Sat 10am–7pm; @www.harrods.com) on Brompton Road. London's most famous department store started out as a family-run grocery store in 1849, with a staff of just two. The current 1905 terracotta building is owned by the Egyptian Mohammed Al Fayed and employs in excess of three thousand staff. Tourists flock to Harrods – it's thought to be one of the city's top-ranking tourist attractions – though if you can do without the sage green and gold carrier bag you can buy most of what the shop stocks more cheaply elsewhere.

The store does, however, have a few sections that are architectural sights in their own right: the Food Hall, with its exquisite Arts and Crafts tiling, and the Egyptian Hall, with its pseudo-hieroglyphs and sphinxes, are particularly striking. Now that a fountain dedicated to Di and Dodi is in place, the Egyptian escalators are an added attraction, and will whisk you to the first-floor "luxury washrooms", where you can splash on free perfume after relieving yourself. Note, too, that the store has a draconian dress code: no shorts, no vest T-shirts and backpacks must be carried in the hand.

Chelsea

Map 3, E8. ⊖ Sloane Square.

It wasn't until the latter part of the nineteenth century that **Chelsea** began to earn its reputation as London's very own Left Bank. Its household fame, however, came through **King's Road**'s role as the unofficial catwalk of the "Swinging Sixties". The road remained a fashion parade for hippies, too, and in the Jubilee Year of 1977 it witnessed the birth of punk, masterminded from a shop called Sex, run by Vivienne Westwood and Malcolm McLaren. These days, it's just another wealthy west London suburb and King's Road is lined with the usual chain stores and interior design shops.

The area's other aspect, oddly enough considering its boho reputation, is a military one. For, among the most nattily attired of all those parading down the King's Road are the scarlet- or navy blue-clad Chelsea Pensioners, army veterans from the nearby **Royal Hospital** (Map 3, E8; Mon–Sat 10am–noon & 2–4pm, Sun 2–4pm; free), founded by

Charles II in 1681. The hospital's majestic red-brick wings and grassy courtyards became a blueprint for institutional and collegiate architecture all over the English-speaking world. The public are allowed to view the austere hospital chapel, and the equally grand, wood-panelled dining hall, opposite, which has a vast allegorical mural of Charles II.

The concrete bunker next door to the Royal Hospital, on Royal Hospital Road, houses the **National Army Museum** (daily 10am–5.30pm; free; @www.national-army -museum.ac.uk). The militarily obsessed are unlikely to be disappointed by the succession of uniforms and medals, but there is very little here for non-enthusiasts. The temporary exhibitions staged on the ground floor are the museum's strong point, but it's rather disappointing overall – you're better off visiting the infinitely superior Imperial War Museum (see p.119).

Cheyne Walk and Cheyne Row

Map 3, D9. ⊖ Sloane Square then any bus heading down King's Road.

The quiet riverside locale of **Cheyne** (pronounced "chainy") drew artists and writers in great numbers during the nineteenth century. Since the building of the Embankment and the increase in the volume of traffic, however, the character of this peaceful haven has been lost. Novelist Henry James, who lived at no. 21, used to take "beguiling drives" in his wheelchair along the Embankment; today, he'd be hospitalized in the process.

The chief reason to come here nowadays is to visit the **Chelsea Physic Garden** (April–Oct Wed noon–5pm, Sun 2–6pm; £6; @www.chelseaphysicgarden.co.uk), which marks the beginning of Cheyne Walk. Founded in 1673 by the Royal Society of Apothecaries, this is the oldest botanical garden in the country. Unfortunately, it's also rather a small garden, and a little too close to Chelsea Embankment to be a peaceful oasis. It's really of most interest to very keen botanists – to learn more, take the free guided walk at 1.30pm. There's also a teahouse, serving afternoon tea and delicious home-made cakes, with exhibitions on the floor above.

It's also worth popping into the nearby **Chelsea Old Church** (Tues–Fri 1.30–5.30pm; ⊛www.chelseaoldchurch .org.uk), halfway down Cheyne Walk, where Thomas More built his own private chapel in the south aisle. The church was badly bombed in World War II, but an impressive number of monuments were retrieved from the rubble and continue to adorn the church's interior.

A short distance inland from Cheyne Walk, at 24 Cheyne Row, is **Carlyle's House** (April–Oct Wed–Fri 2–5pm, Sat & Sun 11am–5pm; £4), where the historian Thomas Carlyle set up home, having moved down from his native Scotland in 1834. Now a National Trust property, the house became a museum just fifteen years after Carlyle's death and is a typically dour Victorian abode, kept much as the Carlyles would have had it – his hat still hanging in the hall, and his socks in the chest of drawers. The top floor contains the garret study where Carlyle tried in vain to escape the din of the neighbours' noisy roosters in order to complete his final magnum opus on Frederick the Great.

Notting Hill

Map 3, A5. ⊖ Notting Hill.

Epicentre of the country's first race riots, when busloads of whites attacked West Indian homes in the area, **Notting Hill** is now more famous for its annual Carnival (see p.309), which began life in direct response to the riots. These days, it's the world's biggest street festival outside Rio, with an estimated two million revellers turning up on the last weekend of August for the two-day extravaganza of parades, steel bands and deafening sound systems.

The rest of the year, Notting Hill is a lot quieter, though its cafés and restaurants are cool enough to pull in folk from all over. On Saturdays, big crowds of Londoners and tourists alike descend on the mile-long **Portobello Road Market**, lined with stalls selling everything from antiques to cheap secondhand clothes and fruit and vegetables.

Within easy walking distance of Portobello Road, on the other side of the railway tracks, gasworks and canal, is **Kensal Green Cemetery** (Map 2, 4F; ⓦwww.kensalgreen.co.uk; ⊖ Kensal Green), opened in 1833 and still a functioning burial ground. Graves of the more famous incumbents – Thackeray, Trollope and Brunel – are less interesting architecturally than those arranged on either side of the Centre Avenue, which leads from the easternmost entrance on Harrow Road. Guided tours of the cemetery take place on selected Sundays at 2pm (£5); the tour includes a trip down the catacombs (bring a torch).

12

North London

This chapter concentrates on just a handful of the capital's satellite villages, now subsumed into the general mass of **north London**. Almost all the northern suburbs are easily accessible by tube from the centre; in fact, it was the expansion of the tube which encouraged the forward march of bricks and mortar into many of these suburbs.

The first section covers one of London's finest parks, **Regent's Park**, framed by Nash-designed architecture and home of **London Zoo**. Close by is **Camden Town**, where the weekend market is one of the city's big attractions – a warren of stalls selling street fashion, books, records and goods from across the globe.

The real highlights of north London, though, for visitors and residents alike, are **Hampstead** and **Highgate**, elegant, largely eighteenth-century developments which still reflect their village origins. They have the added advantage of proximity to one of London's wildest patches of greenery, **Hampstead Heath**, where you can enjoy stupendous views, kite-flying and nude bathing, as well as outdoor concerts and high art in the elegant setting of **Kenwood House**.

Also covered are a handful of sights in more far-flung northern suburbs. These include the **RAF Museum** at Hendon and the **Shri Swaminarayan Mandir**, the largest Hindu temple outside India.

Regent's Park

Map 3, E2. ⓦwww.royalparks.org.uk ⊖ Regent's Park, Baker Street or Great Portland Street.

As with almost all of London's royal parks, Londoners have Henry VIII to thank for **Regent's Park**, which he confiscated from the Church for yet more hunting grounds. However, it wasn't until the reign of the Prince Regent (later George IV) that the park began to take its current form. According to the master plan, devised by John Nash in 1811, the park was to be girded by a continuous belt of terraces, and sprinkled with a total of 56 villas, including a magnificent pleasure palace for the Prince himself, which would be linked by Regent Street to Carlton House in St James's. The plan was never fully realized, due to lack of funds, but enough was built to create something of the idealized garden city that Nash and the Prince Regent envisaged.

To appreciate the special quality of Regent's Park, take a closer look at the architecture, starting with the Nash terraces, which form a near-unbroken horseshoe of cream-coloured stucco around the Outer Circle. Within the Inner Circle is the **Open Air Theatre** (ⓦwww.open-air-theatre.org.uk; see p.262), which puts on summer performances of Shakespeare, opera and ballet, and **Queen Mary's Gardens**, by far the prettiest section of the park. A large slice of the gardens is taken up with a glorious rose garden, featuring some four hundred varieties, surrounded by a ring of ramblers.

Clearly visible on the western edge of the park is the shiny copper dome and minaret of the **London Central Mosque** (Map 3, D2; ⓦwww.islamicculturalcentre.co.uk), an entirely appropriate addition, given the Prince Regent's taste for the Orient. Non-Muslim visitors are welcome to look in at the information centre, and glimpse inside the hall of worship, which is packed out with a diversity of communities for the lunchtime Friday prayers.

London Zoo

Map 3, E1. Daily: March–Oct 10am–5.30pm; Nov–Feb 10am–4pm; £14; ⓦwww.zsl.org/london-zoo ⊖ Camden Town.

The northeastern corner of the park is occupied by **London Zoo**. Founded in 1826 with the remnants of the royal menagerie, the zoo has had to change with the times, and now bills itself as an eco-conscious place whose prime purpose is to save species under threat of extinction. It's still not the most uplifting spot for animal-lovers, though the enclosures are as humane as any inner-city zoo could make them, and kids usually love the place. Most are particularly taken by the children's enclosure, where they can actually handle the animals, and the regular "Animals in Action" live shows. The invertebrate house, now known as BUGS, and the new monkey walk-through forest are both guaranteed winners. The zoo boasts some striking architectural features, too, most notably the modernist, spiral-ramped 1930s concrete

Regent's Canal by boat

Three companies run **boat services** on the **Regent's Canal** between Camden and Little Venice, passing through the Maida Hill tunnel and stopping off at London Zoo on the way. The narrowboat *Jenny Wren* (☎020/7485 4433) starts off at Camden, goes through a canal lock (the only company to do so, and heads for Little Venice, while Jason's narrowboats (☎020/7286 3428, ⓦwww.jasons.co.uk) start off at Little Venice; the London Waterbus Company (☎020/7482 2660, ⓦwww.londonwaterbus. com) sets off from both places. Whichever you choose, you can board at either end; **tickets** cost around £5–6 one-way (and only a little more return) and journey time is 50 minutes one-way.

Those interested in the history of the canal should head off to the **London Canal Museum** (Map 3, I1; Tues–Sun 10am–4.30pm; £3; ⓦwww.canalmuseum.org.uk), on the other side of York Way, down New Wharf Road, ten minutes' walk from King's Cross Station.

penguin pool (where Penguin Books' original colophon was sketched); it was designed by the Tecton partnership, led by Russian émigré Berthold Lubetkin.

Camden Town

Map 2, H3. ⊖ Camden Town.

For all the gentrification of the last twenty years, **Camden Town** retains a gritty aspect, compounded by the canal, the various railway lines that plough through the area, and the large shelter for the homeless on Arlington Street. The market, however, gives the area a positive lift on the weekends, and is now the district's best-known attribute.

Having started out as a tiny crafts market in the cobbled courtyard by the lock, **Camden Market** has since mushroomed out of all proportion. More than 150,000 shoppers turn up here each weekend, and parts of the market now stay open all week long, alongside a similarly oriented crop of shops, cafés and bistros. The sheer variety of what's on offer – from bootleg tapes to furniture, along with a mass of street fashion and clubwear, and plenty of foodstalls – is what makes Camden so special. To avoid the crowds, which can be overpowering on a summer Sunday afternoon, you'll need to get here by 10am – by 4pm, many of the stalls will be packing up to go.

Despite having no significant Jewish associations, Camden is home to London's **Jewish Museum** (Mon–Thurs 10am–4pm, Sun 10am–5pm; £3.50; ⊛www.jewishmuseum .org.uk), at 129 Albert St, just off Parkway. The purpose-built premises are smartly designed, and the collection of Judaica includes treasures from London's Great Synagogue, burnt down by Nazi bombers in 1941, and a sixteenth-century Venetian Ark of the Covenant. More compelling are the temporary exhibitions, discussions and occasional concerts. Excellent temporary exhibitions are also staged in the museum's Finchley branch at 80 East End Rd, N3 (Map 2, F1; Mon–Thurs 10.30am–5pm, Sun 10.30am–4.30pm; £2; ⊕020/8349 1143; ⊖ Finchley Central).

Hampstead

Map 2, G2. ⊖ Hampstead.

Perched on a hill above Camden Town, **Hampstead** village developed into a fashionable spa in the eighteenth century, after Dr Gibbons, a celebrated physician, declared the waters of its spring as being of great medicinal value. Its sloping site, which deterred Victorian property speculators and put off the railway companies, saved much of the Georgian village from destruction, and it's little altered to this day. Later, it became one of the city's most celebrated literary quarters and even now it retains its reputation as a bolt hole of the high-profile intelligentsia. You can get some idea of its tone from the fact that the local Labour MP is currently the actress-turned-politician Glenda Jackson.

The steeply inclined High Street, lined with trendy clothes shops and arty cafés, flaunts the area's ever-increasing wealth without completely losing its picturesqueness. There are several small house museums to explore, but proximity to the Heath is the real joy of Hampstead, for this mixture of woodland, smooth pasture and landscaped garden is quite simply the most exhilarating patch of greenery in London.

Fenton House

Map 2, G2. March Sat & Sun 2–5pm; Easter–Oct Wed–Fri 2–5pm, Sat & Sun 11am–5pm; £4.80 ⊖ Hampstead.

Whichever route you take north of Hampstead tube, you'll probably end up at the small triangular green on Holly Bush Hill, on the north side of which stands the late seventeenth-century **Fenton House**. As well as housing a collection of European and Oriental ceramics, this National Trust house contains the superb Benton-Fletcher collection of early musical instruments, chiefly displayed on the top floor. Among the many spinets, virginals and clavichords are the earliest extant English grand piano, and an Unverdorben lute from 1580 (one of only three in the world). For an extra £1, you can hire a tape of music played on the above instruments, to listen to while you walk round.

Freud Museum

Map 2, G3. Wed–Sun noon–5pm; £5; ⓦ www.freud.org.uk
🚇 Swiss Cottage.

One of the most poignant of London's house museums is the **Freud Museum**, hidden away in the leafy streets of south Hampstead at 20 Maresfield Gardens. Having lived in Vienna for his entire adult life, Freud, by now a semi-invalid with only a year to live, was forced to flee the Nazis, arriving in London in the summer of 1938. The ground-floor study and library look exactly as they did when Freud lived here; the collection of erotic antiquities and the famous couch, sumptuously draped in Persian carpets, were all brought here from Vienna. Upstairs, home movies of family life in Vienna are shown continually, and a small room is dedicated to his daughter, Anna, herself an influential child analyst, who lived in the house until her death in 1982.

Burgh House – the Hampstead Museum

Map 2, G3. Wed–Sun noon–5pm; free; ⓦ www.london-northwest.com
/burghhouse 🚇 Hampstead.

The Queen Anne mansion of **Burgh House**, on New End Square, dates from the halcyon spa days of Hampstead Wells – as Hampstead was briefly known – and was at one time occupied by Dr Gibbons, the physician who discovered the spring's medicinal qualities. Surrounded by council housing, it now serves as the **Hampstead Museum**, an exhibition space and a modest local museum, with special emphasis on such notable locals as Constable and Keats; there's also a nice tearoom in the basement.

2 Willow Road

Map 2, G3. Tours: March & Nov Sat noon–5pm; April–Oct Thurs–Sat
noon–5pm; £4.60; ☎ 020/7435 6166 🚇 Hampstead.

For a fascinating insight into the modernist mind-set, take a look inside **2 Willow Road**, an unassuming red-brick terraced house built in the 1930s by the Hungarian-born architect Ernö Goldfinger. When Goldfinger moved in, this was a state-of-the-art pad and, as he changed little in the house in the following sixty years, what you see is a 1930s avant-garde dwelling preserved in aspic, a house at once both modern and old-fashioned. An added bonus is that the rooms are packed with *objets trouvés* and works of art by the likes of Max Ernst, Marcel Duchamp, Henry Moore and Man Ray. Before 3pm, visits are by hour-long guided tour only (noon, 1 & 2pm), for which you must book in advance; after 3pm the public has unguided, unrestricted access. The house is closed during the day on the first Thursday of the month, but open in the evening instead (5–9pm). Incidentally, James Bond's adversary is indeed named after Ernö – Ian Fleming lived close by and had a deep personal dislike of both Goldfinger and his modernist abode.

Keats' House

Map 2, G3. Tues–Sun: April–Oct noon–5pm; Nov–March noon–4pm; £3 ⊖ Hampstead.

Hampstead's most lustrous figure is celebrated at **Keats' House**, an elegant, whitewashed Regency double villa on Keats Grove, a short walk south of Willow Road. Inspired by the peacefulness of Hampstead and by his passion for girl-next-door Fanny Brawne (whose house is also part of the museum), Keats wrote some of his most famous works here before leaving for Rome, where he died of consumption in 1821. The neat, rather staid interior contains books and letters, Fanny's engagement ring and the four-poster bed in which the poet first coughed up blood, confiding to his companion, Charles Brown, "that drop of blood is my death warrant".

Hampstead Heath

Map 2, G2. ⊖ Hampstead.

North London's "green lung", **Hampstead Heath** is the city's most enjoyable public park. It may not have much of its original heathland left, but it packs a wonderful variety of bucolic scenery into its 800 acres. At its southern end are the rolling green pastures of **Parliament Hill**, north London's premier spot for kite-flying. On either side are numerous ponds, three of which – one for men, one for women and one mixed – you can swim in for free. The thickest woodland is to be found in the **West Heath**, beyond Whitestone Pond, also the site of the most formal section, **Hill Garden**, a secretive and romantic little gem with eccentric balustraded terraces and a ruined pergola. Beyond lies **Golders Hill Park**, where you can gaze at pygmy goats and fallow deer, and inspect the impeccably maintained aviaries, home to flamingos, cranes and other exotic birds.

Finally, don't miss the landscaped grounds of Kenwood, in the north of the Heath, which are focused on the whitewashed Neoclassical mansion of **Kenwood House** (daily: April–Oct 11am–5pm; Nov–March 11am–4pm; free). The house is now home to a collection of seventeenth- and eighteenth-century art, including a handful of real masterpieces by the likes of Vermeer, Rembrandt, Boucher, Gainsborough and Reynolds. Of the house's period interiors, the most spectacular is Robert Adam's sky-blue and gold library, its book-filled apses separated from the central entertaining area by paired columns. Upstairs, you can also view the **Suffolk Collection** (11am–4pm), whose highlights include William Larkin's full-length portraits of a Jacobean wedding party. To the south of the house, a grassy amphitheatre slopes down to a lake where outdoor concerts, mostly classical, are held on summer evenings.

Highgate

Map 2, H2. ⊖ Highgate or bus #210 from Archway.

Northeast of the Heath, and fractionally lower than Hampstead (appearances notwithstanding), **Highgate** lacks the literary cachet of its neighbour, but makes up for it with London's most famous cemetery, resting place of Karl Marx. It also retains more of its village origins, especially around **The Grove**, Highgate's finest row of houses, the oldest dating as far back as 1685.

To get to the cemetery, head south down Highgate High Street and **Highgate Hill**, with its amazing views towards the City. When you get to the copper dome of "Holy Joe", the Roman Catholic church which stands on Highgate Hill, pop into the pleasantly landscaped **Waterlow Park**, next door, with its fine café.

The park provides a through-route to **Highgate Cemetery** (Map 2, H2; ⊛highgate-cemetery.org), which is ranged on both sides of Swain's Lane. Highgate's most famous corpse, that of **Karl Marx**, lies in the **East Cemetery** (April–Oct Mon–Fri 10am–5pm, Sat & Sun 11am–5pm; Nov–March closes 4pm; £2). Marx himself asked for a simple grave topped by a headstone, but by 1954 the Communist movement decided to move his grave to a more prominent position and erect the vulgar bronze bust that now surmounts a granite plinth. Close by lies the much simpler grave of the author George Eliot.

What the East Cemetery lacks in atmosphere is in part compensated for by the fact that you can wander at will through its maze of circuitous paths, whereas to visit the more atmospheric and overgrown **West Cemetery**, with its spooky Egyptian Avenue and sunken catacombs, you must go round with a guided tour (March–Nov Mon–Fri noon, 2pm & 4pm, Sat & Sun hourly 11am–4pm; Dec–Feb Sat & Sun hourly 11am–3pm; £3). Among the prominent graves usually visited are those of artist Dante Gabriel Rossetti and lesbian novelist Radclyffe Hall.

Hendon: The RAF Museum

Map 2, E1. Daily 10am–6pm; free; ⓦ www.rafmuseum.org.uk ⊖ Colindale.

A world-class assembly of historic military aircraft can be seen at the **RAF Museum**, located in a godforsaken part of north London beside the M1 motorway. Enthusiasts won't be disappointed, but those looking for a balanced account of modern aerial warfare will – the overall tone is unashamedly militaristic, not to say jingoistic. Those with children should head for the hands-on Aeronauts gallery; those without might prefer to explore the often overlooked display galleries, ranged around the edge of the Main Aircraft Hall, which contain an art gallery and an exhibition on the history of flight, accompanied by replicas of some of the death-traps of early aviation.

Neasden: the Shri Swaminarayan temple

Map 2, D3. Daily 9am–6pm; free; ⓦ www.mandir.org ⊖ Stonebridge Park or Neasden.

Perhaps the most remarkable building in the whole of London lies just off the North Circular, in the glum suburb of **Neasden**. Here, rising majestically above the surrounding semi-detached houses like a mirage, is the **Shri Swaminarayan Mandir**, a traditional Hindu temple topped with domes and *shikharas*, erected in 1995 in a style and scale unseen outside of India for more than a millennium. To reach the temple, you must enter through the adjacent *haveli*, or cultural complex, with its carved wooden portico and balcony. After taking off your shoes, you can proceed to the **mandir** (temple) itself, carved entirely out of Carrara marble, with every possible surface transformed into a honeycomb of arabesques, flowers and seated gods. Beneath the mandir, an **exhibition** (£2) explains the basic tenets of Hinduism and details the life of Lord Swaminarayan, and includes a video about the history of the building.

⑬

South London

Now largely built up into a patchwork of Victorian terraces, one area of **South London** stands head and shoulders above all the others in terms of sightseeing, and that is **Greenwich**, with its outstanding ensemble of the **Old Royal Naval College** and the Queen's House, courtesy of Christopher Wren and Inigo Jones respectively. Most visitors, it has to be said, come to see the **National Maritime Museum**, the **Royal Observatory** and the beautifully landscaped royal park, though Greenwich also pulls in an ever-increasing volume of Londoners in search of bargains at its Sunday **market**.

The only other suburban sights that stand out are the **Dulwich Picture Gallery**, a public art gallery even older than the National Gallery (see p.29), and the eclectic **Horniman Museum**, in neighbouring Forest Hill.

Dulwich Picture Gallery

Map 2, J7. Tues–Fri 10am–5pm, Sat & Sun 11am–5pm; £4, free on Fri; ⊛ www.dulwichpicturegallery.org.uk ⊖ West Dulwich train station, from Victoria.

Dulwich Picture Gallery, on College Road, is the nation's oldest public art gallery, designed by John Soane (see p.81) and opened in 1817. Soane created a beautifully spacious building, awash with natural light and crammed with superb paintings – elegiac landscapes by Cuyp, one of the world's finest Poussin series, and splendid works by Hogarth, Gainsborough, Van Dyck, Canaletto and Rubens, plus **Rembrandt**'s tiny *Portrait of a Young Man*, a top-class portrait of poet, playwright and Royalist, the future Earl of Bristol. At the centre of the museum is a tiny mausoleum designed by Soane for the sarcophagi of the gallery's founders.

Horniman Museum

Map 2, J7. Daily 10.30am–5.30pm; free; ⓦwww.horniman.ac.uk Forest Hill train station from Victoria or London Bridge.

To the southeast of Dulwich Park, on the busy South Circular road, is the wacky **Horniman Museum**, purpose-built in 1901 by Frederick Horniman, a tea trader with a passion for collecting. In addition to the museum's natural history collection of stuffed birds and animals, there's an amazingly eclectic ethnographic collection, and a musical department with more than 1500 instruments from Chinese gongs to electric guitars. Don't miss the museum's new **aquarium** in the basement, and look out for the special sessions at the **Hands on Base**, which allow you to handle and learn more about a whole range of the museum's artefacts.

Greenwich

Greenwich is one of London's most beguiling spots, and the one place in southeast London that draws large numbers of visitors. In Tudor times, Greenwich boasted a royal palace and, in neighbouring Deptford, the royal naval dockyard. Both have long since disappeared, and in place of the palace stands one of the capital's finest architectural set pieces, the **Old Royal Naval College** overlooking the Thames. To the west lies Greenwich town centre, while to the south you'll find the area's two prime tourist sights, the **National Maritime Museum** and the **Royal Observatory**.

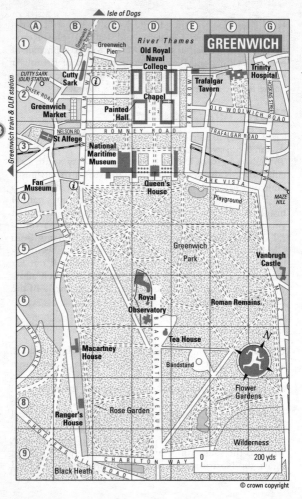

GREENWICH

SOUTH LONDON

13

Isle of Dogs

River Thames

Old Royal Naval College

Trinity Hospital

Cutty Sark (DLR) STATION

Greenwich Pier

Cutty Sark

CREEK ROAD

Greenwich Market

Greenwich train & DLR station

Painted Hall

Chapel

Trafalgar Tavern

HOSKINS STREET

OLD WOOLWICH ROAD

PARK ROW

NELSON RD

St Alfege

ROMNEY ROAD

TRAFALGAR ROAD

National Maritime Museum

Queen's House

Fan Museum

CROOMS HILL

PARK VISTA

MAZE HILL

Playground

MAZE HILL

Greenwich Park

Vanbrugh Castle

Royal Observatory

Roman Remains

HYDE VALE

BLACKHEATH AVENUE

Macartney House

Tea House

Bandstand

MAZE HILL

N

Flower Gardens

Ranger's House

Rose Garden

SHOOTERS HILL ROAD

Black Heath

CHARLTON WAY

Wilderness

0   200 yds

© crown copyright

Getting to Greenwich

If you're heading straight for the National Maritime Museum from central London, the quickest way to get there is to take the **train** from London Bridge (every 30min) to Maze Hill, on the eastern edge of Greenwich Park. Those wanting to start with the town or the *Cutty Sark* should alight at Greenwich station. A more scenic way of getting to Greenwich is to take a **boat** from one of the piers in central London. A third possible option is to take the **Docklands Light Railway** (DLR) to Cutty Sark station. For the best view of the Wren buildings, though, get off the DLR at Island Gardens, admire the view across the river and then take the Greenwich Foot Tunnel under the Thames.

The town centre
See map opposite, B2.

Greenwich town centre, laid out in the 1820s with Nash-style terraces, is nowadays plagued with heavy traffic. To escape the busy streets, head for the original covered section of **Greenwich Market**. There are stalls here from Thursday to Sunday, but the place is at its liveliest at the weekend, when the stalls spill out up the High Road, Stockwell Road and Royal Hill. The best sections are the indoor secondhand book markets, flanking the Central Market on Stockwell Road; the antiques hall, further down on Greenwich High Road; and the flea market on Thames Street.

Greenwich's **tourist office** is in Pepys House in the old Royal Naval College (daily 10am–5pm; ☏0870/608 2000).

A short distance in from the old covered market, on the opposite side of Greenwich Church Street, rises the Doric portico and broken pediment of Nicholas Hawksmoor's **St Alfege's Church** (see map opposite, A3; Mon–Sat 10am–4pm, Sun noon–4pm; ⊕www.st-alfege.org). Built in

155

The Dome

The Dome (⊖ North Greenwich) is clearly visible from the riverside at Greenwich and from the upper parts of Greenwich Park. Built at a cost approaching £800 million of public money, and designed by Richard Rogers, it is by far the world's largest dome – more than half a mile in circumference and 160ft in height – held up by a dozen, 300-foot-tall yellow steel masts. In 2000, for one year only, it housed the nation's chief millennium extravaganza: an array of high-tech themed zones set around a stage, on which a circus-style performance took place twice a day.

Bad reviews and over-optimistic estimates of visitor numbers forced the government to pump in around £150 million of public money just to keep it open. Nevertheless, millions paid up £20 each to visit, and millions went away happy.

Entertainment giants, AEG, have now agreed to spend yet more millions to turn the Dome into a six-floor, 23,000-seater music and sports arena, and the O2 mobile company have paid up to rebrand it "the O2". The venue will re-open in 2007, host the 2009 World Gymnastics Championships and be the 2012 Olympic venue for artistic gymnastics, trampolining and basketball.

1712–18, the church was flattened in the Blitz, but it has been magnificently restored to its former glory.

Wedged in a dry dock by the Greenwich Foot Tunnel is the majestic **Cutty Sark** (see map on p.154, B2; daily 10am–5pm; £4.50; ⊛www.cuttysark.org.uk), the world's last surviving tea clipper, built in 1869. The *Cutty Sark* lasted just eight years in the China tea trade, and it was as a wool clipper that it actually made its name, returning from Australia in just 72 days. Inside, there's little to see beyond an exhibition in the main hold which tells the ship's story, from its inception to its arrival in Greenwich in 1954.

Old Royal Naval College

See map on p.154, D2. Daily 10am–5pm; free; ⊛www.greenwich foundation.org.uk

It's entirely appropriate that the one London building that makes the most of its riverbank location should be the **Old Royal Naval College**. Wren's beautifully symmetrical Baroque ensemble was initially built as a royal palace, but eventually converted into a hospital for disabled seamen. From 1873 until 1998 it was home to the Royal Naval College, and now houses the University of Greenwich and the Trinity College of Music.

The two grandest rooms, situated underneath Wren's twin domes, are open to the public and well worth visiting. The entrance to the college is on King William Walk, and visitors are ushered first into the **Chapel** in the east wing. The exquisite pastel-shaded plasterwork and spectacular, decorative detailing on the ceiling were designed by James "Athenian" Stuart after a fire in 1799 destroyed the original interior. From the chapel, you can take the underground Chalk Walk to gain access to the magnificent **Painted Hall** in the west wing, which is dominated by James Thornhill's gargantuan allegorical ceiling painting, and his trompe l'oeil fluted pilasters.

National Maritime Museum

See map on p.154, C3. Daily 10am–5pm; July & Aug closes 6pm; free; Ⓦ www.nmm.ac.uk

The main entrance to the excellent **National Maritime Museum**, which occupies the old Naval Asylum, is on Romney Road. From here, you enter the spectacular glass-roofed central courtyard, which houses the museum's largest artefacts, among them the splendid 63-foot-long gilded **Royal Barge**, designed in Rococo style by William Kent for Prince Frederick, the much-unloved eldest son of George II.

The various themed galleries are superbly designed to appeal to visitors of all ages. In **Explorers**, on Level 1, you get to view some Titanic relics; **Passengers** re-lives the glory days of transatlantic shipping, which officially came to an end in 1957 when more people went by air than by sea; **Trade & Empire,** on Level 2, is a gallery devoted to the legacy of the British Empire, warts and all, from the slave trade to the opium wars; **Oceans of Discovery**, on Level 3, boasts Captain Cook's sextant and K1 marine clock, Shackleton's compass, and **Captain Scott**'s overshoes, watch and funky sledging goggles.

Level 3 also boasts two hands-on galleries: **The Bridge**, where you can attempt to navigate a catamaran, a paddle steamer and a rowing boat to shore; and **All Hands**, where children can have a go at radio transmission, loading miniature cargo, firing a cannon and so forth. Finally, there's the **Nelson Gallery**, which contains the museum's vast collection of Nelson-related memorabilia, including Turner's *Battle of Trafalgar, 21st October, 1805*, his largest work and only royal commission.

Inigo Jones's **Queen's House**, originally built amidst a rambling Tudor royal palace, is now the focal point of the Greenwich ensemble, and is an integral part of the Maritime Museum. As royal residences go, it's an unassuming country house, but as the first Neoclassical building in the country, it has enormous architectural significance. The interior is currently used for temporary exhibitions. Nevertheless, one or two features survive (or have been reinstated) from Stuart times. Off the Great Hall, a perfect cube, lies the beautiful Tulip Staircase, Britain's earliest cantilevered spiral staircase – its name derives from the floral patterning in the wrought-iron balustrade.

Royal Observatory

See map on p.154, D6. Daily 10am–5pm; July & Aug closes 6pm; free; ⓦwww.rog.nmm.ac.uk

Crowning the highest hill in Greenwich Park, behind the National Maritime Museum, the **Royal Observatory** was established in 1675 by Charles II to house the first Astronomer Royal, John Flamsteed. Flamsteed's chief task was to study the night sky in order to discover an astronomical method of finding the longitude of a ship at sea, the lack of which was causing enormous problems for the emerging British Empire. Astrologers continued to work here at Greenwich until the postwar smog forced them to decamp to Herstmonceux Castle and the clearer skies of Sussex (they've since moved to the Pacific); the old observatory, meanwhile, is now a very popular museum.

Greenwich's greatest claim to fame is, of course, as the home of **Greenwich Mean Time** (GMT) and the Prime Meridian. Since 1884, Greenwich has occupied zero longitude, which means the entire world sets its clocks by GMT. What the Royal Observatory doesn't tell you is that the meridian has, in fact, moved. Nowadays, navigators tend to use the Global Positioning System (GPS), served by several US military satellites, which place the meridian 336ft to the east of the brass strip in the courtyard that marks the Greenwich Meridian.

The oldest part of the observatory is the Wren-built **Flamsteed House**, whose northeastern turret sports a bright red time-ball that climbs the mast at 12.58pm and drops at 1pm GMT precisely; it was added in 1833, to allow ships on the Thames to set their clocks. Passing quickly through Flamsteed's restored apartments and the Octagon Room, where the king used to show off to his guests, you reach the Chronometer Gallery, which focuses on the search for the precise measurement of longitude, and displays four of the marine clocks designed by John Harrison, including "H4", which helped win the Longitude Prize in 1763.

The observatory is now in the process of massive redevelopment, which will eventually see the redesigning of some of the galleries described above and the creation of a state-of-the-art **Planetarium**, housed in the South Building.

The Ranger's House

See map on p.154, B8. April–Sept Wed–Sun 10am–6pm; £5.30.
Southwest of the observatory, and backing onto Greenwich park's rose garden, is the **Ranger's House**, a red-brick

Georgian villa that houses an art collection amassed by Julius Wernher, the German-born millionaire who made his money by exploiting the diamond deposits of South Africa. His taste in art is eclectic, ranging from medieval ivory miniatures to Iznik pottery, though he was definitely a man who placed technical virtuosity above artistic merit. The high points of the collection are Memlinc's *Virgin and Child*, the pair of sixteenth-century majolica dishes decorated with mythological scenes for Isabella d'Este, both located upstairs, and the Reynolds portraits and de Hooch interior, located downstairs.

The Fan Museum

See map on p.154, A4. Tues–Sat 11am–5pm, Sun noon–5pm; £3.50; ⓦ www.fan-museum.org

Croom's Hill boasts some of Greenwich's finest Georgian buildings, one of which houses the **Fan Museum** at no. 12. It's a fascinating little place (and an extremely beautiful house), revealing the importance of the fan as a social and political document. The permanent exhibition on the ground floor traces the history of the materials employed, from peacock feathers to straw, while temporary exhibitions on the first floor explore such subjects as techniques of production and changing fashion.

14

Chiswick to Windsor

Most people experience west London en route to or from Heathrow airport, either from the confines of the train or tube (which runs overground most of the way) or the motorway. The city and its satellites seem to continue unabated, with only fleeting glimpses of the countryside. However, in the five-mile stretch from Chiswick to Osterley there are several former country retreats, now surrounded by suburbia, which are definitely worth digging out.

The Palladian villa of **Chiswick House** is perhaps the best known of these attractions, though it draws nothing like as many visitors as **Syon House**, most of whom come for the gardening centre rather than for the house itself, a showcase for the talents of Robert Adam, who also worked at **Osterley**

River transport

From April to September Westminster Passenger Services (℡020/7930 2062, ⓦwww.wpsa.co.uk) runs four **boats** daily from Westminster Pier to Kew, and two boats to Richmond and Hampton Court. The full trip takes 3hr one way, and costs £13.50 single, £19.50 return. In addition, Turks (℡020/8546 2434, ⓦwww.turks.co.uk) run a regular service from Richmond to Hampton Court (April to mid-Sept Tues–Sun) which costs £5.50 single or £7 return.

House, another Elizabethan conversion, now owned by the National Trust.

Running through much of this chapter is the **River Thames**, once known as the "Great Highway of London" and still the most pleasant way to travel in these parts during the summer. Boats plough up the Thames all the way from central London, via the **Royal Botanic Gardens of Kew** and the picturesque riverside at **Richmond**, as far as **Hampton Court**, home of the country's largest and most impressive royal residence (and the famous maze). To reach the heavily touristed royal outpost of **Windsor Castle**, however, you really need to take the train.

Chiswick House

Map 2, E6. Daily: April–Sept 10am–6pm; Oct 10am–5pm; £3.50. Chiswick train station, from Waterloo.

Chiswick House is a perfect little Neoclassical villa, designed by the third Earl of Burlington in the 1720s, and set in one of the most beautifully landscaped gardens in London. Like its Palladian prototype, the house was purpose-built as a "temple to the arts" – here, amid his fine art collection, Lord Burlington could entertain artistic friends such as Swift, Handel and Pope. Visitors enter via the lower floor, where you can pick up an audioguide, before heading up to the floor above, a series of cleverly interconnecting rooms, each enjoying a wonderful view out onto the gardens – all, that is, except the Tribunal, the central octagonal hall, where the earl's finest paintings and sculptures would have been displayed.

To do a quick circuit of the **gardens**, head across the smooth carpet of grass, punctuated by urns and sphinxes, that sit under the shadow of two giant cedars of Lebanon. A great place from which to admire the northwest side of the house is from the stone benches of the exedra, a set of yew-hedge niches harbouring lions and copies of Roman statuary, situated beyond the cedars. Elsewhere, there's an

Italian garden, a maze of high-hedge alleyways, a lake and a grassy amphitheatre, centred on an obelisk in a pond and overlooked by an Ionic temple.

Hogarth's House

Map 2, E5. April–Oct Tues–Fri 1–5pm, Sat & Sun 1–6pm; Nov–March Tues–Fri 1–4pm, Sat & Sun 1–5pm; closed Jan; free.

If you leave Chiswick House gardens by the northernmost exit, beyond the Italian garden, it's just a short walk along the thunderous A4 road to **Hogarth's House**, where the artist spent each summer from 1749 until his death in 1764. Nowadays it's difficult to believe Hogarth came here for "peace and quiet", but in the eighteenth century the house was almost entirely surrounded by countryside. Amongst the scores of Hogarth's engravings, you can see copies of his satirical series – *An Election, Marriage à la Mode, A Rake's Progress* and *A Harlot's Progress* – and compare the modern view from the parlour with the more idyllic scene in *Mr Ranby's House*.

The Wetland Centre

Map 2, E6. Mon–Sat: summer 9.30am–6pm; winter 9.30am–5pm; open Sun for WWT members only; £6.75; ℡020/8409 4400, ⓦwww .wwt.org.uk ⊖ Hammersmith, then bus #283, or walk from Barnes train station.

For anyone even remotely interested in wildlife, the **Wetland Centre** in well-to-do Barnes is an absolute must. On the site of four disused reservoirs, across the river from Hammersmith, the Wildfowl & Wetland Trust (WWT) has created a high-tech 105-acre mosaic of wetland habitats, a stone's throw from central London. The centre serves a dual function: to attract native species of bird to its watery lagoons, and to assist in the WWT's programme of breeding rare wildfowl in captivity. On arrival – unless it's raining – you might as well skip the (albeit superbly produced) introductory audiovisual in the theatre, and head straight out to the ponds. If the weather's bad, or you've children with you, however, it's definitely worth visiting the **Discovery Centre**, where kids can take part in a swan identification parade, or take a duck's-eye view of the world, while their minders check out the WWT website.

Kew Bridge Steam Museum

Map 2, D5. Daily 11am–5pm; Mon–Fri £4.25, Sat & Sun £5.75; ⓦwww.kbsm.org Kew Bridge train station from Waterloo, or bus #237 or #267 from Gunnersbury.

Difficult to miss thanks to its stylish Italianate standpipe tower, **Kew Bridge Steam Museum** occupies a former pumping station, on the corner of Kew Bridge Road and Green Dragon Lane, 100 yards west of the bridge itself. At the heart of the museum is the Steam Hall, which contains a triple expansion steam engine and four gigantic nineteenth-century Cornish beam engines, while two adjoining rooms house the pumping station's original beam engines, one of which is the largest in the world. The steam engines may be things of great beauty, but they are primarily of interest to enthusiasts. Not so the museum's **Water for Life** gallery in the basement, devoted to the history of the capital's water supply. The best time to visit is at weekends, when each of the museum's industrial dinosaurs is put through its paces, and the small narrow-gauge steam railway runs back and forth round the yard (March–Nov Sun).

Syon House

Map 2, C6. April–Oct Wed, Thurs & Sun 11am–5pm; £7.50; ⓦwww .syonpark.co.uk Kew Bridge train station froom Waterloo, or bus #237 or #267 from Gunnersbury.

Syon, London seat of the Percy family (aka the Dukes of Northumberland) since Elizabethan times, is now more of a working commercial concern than a family home, embracing a garden centre, a wholefood shop, a trout fishery, an aquatic centre stocked with tropical fish, a mini-zoo and a butterfly house, as well as the old aristocratic mansion and its gardens.

From its rather plain, castellated exterior, you'd never guess that **Syon House** contains the most opulent eighteenth-century interiors in the whole of London. The splendour of Robert Adam's refurbishment is immediately revealed, however, in the pristine Great Hall, an apsed double cube with a screen of Doric columns at one end and classical statuary dotted around the edges. There are several more Adam-designed rooms to admire in the house, plus a smattering of works by Van Dyck, Lely, Gainsborough and Reynolds.

While Adam beautified Syon House, Capability Brown laid out its **gardens** (daily 10.30am–5.30pm; £3.75) around an artificial lake, surrounding the water with oaks, beeches, limes and cedars. The gardens' chief focus now, however, is the crescent-shaped **Great Conservatory**, an early nineteenth-century addition which is said to have inspired Joseph Paxton, architect of the Crystal Palace. Those with young children will be compelled to make use of the **miniature steam train** that runs through the park at weekends from April to October, and on Wednesdays during the school holidays.

Another plus point for kids is Syon's **Butterfly House** (daily: April–Sept 10am–5pm; Oct–March 10am–3.30pm; £5.25; ⓦwww.londonbutterflyhouse.com), a small, mesh-covered hothouse, where you can walk amid hundreds of exotic butterflies from all over the world, as they flit about the foliage. An adjoining room houses a collection of iguanas, millipedes, tarantulas and giant hissing Tanzanian cockroaches.

If your kids show more enthusiasm for life-threatening reptiles than delicate insects, then you could skip the butterflies and go instead for the adjacent **London Aquatic Experience** (daily: April–Sept 10am–6pm; Oct–March 10am–5pm;

£5; ⓦwww.aquatic-experience.org), a purpose-built centre with a mixed range of aquatic creatures from the mysterious basilisk, which can walk on water, to the perennially popular piranhas and crocodiles.

Osterley

Map 2, B5. Park: daily 9am–7.30pm or dusk; free. House: March Sat & Sun 1–4.30pm; Easter–Oct Wed–Sun 1–4.30pm; £4.90 ⊖ Osterley.

Robert Adam redesigned another colossal Elizabethan mansion – this time for the Child family – three miles northwest of Syon at **Osterley Park**, which maintains the impression of being in the middle of the countryside, despite the presence of the M4 to the north of the house. The park itself is well worth exploring, and there's a great café in the Tudor stables, but anyone with a passing interest in Adam's work should pay a visit to **Osterley House** itself.

From the outside, Osterley bears some similarity to Syon, the big difference being Adam's grand entrance portico, with its tall, Ionic colonnade. From here, you enter a characteristically cool Entrance Hall, followed by the so-called State Rooms of the south wing. Highlights include the Drawing Room, with Reynolds portraits on the damask walls and a coffered ceiling centred on a giant marigold, and the Etruscan Dressing Room, in which every surface is covered in delicate painted trelliswork, sphinxes and urns, a style that Adam (and Wedgwood) dubbed "Etruscan", though it is in fact derived from Greek vases found at Pompeii.

Kew Gardens

Map 2, C6. Daily 9.30am–7.30pm or dusk; £10; ⓦwww.kew.org ⊖ Kew Gardens.

Established in 1759, the **Royal Botanic Gardens** have grown from their original eight acres into a 300-acre site in which more than 33,000 species are grown in plantations and glasshouses, a display that attracts over a million visitors every year, most of them with no specialist interest at all. There's always something to see, whatever the season, but to get the most out of the place come sometime between spring and autumn, bring a picnic and stay for the day. The only drawback to Kew is the fact that it lies on the main flight path to Heathrow.

There are four entry points to the gardens, but the majority of people arrive at Kew Gardens tube and train station, a few minutes' walk east of the **Victoria Gate**. Of all the glasshouses, by far the most celebrated is the **Palm House**, a curvaceous mound of glass and wrought iron designed by Decimus Burton in the 1840s. Its drippingly humid atmosphere nurtures most of the known palm species, while there's a small but excellent tropical aquarium in the basement. South of here is the largest of the glasshouses, the **Temperate House**, which contains plants from every continent, including one of the largest indoor palms in the world, the sixty-foot Chilean Wine Palm.

Kew's origins as an eighteenth-century royal pleasure garden are evident in the numerous follies dotted about the gardens, the most conspicuous of which is the ten-storey, 163-foot-high **Pagoda**, visible to the south of the Temperate House. The three-storey red-brick mansion of **Kew Palace**, to the northwest of the Palm House, was bought by George II as a nursery for his umpteen children (sadly, it's been closed for renovation for some years now). A sure way to lose the crowds is to head for the thickly wooded, southwestern section of the park around **Queen Charlotte's Cottage** (April–Sept Sat & Sun 10.30am–4pm; free), a tiny thatched summerhouse built in the 1770s as a royal picnic spot for George III's queen.

Richmond

Map 2, D7. ⊖ Richmond.

On emerging from the station at **Richmond**, you'd be forgiven for wondering why you're here, but the procession of chain stores spread out along the one-way system is only half the story. To see the area's more interesting side, take one of the narrow pedestrianized alleyways off busy George Street, which bring you to the wide, open space of **Richmond Green**, one of the finest village greens in London, and no doubt one of the most peaceful before it found itself on the main flight path into Heathrow. Handsome seventeenth- and eighteenth-century houses line the south side of the Green, where the medieval royal palace of Richmond once stood, though only the unspectacular **Tudor Gateway** survives today.

The other place to head for in Richmond is the **Riverside**, pedestrianized, terraced and redeveloped in ersatz classical style in the 1980s. The real joy of the waterfront, however, is **Richmond Bridge**, London's oldest extant bridge, an elegant span of five arches made from Purbeck stone in 1777. The old town hall, set back from the new development, houses the **tourist office** (Mon–Fri 10am–5pm; Easter–Sept daily 10am–5pm; ☎020/8940 9125, ⊛www .guidetorichmond.co.uk) and, on the second floor, the **Richmond Museum** (Tues–Sat 11am–5pm; May–Oct also Sun 1–4pm; free; ⊛www.museumofrichmond.com), but most folk prefer to ensconce themselves in the riverside pubs, or head for the numerous boat- and bike-rental outlets.

Richmond's greatest attraction is the enormous **Richmond Park** (daily: March–Sept 7am–dusk; Oct–Feb 7.30am–dusk; free; ⊛www.royalparks.gov.uk), at the top of Richmond Hill – 2500 acres of undulating grassland and bracken, dotted with coppiced woodland and as wild as anything in London. Eight miles across at its widest point, this is Europe's largest city park, famed for its red and fallow deer, which roam freely, and for its ancient oaks. For the most part untamed, the park does have a couple of deliberately landscaped plantations which feature splendid springtime azaleas and rhododendrons, in particular the **Isabella Plantation**.

Ham House

Map 2, C7. April–Oct Mon–Wed, Sat & Sun 1–5pm; £7.50 including gardens. Bus #371, or walk from Richmond.

Continuing along the towpath beyond Richmond Bridge, you'll arrive at **Ham House** after a mile or so, home to the Earls of Dysart for nearly three hundred years. Expensively furnished in the seventeenth century, and little altered since then, the house boasts one of the finest Stuart interiors in the country, from the stupendously ornate Great Staircase to the Long Gallery, featuring six "Court Beauties" by Peter Lely. Elsewhere, there are several fine ceiling paintings, some exquisite parquet flooring, and works by Van Dyck and Reynolds. Another bonus are the formal seventeenth-century **gardens** (open all year Mon–Wed, Sat & Sun 11am–6pm; £3.50, free with ticket for house), especially the Cherry Garden, laid out with a pungent lavender parterre, and surrounded by yew hedges and pleached hornbeam arbours. The Orangery, overlooking the original kitchen garden, serves as a tearoom.

Hampton Court Palace

Map 2, B9. Daily: April–Oct 10am–6pm; Nov–March 10am–4.30pm; £12; ⓦwww.hrp.org.uk Hampton Court train station from Waterloo.

Hampton Court Palace, a sprawling red-brick ensemble on the banks of the Thames, thirteen miles southwest of London, is the finest of England's royal abodes. Built in 1516 by the upwardly mobile **Cardinal Wolsey**, Henry VIII's Lord Chancellor, it was purloined by Henry himself after Wolsey fell from favour. In the second half of the seventeenth century, Charles II laid out the gardens, inspired by what he had seen at Versailles, while William and Mary had large sections of the palace remodelled by Wren a few years later.

The **Royal Apartments** are divided into six thematic walking tours. There's not a lot of information in any of the rooms, but the palace staff are very knowledgeable,

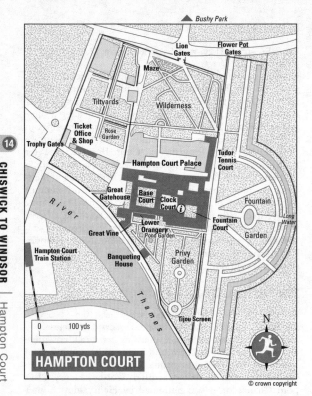

▲ Bushy Park

Lion Gates
Flower Pot Gates
Maze
Tiltyards
Wilderness
Ticket Office & Shop
Rose Garden
Trophy Gates
Hampton Court Palace
Tudor Tennis Court
River
Great Gatehouse
Base Court
Clock Court ℹ
Fountain Court
Fountain
Long Water
Lower Orangery
Pond Garden
Great Vine
Garden
Hampton Court Train Station
Banqueting House
Privy Garden
Thames
Tijou Screen
N

0   100 yds

HAMPTON COURT

© crown copyright

and guided tours, each lasting 45 minutes, are available at no extra charge for Henry VIII's and the King's apartments; all are led by period-costumed historians, who do a fine job of bringing the place to life. If your energy is lacking – and Hampton Court is huge – the most rewarding sections are **Henry VIII's State Apartments**, which feature the glorious double hammer-beamed Great Hall, the **King's Apartments** (remodelled by William III), and the vast **Tudor Kitchens**. The last two are also served by audio tours. Part of the Royal Collection is housed in the **Renaissance Picture Gallery** and is chock-full of treasures, among them paintings by Tintoretto, Lotto, Titian, Cranach, Bruegel and Holbein.

Tickets to the Royal Apartments cover entry to the rest of the sites in the grounds. Those who don't wish to visit the apartments are free to wander around the gardens, but have to pay extra to visit the curious **Royal Tennis Courts** (50p), the palace's famously tricky yew-hedge **Maze** (£3), and the **Privy Garden** (£3), where you can view Andrea Mantegna's colourful, heroic canvases, *The Triumphs of Caesar*, housed in the Lower Orangery, and the celebrated **Great Vine**, whose grapes are sold at the palace each year in September.

Windsor and Eton

Every weekend, trains from Waterloo and Paddington are packed with people heading for **Windsor**, the royal enclave 21 miles west of London, where they join the human

Getting to Windsor

Windsor has two **train stations**, both very close to the centre. Direct trains from Waterloo (every 30min; journey time 50min–1hr) arrive at **Windsor & Eton Riverside**, five minutes' walk from the centre; trains from Paddington require a change at Slough (Mon–Fri every 20min, Sat & Sun every 30min; journey time 30–40min), and arrive at **Windsor & Eton Central**, directly opposite the castle. The latter styles itself "Windsor Royal Station", though Queen Victoria herself was very particular to favour neither train station (and therefore train company) over the other. Note that you must arrive and depart from the same station, as tickets are not interchangeable. The **tourist office** (daily 10am–5pm; longer hours in summer; ☏01753/743900, ⊛www.windsor.gov.uk) is at 24 High St, opposite the Guildhall.

conveyor belt round Windsor Castle. Though almost as famous as Windsor, **Eton** (across the river from the castle) receives a mere fraction of the tourists, yet the guided tours of the school give an eye-opening glimpse of life as lived by the offspring of Britain's moneyed classes.

Windsor Castle

Daily: March–Oct 9.45am–5.15pm; Nov–Feb 9.45am–4.15pm; £12.50; ⓦ www.royal.gov.uk

Towering above the town on a steep chalk bluff, **Windsor Castle** is an undeniably awesome sight, its chilly grey walls, punctuated by mighty medieval bastions, continuing as far as the eye can see. Once there, the small selection of state rooms open to the public is unexciting, though the magnificent St George's Chapel and the chance to see another small selection of the Queen's private art collection make the trip worthwhile. On a fine day, it pays to put aside some time for exploring **Windsor Great Park**, which stretches for several miles to the south of the castle.

Once inside the castle, it's best to head straight for **St George's Chapel** (Mon–Sat 10am–4pm), a glorious Gothic Perpendicular structure ranking with Henry VII's chapel in Westminster Abbey, and the second most important resting place for royal corpses after the Abbey – the Queen Mum and (the ashes of) Princess Margaret are buried here. Entry is via the south door and a one-way system operates, which brings you out by the **Albert Memorial Chapel**, built by Henry VII as a burial place for Henry VI, completed by Cardinal Wolsey for his own burial, but eventually converted for Queen Victoria into a high-Victorian memorial to her husband, Prince Albert.

- -

The **Changing of the Guard** (see p.32) takes place at
Windsor April–June Mon–Sat at 11am;
alternate days the rest of the year.

- -

Before entering the State Apartments, pay a quick visit to **Queen Mary's Dolls' House**, a palatial micro-residence designed for the amusement of the wife of George V, and the **Gallery**, where special exhibitions culled from the Royal Collection are staged. Most visitors just gape in awe at the gilded grandeur of the **State Apartments**, while the real highlights – the paintings from the Royal Collection that line the walls – are rarely given a second glance. The **King's Dressing Room**, for example, despite its small size, contains a feast of art treasures, including a dapper Rubens self-portrait, Van Dyck's famous triple portrait of Charles I, and *The Artist's Mother*, a perfectly observed study of old age by Rembrandt.

You'd hardly know that Windsor suffered the most devastating **fire** in its history in 1992, so thorough (and uninspired) has the restoration been in rooms such as **St George's Hall**. By contrast, the octagonal **Lantern Lobby**, beyond, is clearly an entirely new room, a safe neo-Gothic design replacing the old chapel. At this point, those visiting during the winter season (Oct–March) are given the privilege of seeing four **Semi-State Rooms**, created in the 1820s by George IV, and still used in the summer months by the Royal Family.

Most tourists are put off going to **Windsor Great Park** due to its sheer scale. With the Home Park – including Victoria and Albert's mausoleum of Frogmore – off limits to the public, except for a very few days in each year, visitors can only enter the park via the three-mile Long Walk. Another mile or so to the south is **Savill Garden** (daily: March–Oct 10am–6pm; Nov–Feb 10am–4pm; £3.50–5.50 depending on season; ⓦwww.savillgarden.co.uk), a 35-acre patch of woodland that has one of the finest floral displays in and around London.

Eton College

Easter, July & Aug daily 10.30am–4.30pm; after Easter to June & Sept daily 2–4.30pm; £3.80; ⓦwww.etoncollege.com

Crossing the bridge at the end of Thames Avenue in Windsor town brings you to **Eton**, a one-street village lined with bookshops and antique dealers, but famous all over the world for **Eton College**, a ten-minute walk from the river. When the school was founded in 1440, its aim was to give free education to seventy poor scholars and choristers – how times have changed. The original fifteenth-century **schoolroom**, gnarled with centuries of graffiti, survives, but the real highlight is the **College Chapel**, completed in 1482, a wonderful example of English Perpendicular architecture. The self-congratulatory **Museum of Eton Life**, where you're deposited at the end of the tour, is well worth missing unless you have a fascination with flogging, fagging and bragging about the school's facilities and alumni.

Listings

Listings

Accommodation

There's no getting away from the fact that **accommodation** in London is expensive. Compared with most European cities, you pay over the odds in every category. The city's hostels are among the most expensive in the world, while venerable institutions such as the *Ritz*, the *Dorchester* and the *Savoy* charge guests the very top international prices – up to £300 or more per luxurious night.

The cheapest places to stay are the dorm beds of the city's numerous **hostels**: one in an independent hostel will cost you £12, while official YHA hostels will charge £20 or more. Even the most basic **B&Bs** struggle to bring their tariffs down to £45 for a double with shared facilities, and you're more likely to find yourself paying £60 or more. In addition to hotels and B&Bs, there's also a growing trend of **apartment complexes**. Like hotels, they can be booked by the night, but for the price they are generally of a higher standard than other accommodation in the same price band, and are particularly good value for families or groups.

We've given phone numbers and websites or email addresses for all our listed accommodation, but if you fail to find a bed you could turn to one of the various **accommodation agencies**. All London tourist offices (listed on p.17) operate a room-booking service, for which a small fee is levied (they also take the first night's fee in advance). There

London postcodes

A brief word on **London postcodes**: the name of each street is followed by a letter giving the geographical location (E for "east", WC for "west central" and so on) and a number that specifies the postal area. However, this is not a reliable indication of the remoteness of the locale – W5, for example, lies beyond the more remote sounding NW10 – so it's always best to check a map before taking a room in what may sound like a fairly central area.

are **British Hotel Reservation Centre** (BHRC; Ⓦwww .bhrc.co.uk) desks at Heathrow arrivals terminal, and at both Heathrow underground stations (Ⓣ020/8564 8808 or 8564 8211), and both terminals of Gatwick Airport (Ⓣ01293/502 433); there are also four desks in and around Victoria: at the train station (Ⓣ020/7828 1027), coach station (Ⓣ020/7824 8232), underground (Ⓣ020/7828 2262) and at 13 Grosvenor Gardens, SW1 (Ⓣ020/7828 2425). Most offices are open daily from 6am till midnight, and there's no booking fee.

You can also book for free **online** at Ⓦwww.londontown .com; payment is made directly to the hotel on checking out and they can offer discounts of up to fifty percent. Other useful websites include Ⓦwww.lastminute.com, Ⓦwww .hotelsengland.com, and Ⓦwww.laterooms.com, which has great deals if you book right at the last moment.

Hostels

London's official **Youth Hostel Association (YHA) hostels** are generally the cleanest, most efficiently run hostels in the capital. However, they charge around fifty percent or more above the rates of private hostels, and tend to get booked up several months in advance. **Independent hostels** are cheaper and more relaxed, but can be less reliable in terms of facilities. Typical of this laid-back brand of hostel is the Astor chain of five hostels, run exclusively for the 18–30 age group. A good website for booking independent hostels **online** is Ⓦwww.hostellondon.com.

YHA hostels

City of London

Map 5, H4. 36 Carter Lane, EC4 Ⓣ020/7236 4965, Ⓔcity@yha.org.ukↈ St Paul's. 200-bed hostel in superb location opposite St Paul's Cathedral. Some twins at £50 a room, but mostly four- to eight-bed dorms for £17.20 per person. There's no kitchen, but a café for lunch and dinner. No groups.

Earl's Court

Map 3, A8. 38 Bolton Gardens, SW5 Ⓣ020/7373 7083, Ⓔearlscourt@yha.org.ukↈ Earl's Court. Better than a lot of accommodation in Earl's Court, but only offering dorms with usually 10 beds – and the triple bunks take some getting used to. Kitchen, café and patio garden. No groups. £19.50 per person.

Hampstead Heath

Map 2, G2. 4 Wellgarth Rd, NW11 Ⓣ020/8458 9054, Ⓔhampstead@yha.org.uk ↈ Golders Green. One of London's biggest and best-appointed YHA hostels, with its own garden and the wilds of Hampstead Heath

nearby. Rooms with 3–6 beds cost £20.40 per person; family rooms with 2–5 beds are also available, starting at £35 for one adult and one child or £45 for two adults.

Holland House

Map 2, F5. Holland Walk, W8 Ⓣ020/7937 0748, Ⓦwww.hollhse .btinternet.co.ukↈ Holland Park or High Street Kensington. Idyllically situated in the wooded expanse of Holland Park and fairly convenient for the centre, this extensive hostel offers a decent kitchen and an inexpensive café, but tends to be popular with school groups. Dorms only (8–20 beds), at £21.60 per person.

Oxford Street

Map 3, G4. 14 Noel St, W1 Ⓣ020/7734 1618, Ⓔoxfordst@yha .org.ukↈ Oxford Circus or Tottenham Court Road. Its West End location and modest size (75 beds in rooms of 2, 3 and 4 beds) mean that this hostel tends to be full year round. No children under 6, no groups, and no café, but there is a large kitchen. From £22.60 per person.

Rotherhithe

Map 2, K5. 20 Salter Rd, SE16 ☎ **020/7232 2114,** ⓔ **rotherhithe@yha.org.uk** ⊖ **Rotherhithe or Canada Water.** London's largest purpose-built hostel can feel a little out of things, but it's well-connected to central London, and often has space when more central places are full. Breakfast, packed lunch and evening meals available. Rooms have 2, 4, 6 or 10 beds and cost from £24.60 per person.

St Pancras

Map 3, H2. 79–81 Euston Rd, NW1 ☎ **020/7388 9998,** ⓔ **stpancras@yha.org.uk** ⊖ **King's Cross or Euston.** Housed on six floors of a former police station, directly opposite the British Library, on the busy Euston Road. Beds costs £24.60 per person, and rooms are very clean, bright, triple glazed and air conditioned – some, including all doubles, even have en-suite facilities. Family rooms are available, all with TVs, from £50.50. No groups.

Private hostels

Ashlee House

Map 3, I2. 261–265 Gray's Inn Rd, WC1 ☎ **020/7833 9400,** ⓦ **www .ashleehouse.co.uk** ⊖ **King's Cross.** Clean and friendly hostel in a converted office block near King's Cross Station. Internet access, laundry and kitchen facilities are provided. Dorms, which vary in size from four to sixteen beds, start at £16; there are also a few private singles and twins, starting at £25 per person. Breakfast is included.

Generator

Map 3, H2. Compton Place, off Tavistock Place, WC1 ☎ **020/7388 7666,** ⓦ **www.the-generator.co.uk** ⊖ **Russell Square or Euston.** A huge, funky 800-bed hostel, tucked away down a cobbled street. The neon and UV lighting and post-industrial décor may not be to everyone's taste, but with prices starting at just £12.50 a night for a dorm bed and breakfast, this is the best bargain in this part of town. Facilities include Internet access, games rooms, movie nights, a bar and a canteen serving breakfast and evening meals for just £3. Over 800 beds, with prices ranging from £35 for a single, to £25 per person for a double, £20 per person for a triple, and £12.50 (12 beds) to £17 (4 beds) in a dorm.

Leinster Inn

Map 3, A5. 7–12 Leinster Square, W2 ☎ **020/7229 9641,** ⓦ **www .astorhostels.com** ⊖ **Queensway or**

Notting Hill Gate. With 360 beds, this is the biggest and liveliest of the Astor hostels (under-30s only), with a party atmosphere and two bars open until the small hours. Dorm beds (4–8 per room) £14–18, singles from £26, doubles from £45.

Museum Inn

Map 3, I3. 27 Montague St, W1 ☎020/7580 5360, ⓦwww.astorhostels.com⊖ Russell Square. In a lovely Georgian house by the British Museum, this is the quietest of the Astor hostels. There's no bar, but it's a sociable, laid-back place, and well situated. Small kitchen, TV lounge, and baths as well as showers. Dorms with 4–10 beds from £16, including breakfast.

St Christopher's Village

Map 7, E9. 161–165 Borough High St, SE1 ☎020/7407 1856, ⓦwww.st-christophers.co.uk⊖ London Bridge. Flagship of a chain of independent hostels, with no fewer than three properties on Borough High Street (and branches in Camden, Greenwich and Shepherd's Bush). The décor is upbeat and cheerful, the place is efficiently run and there's a party-animal ambience, fuelled by the neighbouring bar and the rooftop sauna and hot tub. Beds in dorms with 4–14 beds £13–22, twins £44!

wake up! London

Map 3, B4. 1 Queens Gardens, W2 ☎020/7262 4471, ⓦwww.wakeuplondon.co.uk ⊖ Paddington or Lancaster Gate. New and funky hostel with great facilities, including an information desk, 24hr reception and a basement bar (with pool table) that's open daily until 3am. A good choice if you want a party atmosphere. Beds, in single and twin rooms or in 8-bed dorms, cost from £15.

Hotels and B&Bs

Most **B&Bs and hotels** are housed in former residential properties, which means that rooms tend to be on the small side, and only the more upmarket properties have elevators. That said, most rooms have TVs, tea- and coffee-making facilities and telephones, and breakfast is nearly always included in the price.

The recommendations below cover every category from budget to luxury, though you're unlikely to find anything at all for under £50 – most accommodation falls between £50 and £100 per double. Bear in mind that many of the plush hotels listed slash their advertised rates at the weekend, when the business types have gone home.

When choosing your **area**, bear in mind that the West End – Soho, Covent Garden, St James's, Mayfair and Marylebone – and the western districts of Knightsbridge and Kensington, are dominated by expensive, upmarket hotels, whereas Bloomsbury is both inexpensive and very central. For cheaper rooms, the widest choice is close to the main train termini of Victoria and Paddington, and the budget B&Bs of Earl's Court.

St James's, Mayfair and Marylebone

Edward Lear Hotel
Map 3, E4. 28–30 Seymour St, W1
⊕ 020/7402 5401, ⊛ www.edlear
.com⊖ Marble Arch. Lear's former home enjoys a great location close to Oxford Street and Hyde Park, lovely flower boxes and a plush foyer. Rooms themselves need a bit of a make-over, but the low prices reflect both this and the fact that most only have shared facilities. £66.50.

Lincoln House Hotel
Map 3, E4. 33 Gloucester Place, W1 ⊕ 020/7486 7630, ⊛ www .lincoln-house-hotel.co.uk ⊖ Marble Arch. Dark wood panelling gives this Georgian B&B in Marylebone a ship's-cabin feel,

while all the rooms are en suite and well equipped. Rates vary according to the size of the bed and length of stay. £79.

Palace Hotel
Map 3, E4. 31 Great Cumberland Place, W1 ⊕ 020/7262 5585 ⊖ Marble Arch. Small but luxurious hotel close to Marble Arch which oozes class, from the hand-painted friezes on the staircase to the four-poster beds in many of the rooms. Continental breakfast included. £70.

The Ritz
Map 4, C9. 150 Piccadilly, W1
⊕ 020/7300 2308, ⊛ www
.theritzhotel.co.uk⊖ Green Park. In a class of its own with its extravagant Louis XVI interiors and overall air of decadent luxury. Rooms,

which start at around £350 for a double, maintain the opulent French theme, with the west-facing accommodation, overlooking Green Park, in greatest demand. Ask about the special weekend packages, including breakfast and champagne.

Wigmore Court Hotel
Map 3, E4. 23 Gloucester Place, W1 ☏020/7935 0928, ⓦwww.wigmore -court-hotel.co.uk⊖ Marble Arch or Baker Street. The chintzy décor may not be to everyone's taste, but this Georgian town house is a better than average B&B, boasting a high tally of returning clients. Comfortable rooms with en-suite facilities, plus two doubles with shared facilities at a price code lower. Unusually, there's also a laundry and basic kitchen for guests' use. £89.

Soho, Covent Garden and the Strand

The Fielding Hotel
Map 4, I6. 4 Broad Court, Bow St, WC2 ☏020/7836 8305, ⓦwww.the-fielding-hotel.co.uk ⊖ Covent Garden. Quietly and perfectly situated on a traffic-free and gas-lit court, this excellent hotel is one of Covent Garden's hidden gems. It's footsteps away from the Royal Opera House, and its en-suite rooms are a firm

favourite with visiting performers. Breakfast is extra. £100.

Hazlitt's
Map 4, F5. 6 Frith St, W1 ☏020/7434 1771, ⓦwww.hazlittshotel.co.uk ⊖ Tottenham Court Road. Located off the south side of Soho Square, this early-eighteenth-century building is a hotel of real character and charm, offering en-suite rooms decorated and furnished as close to period style as convenience and comfort allow. There's a small sitting room, but no dining room (although some of London's best restaurants are a stone's throw away). Continental breakfast (served in the rooms) is available, but isn't included in the rates. £205.

Manzi's
Map 4, F7. 1–2 Leicester St, WC2 ☏020/7734 0224, ⓦwww.manzis .co.uk⊖ Leicester Square. Set over the Italian and seafood restaurant of the same name, *Manzi's* is one of very few West End hotels in this price range. It's certainly right in the thick of things, although noise might prove to be a nuisance. Continental breakfast included. £83.

St Martin's Lane
Map 4, G7. 45 St Martin's Lane, WC2 ☏020/7300 5500, ⓦwww .morganshotelgroup.com

⊖ Leicester Square. This self-consciously chic boutique hotel with a bafflingly anonymous glass facade is a big hit with the media crowd. The *Light Bar* is the most startling of the hotel's eating and drinking outlets. Rooms currently start at around £250 a double, but rates come down at the weekend.

Seven Dials Hotel
Map 4, G6. 7 Monmouth St, WC2 ☎020/7681 0791, ⍾www.smoothhound.co.uk/hotels/sevendials ⊖ Covent Garden. Pleasant family-run hotel in the heart of theatreland. All rooms are en suite and have TV, tea/coffee-making facilities and direct-dial phones. £65.

Soho Hotel
Map 4, F5. 4 Richmond Mews, W1 ☎020/7559 3000, ⍾www.sohohotel.com ⊖ Tottenham Court Road. An ex-NCP car park made over by designer of the moment Kit Kemp. No two spaces are the same, and the result is eclecticism bordering on schizophrenia, from the Oriental lobby to the camp fuchsia boudoirs and a screening room done out in fake fur and scarlet leather. The penthouse suites (£795 a night, anyone?) have wonderful wraparound terraces and rooftop views, and facilities are, as you'd expect, top-notch. £275.

Bloomsbury

Hotel Cavendish
Map 3, H3. 75 Gower St, WC1, ☎020/7636 9079, ⍾www.hotelcavendish.com ⊖ Goodge Street. Gower Street is very busy with traffic, but get a room at the back of the property and you'll have a peaceful night. This is a real bargain, with lovely owners, a walled garden and some original features. All rooms have shared facilities, and there are some good-value family rooms, too. £48.

Crescent Hotel
Map 3, H2. 49–50 Cartwright Gardens, WC1 ☎020/7387 1515, ⍾www.crescenthoteloflondon.com ⊖ Euston or Russell Square. Comfortable and clean B&B, with pink furnishings. All doubles are en suite, but there are a few bargain singles with shared facilities. £93.

myhotel
Map 3, H3. 11–13 Bayley St, Bedford Square, WC1 ☎020/7667 6000, ⍾www.myhotels.co.uk ⊖ Tottenham Court Road. The aquarium in the lobby is the telltale sign that this is a feng shui hotel. Despite the positive vibes, and the Conran-designed look, the double-glazed, air-conditioned rooms are on the small side for the price. Still, there's a gym, a

pleasant library and a restaurant – and the location is great for the West End. £270.

Ridgemount Private Hotel
Map 4, F1. 65–67 Gower St, WC1 ①020/7636 1141, ⑩www .ridgemounthotel.co.uk⊖ Goode Street. Old fashioned, very friendly family-run place, with small rooms, half of them with shared facilities, a garden, free hot-drinks machine and laundry service. A reliable, basic bargain for Bloomsbury; cash only. £52.

Hotel Russell
Map 4 H1. Russell Square, WC1 ①020/7837 6470, ⑩www.principal -hotels.com⊖ Russell Square. From its grand 1898 exterior to its opulent interiors of marble, wood and crystal, this late-Victorian landmark fully retains its period atmosphere in all its public areas. The rooms live up to the grandeur of the lobby, if not necessarily to its style. Expensive, but various deals are available; check their website. Breakfast is not included. £229.

Clerkenwell and the City

City Hotel
Map 7, M2. 12 Osborn St, E1 ①020/7247 3313, ⑩www .cityhotellondon.co.uk⊖ Aldgate East. Spacious and clean, this modern hotel stands on the eastern edge of the City, in the heart of the Bengali East End at the bottom of Brick Lane. The plain rooms are all en suite, and many have kitchens, too; four-person rooms are a bargain for families or small groups. £85.

The King's Wardrobe
Map 5, H5. 6 Wardrobe Place, Carter Lane, EC4 ①020/7792 2222, ⑩www.bridgestreet.com ⊖ St Paul's. Wonderfully located in a quiet courtyard just behind St Paul's Cathedral, this place is part of an international chain that caters largely for a business clientele. The apartments (one-to three-bed) offer fully equipped kitchens and workstations, a concierge service and housekeeping, and offer great value if you're sharing. Though housed in a fourteenth-century building that once contained Edward III's royal regalia, the interior is unrelentingly modern. £130–160 per night per apartment.

The Rookery
Map 3, K3. 12 Peter's Lane, Cowcross St, EC1 ①020/7336 0931, ⑩www .rookeryhotel.com⊖ Farringdon. Rambling Georgian town house that makes a fantastically discreet little hideaway on the edge of the City in trendy Clerken-

well. The rooms start at around £245 a double; each one has been individually designed in a deliciously camp, modern take on Baroque, and all have super bathrooms with lots of character.

Zetter Hotel
Map 3, K3. 86–88 Clerkenwell Rd, EC1 ⊕020/7324 4444, ⓦwww .thezetter.com⊖ Farringdon.
A warehouse converted with real style and a dash of 1960s glamour. Rooms are simple and minimalist, with decorative floral panels and lights that change colour; ask for a room at the back overlooking cobbled St John's Square. The attached restaurant serves good modern Italian food, and water for guests is supplied from the *Zetter's* own well. £158.

South Bank and Southwark

Mad Hatter
Map 6, F2. 3–7 Stamford St, SE1 ⊕020/7401 9222, ⓦwww.fullers .co.uk⊖ Southwark or Blackfriars.
Situated above a Fuller's pub on the corner of Blackfriars Road, and run by the Fuller's brewery. Breakfast is extra on weekdays, and is served in the pub, but this is a great location, a short walk from the Tate Modern and the South Bank. Ask about the weekend deals. £125.

Southwark Rose Hotel
Map 7, C9. 43–47 Southwark Bridge Rd, SE1 ⊕020/7015 1490, ⓦwww .southwarkrosehotel.co.uk
⊖ London Bridge. The *Southwark Rose* markets itself as a budget hotel with boutique style – nice design touches raise the rooms several notches above the bland chain hotels in the area. Giant aluminium lamps hover over the lobby, which is lined with funky photographs, while the penthouse restaurant offers breakfast with a rooftop view and free Internet access. £120.

Victoria

B&B Belgravia
Map 3 E7. 64–66 Ebury St, SW1 ⊕020/7823 4928, ⓦwww.bb-belgravia.com
⊖ Victoria. A rarity in this neck of the woods – a B&B with flair. The 17 rooms are of boutique hotel quality, with original cornices and large sash windows along with stylish modern touches – all have flatscreen TVs and slick bathrooms. Communal spaces are light and similarly well designed, and staff are welcoming and enthusiastic. Full English breakfast and Internet access included. £94.

Luna & Simone Hotel

Map 3, G8. 47–49 Belgrave Rd, SW1 ⓣ020/7834 5897, ⓦwww .lunasimonehotel.com ⊖ Victoria. Inexpensive B&B with a bright foyer, friendly staff and plain, well-maintained rooms – most of them en suite – with TVs and telephones. Internet access. £75.

Oxford House Hotel

Map 3, F8. 92–94 Cambridge St, SW1 ⓣ020/7834 6467, ⓕ020/7834 0225 ⊖ Victoria. Probably the best-value rooms you can get near Victoria station, though not otherwise distinguished. Showers and toilets are shared, but kept pristine. Full English breakfast included. £45.

Sanctuary House Hotel

Map 4, F13. 33 Tothill St, SW1 ⓣ020/7799 4044, ⓦwww.fullers hotels.co.uk ⊖ St James's Park. Run by Fuller's Brewery, situated above a Fuller's pub, and decked out like one, too, in gaudy pseudo-Victoriana. Breakfast is extra, and is served in the pub, but the location, right by St James's Park, is terrific. Ask about weekend deals. £135.

Paddington, Bayswater and Notting Hill

Columbia Hotel

Map 3, C5. 95–99 Lancaster Gate, W2 ⓣ020/7402 0021, ⓦwww.columbiahotel.co.uk ⊖ Lancaster Gate. This large hotel, once five Victorian houses, offers simply decorated en-suite rooms – some with views over Hyde Park – a spacious public lounge with a vaguely Deco feel, and a cocktail bar. Said to be a rock-star favourite, but surprisingly good value for all that. £86.

Garden Court Hotel

Map 3, A4. 30–31 Kensington Gardens Square, W2 ⓣ020/7229 2553, ⓦwww.gardencourthotel.co.uk ⊖ Bayswater or Queensway. Presentable, family-run B&B on a quiet square close to Portobello market; half the rooms have shared facilities, half are en suite. Full English breakfast included. £64, en suite £92.

The Gresham Hotel

Map 3, C4. 116 Sussex Gardens, W2 ⓣ020/7402 2920, ⓦwww .the-gresham-hotel.co.uk ⊖ Paddington. B&B with a touch more class than many in the area. Rooms are small but tastefully kitted out, and all have TV. Continental breakfast included. £95.

The Hempel

Map 3, B5. 31–35 Craven Hill Gardens, W2 ⓣ020/7298 9000, ⓦwww.the-hempel.co.uk ⊖ Lancaster Gate or Queensway.

Deeply fashionable minimalist hotel, designed by the actress turned designer Anoushka Hempel, with a huge and very empty atrium entrance and an excellent postmodern Italian/Thai restaurant – *I-Thai* – on site. White-on-white rooms start at around £245.

Pavilion Hotel

Map 3, C4. 34–36 Sussex Gardens, W2 ☎ 020/7262 0905, ⓦ www .pavilion.hotel.co.uk ⊖ Paddington. A decadent rock star's home from home, with outrageously over-the-top décor and every room individually themed, from "honky tonk Afro" to "Highland Fling". £100.

Portobello Gold

Map 2, F4. 95–97 Portobello Rd, W1 ☎ 020/7460 4900, ⓦ www.portobellogold.com ⊖ Notting Hill Gate or Holland Park. Fun and friendly option above a cheery modern pub. Rooms are plain, and some are tiny, with miniature en-suite bathrooms, but all are fairly priced. Best is the apartment which sleeps 6 (at a pinch) and costs just £150 a night. It has the feel of a cosy, down-at-heel holiday home, with a dinky Caribbean-themed bathroom and a fantastic roof terrace with putting green. £70.

Knightsbridge, Kensington and Chelsea

Abbey House

Map 3, A6. 11 Vicarage Gate, W8 ☎ 020/7721 7395, ⓦ www .abbeyhousekensington.com ⊖ High Street Kensington or Notting Hill. Inexpensive Victorian B&B in a quiet street just north of Kensington High Street, maintained to a very high standard by its attentive owners. Rooms are large and bright – prices are kept down by offering shared facilities rather than fitting the usual cramped bathroom unit. Full English breakfast included, and free tea and coffee available all day. Cash only. £74.

Aster House

Map 3, C8. 3 Sumner Place, SW7 ☎ 020/7581 5888, ⓦ www.asterhouse.com ⊖ South Kensington. Pleasant, non-smoking and award-winning B&B in a luxurious white-stuccoed South Ken street; there's a lovely garden at the back and a large conservatory, where breakfast is served. Singles with shared facilities start at around £90 a night; doubles from £140.

Blakes Hotel

Map 3, B8. 33 Roland Gardens, SW7 ☎ 020/7370 6701, ⓦ www .blakeshotel.com ⊖ Gloucester

Road. *Blakes'* dramatic interior – another one designed by Anoushka Hempel – and glamorous suites have long attracted visiting celebs. A faintly *Raffles*-esque flavour pervades, with bamboo furniture and old travelling trunks mixing with unusual objects, tapestries and prints. Doubles from £275 are smart but small, the restaurant and bar are excellent, and service is of a very high standard. Singles from £170.

Five Sumner Place
Map 3, C8. 5 Sumner Place, SW7 ℡020/7584 7586, ⓦwww.sumner place.com ⊖ South Kensington. Another discreetly luxurious B&B (see *Aster House* above) on this attractive white-stuccoed terrace. As at *Aster House*, all rooms are en suite and breakfast is served in the lovely conservatory. £130.

The Gore
Map 3, B7. 189 Queen's Gate, SW7 ℡020/7584 6601, ⓦwww .gorehotel.com ⊖ South Kensington, Gloucester Road or High Street Kensington. Popular, privately owned century-old hotel, awash with Oriental rugs, rich mahogany, walnut panelling and other Victoriana. A pricey, but excellent bistro restaurant adds to its allure, and it's only a step away from Hyde Park. Rooms, some

with four-poster beds, from £190.

Hotel 167
Map 3, B8. 167 Old Brompton Rd, SW5 ℡020/7373 3221, ⓦwww .hotel167.com⊖ Gloucester Road. Small, stylishly furnished B&B with en-suite facilities, double glazing and a fridge in all rooms. Continental buffet-style breakfast is served in the attractive morning room/reception. £100.

Vicarage Private Hotel
Map 3, A6. 10 Vicarage Gate, W8 ℡020/7229 4030, ⓦwww.london vicaragehotel.com⊖ High Street Kensington or Notting Hill. Ideally located B&B a step away from Hyde Park. Clean rooms with shared facilities, and full English breakfast included in the price. Cash/travellers' cheques only. £78.

Hampstead

Hampstead Village Guesthouse
🏃 Map G3. 2 Kemplay Rd, NW3 ℡020/7435 8679, ⓦww .HampsteadGuesthouse.com ⊖ Hampstead. Lovely B&B in a freestanding Victorian house on a quiet backstreet between Hampstead village and the Heath. Rooms (most en suite, all non smoking) are wonderfully

characterful, crammed with books, pictures and handmade and antique furniture. Cute cabin-like single for £48, and a self-contained studio for £90. Meals to order.

La Gaffe

Map 2, G3. 107–111 Heath St, NW3 ☏**020/7435 8965,** ⓦ**www .lagaffe.co.uk** ⊖ **Hampstead.** Small, warren-like hotel situated over an Italian restaurant and bar in the heart of Hampstead village. All rooms are en suite, if a little cramped, and there's a roof terrace for use in fine weather. £95.

Earl's Court

Mayflower Hotel

Map 3, A8. 26–28 Trebovir Rd, SW5 ☏**020/7370 0991,** ⓦ**www.mayflower-group.co.uk** ⊖ **Earl's Court.** In an area of bog-standard B&Bs, this is a real winner, decked out in bold warm colours and strewn with Indian antiques; there's a stylish water feature in reception and parrots in the lounge. All rooms are en suite, with singles from £60, doubles £120, and apartments (£130) that work out economical if you're in a group.

Richmond and Greenwich

Doughty Cottage B&B

Map 2 C7. 142a Richmond Hill, TW10 6RH ☏**020/8332 9434,** ⓦ**www.doughtycottage.com** ⊖ **Richmond.** A walled cottage at the top of Richmond Hill. The en-suite rooms are fantastically comfortable, decked out in ornate Italianate style. Latticed windows look down to the Thames and Petersham Meadows. £70.

16

Cafés and snacks

T his chapter covers the full range of **cafés** from unreconstructed "greasy spoons", where you can get traditional English breakfasts – fried egg, sausage and bacon and the like – fish and chips, pies and other calorific treats, to the refined salons of London's top hotels, where you can enjoy an afternoon tea blowout. In between, you'll find bakeries, brasseries, sandwich bars, coffee shops and ice cream parlours, all of which are open during the day for light meals, snacks or just a drink. We've also included several **ethnic eating** places where speedy service and low prices are the priority – places perfect for an inexpensive or quick bite before going out to a theatre, cinema or club. Wherever you go, you should be able to fill up for less than £10.

If you want to surf while you slurp, you'll find that London has nothing like the number and variety of **Internet cafés** as other capital cities. Your best bet is to head for a branch of *easyInternetcafé* (Ⓦ www.easy.everything.com), the no-frills Internet café chain (see Directory, p.319, for a list of branches). Alternatively, there's the more congenial *Be the*

Reds! (☎020/7209 0984; Mon–Sat 10.30am–2am) at 39 Whitfield St, just off Tottenham Court Road (⊖ Goodge Street) – a Korean-run place serving *kimbab* and coffee, with billiards in the basement.

Mayfair and Marylebone

Apostrophe
Map 4, A5. 23 Barrett St, W1 ☎020/7355 1001⊖ Bond Street. Mon–Fri 7.30am–8pm, Sat & Sun 9.30am–8pm. Modern take on the French boulangerie/patisserie, with tables looking out onto pedestrianized St Christopher's Place, just off Oxford Street. Serves up delicious sandwiches and coffee, and sells the legendary Poilâne bread.

Mômo Tearoom
Map 4, D7. 25 Heddon St, W1 ☎020/7434 4040⊖ Piccadilly Circus. Mon–Sat noon–1am, Sun noon–10.30pm. The ultimate Arabic pastiche and a successful one. The adjacent restaurant (*Momo*) is expensive, while the tearoom serves more reasonably priced, equally delicious snacks. It's a great place to hang out, with tables and hookahs spilling out onto the pavement of this little Mayfair alleyway behind Regent Street.

Patisserie Valerie at Sagne
Map 3, E3. 105 Marylebone High St, W1 ☎020/7935 6240, ⓦwww.patisserie-valerie .co.uk⊖ Bond Street or Baker Street. Mon–Fri 7.30am–7pm, Sat 8am–7pm, Sun 9am–6pm. Founded as *Maison Sagne* in the 1920s, and preserving its wonderful décor from those days, the café is now run by Soho's fab patisserie makers, and is, without doubt, Marylebone's finest.

Paul Rothe & Son
Map 4 A4. 35 Marylebone Lane, W1 ☎020/7935 6783⊖ Bond Street. Mon–Fri 8am–6pm, Sat 11.30am–5.30pm. Old-fashioned deli selling "English & Foreign Provisions", established in 1900, and serving soups, toasties and sandwiches to customers at formica tables inside the shop.

Soho

Bar du Marché
Map 4, E6. 19 Berwick St, W1 ☎020/7734 4606⊖ Tottenham Court Road, Piccadilly Circus or Leicester Square. Mon–Sat noon–11pm. A weird find in the middle of raucous Berwick Street market: a licensed French café serving quick snacks, brasserie

staples and set meals for less than £10.

Bar Italia

Map 4, F6. 22 Frith St, W1 ☎020/7437 4520 ⊖ Leicester Square. Nearly 24hr; closed Mon–Fri 4–6am. Tiny café that's a Soho institution, serving coffee, croissants and sandwiches more or less around the clock – as it has done since 1949. Popular with late-night clubbers and those here to watch the Italian-league soccer on the giant screen.

Beatroot

Map 4, E6. 92 Berwick St, W1 ☎020/7437 8591 ⊖ Piccadilly Circus. Mon–Sat 9am–9pm, Sun noon–7.30pm. Great little veggie café by the market, doling out hot savoury bakes, stews and salads (plus delicious cakes) in boxes of varying sizes – all under £5.

Brasil by Kilo

Map 4, F4. 17 Oxford St, W1 ☎020/7287 7161 ⊖ Tottenham Court Road. Daily noon–9pm. Basic and friendly refueling stop on Oxford Street, serving Brazilian food for around 99p per kilo. Head upstairs for the array of hot food and salads, or for the coffee bar downstairs for traditional snacks and sweets.

Maison Bertaux

Map 4, F6. 28 Greek St, W1 ☎020/7437 6007 ⊖ Leicester Square. Daily 8.30am–late. Long-standing, old-fashioned Soho patisserie, with tables on two floors (and one or two outside). The wonderful pastries here are among the best in the West End and a loyal clientele keeps the place busy all day long.

Patisserie Valerie

Map 4, F6. 44 Old Compton St, W1 ☎020/7437 3466, ⊛www .patisserie-valerie.co.uk ⊖ Leicester Square or Piccadilly Circus. Mon–Fri 7.30am–9pm, Sat 8am–9pm, Sun 9.30am–7pm. Popular coffee, croissant and cake emporium dating from the 1950s and attracting a loud-talking, arty Soho crowd. The same outfit runs *Patisserie Valerie at Sagne* in Marylebone (see opposite) and *Café Valerie* at 8 Russell Street, Covent Garden.

Randall and Aubin

Map 4, E6. 16 Brewer St, W1 ☎020/7287 4447 ⊖ Piccadilly Circus. Mon–Sat noon–11pm, Sun 4–10.30pm. Converted butcher's, now an excellent (but by no means cheap) champagne-oyster bar, rotisserie, sandwich shop and charcuterie, where diners perch at old marble-top counters.

Chinatown

Kopi-Tiam
Map 4, F7. 9 Wardour St, W1
⊖ Leicester Square. Daily 11am–11pm. Bright, cheap Malaysian café serving up curries, coconut rice, juices and "herbal soups" to local Malays, all for around a fiver.

Lee Ho Fook
Map 4, F7. 4 Macclesfield St, W1
⊖ Leicester Square. Mon–Thurs & Sun 11am–midnight, Fri & Sat 11am–1am. A genuine Chinese barbecue house – small, spartan and cheap – that's very difficult to find. So here are the directions: on the west side of the street is Dansey Place, and on the corner is a red-and-gold sign in Chinese and a host of ducks hanging on a rack.

Misato
Map 4, F7. 11 Wardour St, W1
⊖ Leicester Square. Daily noon–3pm & 5–10.30pm. Modern, canteen-style Japanese café serving stomach-filling rice and noodle dishes for around a fiver, plus miso soup, sushi and bento boxes.

Covent Garden and the Strand

Café in the Crypt
Map 4, H8. St Martin-in-the-Fields, Duncannon St, WC2 ☎020/7766 1129⊖ Charing Cross. Mon–Wed 10am–8pm, Thurs–Sat 10am–11pm, Sun noon–8pm. The self-service buffet, which has regular veggie dishes, usually hits the spot and the handy and atmospheric location – below the church – makes

London for veggies

Most restaurants in London will make some attempt to cater for **vegetarians**. Below is a list of exclusively vegetarian places recommended in this chapter and the "Restaurants" chapter.

Beatroot
92 Berwick St, W1 (see p.193)
Food for Thought
31 Neal St, WC2 (see p.195)
The Gate
51 Queen Caroline St, W6 (see p.210)

Manna
4 Erskine Rd, NW3 (see p.210)
Mildred's
45 Lexington St, W1 (see p.204)
The Place Below
Church of St Mary-le-Bow, Cheapside, EC2 (see p.196)

this an ideal spot to fill up before hitting the West End.

Food for Thought
Map 4, H5. 31 Neal St, WC2 ☎020/7836 9072 ⊖ Covent Garden. Mon–Sat noon–8.30pm, Sun noon–5pm. Long-established, minuscule bargain veggie restaurant with takeaway counter – the food is delicious, with the menu changing twice daily, and there are regular vegan and wheat-free options. Expect to queue and not to linger at peak times.

Gaby's
Map 4, G7. 30 Charing Cross Rd, WC2 ☎020/7836 4233⊖ Leicester Square. Mon–Sat 10am–midnight. Busy café and takeaway joint serving a wide range of home-cooked veggie and Middle Eastern specialities. Hard to beat for value, choice, location or long hours – it's licensed, too. The takeaway falafel is a central London bargain.

India Club
Map 3, I5. 143 Strand, WC2 ☎020/7836 0650⊖ Covent Garden or Temple. Daily noon–2.30pm & 6–10.50pm. There's a very faded charm to this long-established, inexpensive Anglo-Indian eatery, sandwiched between floors of the budget *Strand Continental*

Hotel. The chilli *bhajis* are to be taken very seriously.

Monmouth Coffee Company
Map 4, G5. 27 Monmouth St, WC2 ☎020/7645 3561⊖ Covent Garden or Leicester Square. Mon–Sat 8am–6.30pm. The marvellous aroma is the first thing you notice here, while the cramped wooden booths and daily newspapers on hand evoke an eighteenth-century coffee-house atmosphere – pick and mix your coffee from a fine selection (or buy the beans to take home).

Rock & Sole Plaice
Map 4, H5. 47 Endell St, WC2 ☎020/7836 3785⊖ Covent Garden. Daily 11.30am–10pm. A rare survivor: a no-nonsense traditional fish and chip shop in central London. Takeaway, eat in or sit out at one of the pavement tables.

Bloomsbury

Coffee Gallery
Map 4, H4. 23 Museum St, WC1 ☎020/7436 0455⊖ Tottenham Court Road. Mon–Fri 8.30am–5.30pm, Sat 10am–7pm, Sun noon–7pm. An excellent small café close to the British Museum, serving mouthwatering Italian sandwiches and a few more substantial dishes at lunchtime. Get there early to grab a seat.

Wagamama

🏃 Map 4, G4. 4 Streatham St, WC1 ☎020/7323 9223, 🌐www.wagamama.com⊖ Tottenham Court Road. Mon–Sat noon–11pm, Sun 12.30–10pm. Much copied since, *Wagamama* was the pioneer when it came to austere, minimalist, canteen-style noodle bars. Diners share long benches and slurp from huge bowls of noodle soup or stir-fried plates. Don't be put off if there's a queue, as the rapid turnover means it moves pretty fast, even at peak times. There are around twenty other branches in London, including a new outlet at the Royal Festival Hall on the South Bank.

Clerkenwell and Hoxton

Al's Café Bar

Map 3, J2. 11–13 Exmouth Market, EC1 ☎020/7837 4821 ⊖ Angel or Farringdon. Mon, Tues & Sun 8am–11pm, Wed–Sat 8am–2am. This is a trendy little spot – a greasy spoon with designer Formica tables and a local media-luvvie clientele who adore the Italian breads, Mediterranean dishes, nachos, decent coffee and good soups alongside the chips and grills. In the evening, it's more club-bar than café.

Clark & Sons

🏃 Map 3 J2. 46 Exmouth Market, EC1 ☎020/7837 1974 ⊖ Angel or Farringdon. Mon–Thurs 10.30am–4pm, Fri 10.30am–5.30pm, Sat 10.30am–5pm. It's a welcome surprise to find this genuine pie-and-mash shop still going strong in increasingly trendy Exmouth Market, and it's the most central one in the capital.

The City

De Gustibus

Map 5, H5. 53–55 Carter Lane, EC2 ☎020/7236 0056, 🌐www.degustibus.co.uk⊖ St Paul's or Blackfriars. Mon–Fri 7am–5pm. Award-winning bakery that constructs a wide variety of sandwiches, bruschetta, croques monsieur and quiches to eat in, perched on stools, or take away.

K10

Map 7, F2. 20 Copthall Ave, EC2 ☎020/7562 8510⊖ Moorgate. Mon–Fri 11.30am–3pm; takeaway till 6pm. Remarkably good, inexpensive City sushi outlet, with busy takeaway upstairs, and a *kaiten* (conveyor-belt) restaurant downstairs.

The Place Below

Map 7, D4. Church of St Mary-le-Bow, Cheapside, EC2 ☎020/7329

0789, Ⓦ www.theplacebelow
.co.uk ⊖ St Paul's or Bank. Mon–Fri
7.30am–3.30pm. Something of a

find in the midst of the City – a
café serving imaginative vegetarian dishes. Added to that, the

Afternoon tea

The classic English **afternoon tea** – assorted sandwiches, scones
and cream, cakes and tarts and, of course, pots of hot tea – is
available all over London. The best venues are the capital's top
hotels and most fashionable department stores; a selection of the
best is picked out below. To avoid disappointment it's best to book
in advance. Expect to spend £15–30 a head, and leave your jeans
and trainers at home – most hotels will expect men to wear a jacket
of some sort, though only *The Ritz* insists on jacket and tie.

Brown's
Map 4, C8. 33–34 Albemarle
St, W1 Ⓣ020/7493 6020,
Ⓦwww.brownshotel.com
⊖ Green Park. Daily 2–6pm.
Claridge's
Map 3, A5. Brook Street, W1
Ⓣ020/7629 8860, Ⓦwww
.savoy-group.co.uk⊖ Bond
Street. Daily 3–5.30pm.
The Dorchester
Map 3, E5. 54 Park Lane, W1
Ⓣ020/7629 8888, Ⓦwww
.dorchesterhotel.co.uk⊖ Hyde
Park Corner. Daily 3–6pm.
Fortnum & Mason
Map 4, D9. 181 Piccadilly, W1
Ⓣ020/7734 8040, Ⓦwww
.fortnumandmason.com
⊖ Green Park or Piccadilly
Circus. Daily 3–5.30pm.
Lanesborough
Map 3, E6. Hyde Park

Corner, SW1 Ⓣ020/7259
5599, Ⓦwww.lanesborough.
com⊖ Green Park. Mon–Sat
3.30–6pm, Sun 4–6pm.
The Ritz
Map 4, C9. Piccadilly, W1
Ⓣ020/7493 8181, Ⓦwww
.theritzhotel.co.uk⊖ Green
Park. Daily 11.30am, 1.30,
3.30 & 5.30pm.
The Savoy
Map 4, I8. Strand, WC2
Ⓣ020/7836 4343, Ⓦwww
.savoy-group.co.uk⊖ Char-
ing Cross. Mon–Fri 2–3.30pm
& 4–6pm, Sat & Sun noon–
1.30pm, 2–3.30pm & 4–6pm.
The Wolsely
Map 4, C9. 160 Piccadilly,
W1 Ⓣ020/7499 699, Ⓦwww
.thewolsely.com⊖ Green
Park. Mon–Fri 3–5.30pm, Sat
& Sun 3.30–6pm.

wonderful Norman crypt makes for a very pleasant place in which to sample them.

The East End

Arkansas Café

Map 3, N3. Unit 12, Old Spitalfields Market, E1 ☎020/7377 6999 ⊖ Liverpool Street. Mon–Fri noon–2.30pm, Sun noon–4pm. American barbecue fuel stop, using only the very best free-range ingredients. Try chef Bubb's own smoked beef brisket and ribs, and be sure to taste his home-made barbie sauce (made to a secret formula).

Brick Lane Beigel Bake

Map 2, J4. 159 Brick Lane, E1 ☎020/7729 0616⊖ Shoreditch or Aldgate East. Daily 24hr. The bagels at this no-frills takeaway in the heart of the East End are freshly made and unbelievably cheap, even when stuffed with smoked salmon and cream cheese.

Frizzante Café at Hackney City Farm

Map 2, J3. 1a Goldsmith's Row, E2 ☎020/7729 2266 ⊖ Bethnal Green. Tues–Sun 10am–4.30pm. The best home-made family-friendly breakfasts and lunches this side of Bologna. Generous all-day "Big Farm" or veggie breakfasts, risottos and delicious pizza-like piadinas, all for around a fiver.

Lambeth and Southwark

El Vergel

Map 3, L6. 8 Lant Rd, SE1 ☎020/7357 0057, ⓦ www.elvergel .co.uk⊖ Borough. Mon–Fri 8.30am–3pm, Sat 10am–3pm. Small, very busy weekday café at the west end of Lant Street, worth the quick stroll from Borough tube. They do all the usual lunchtime takeaways, but you're really here to sample the Latin American specialities.

Konditor & Cook

Map 6, D4. 22 Cornwall Rd, SE1 ☎020/7261 0456 ⊖ Waterloo. Mon–Fri 7.30am–6.30pm, Sat 8.30am–2.30pm. A cut above your average bakery, *Konditor & Cook* make wonderful cakes and biscuits, as well as offering a choice of sandwiches and coffee and tea. With only a few tables inside, most folk take away. There are other branches on the south side of the Thames at 10 Stoney St by Borough Market and in the Design Museum.

Monmouth Café

Map 7, E8. 2 Park St, SE1 ☎020/7645 3585⊖ London Bridge. Mon–Sat 7.30am–6pm. In the foodie heart of Borough Market, the *Monmouth Café* (sister of the Covent Garden outlet) spills out onto the pavement, offering delicious croissants, bread and jam, and excelling in serving up single-estate coffee.

Kensington, Chelsea and Notting Hill

Books for Cooks
Map 2, F4. 4 Blenheim Crescent, W11 ☎020/7221 1992, ⓦwww .booksforcooks.com⊖ Ladbroke Grove or Notting Hill Gate. Tues–Sat 10am–3.30pm, closed 3 weeks in Aug. Tiny café/restaurant within London's top cookery book-shop. Conditions are cramped, but this is an experience not to be missed: in the test kitchen, resident chefs experiment with recipes from the cookbooks, so you never know what might be on the menu. Alternatively, pop in for an excellent coffee and a home-made cake.

Chelsea Kitchen
Map 3, E8. 98 King's Rd, SW3 ☎020/7589 1330⊖ Sloane Square. Daily noon–11pm. A useful, cheap café in Chelsea (now part of the no-nonsense *Stockpot* chain). Don't expect anything remark-able – just budget stomach-fillers in the form of steaks, spag bol and the like.

Daquise
Map 8, D8. 20 Thurloe St, SW7 ☎020/7589 6117⊖ South Kensing-ton. Daily 11.30am–11pm. This cosy, old-fashioned Polish café right by the tube is something of a South Ken institution, serving Polish home cooking or simple coffee, tea and cakes depending on the time of day.

Gloriette
Map 8, G6. 128 Brompton Rd, SW7 ☎020/7589 4635⊖ South Kensing-ton or Knightsbridge. Mon–Fri 7am–8pm, Sat 8am–8pm, Sun 9am–6pm. Long-established Viennese café that makes a perfect post-muse-um halt for coffee and outrageous cakes; also serves sandwiches, Wiener schnitzel, pasta dishes, goulash and fish and chips.

Lisboa Patisserie
 Map 2, F4. 57 Golborne Rd, W10 ☎020/8968 5242 ⊖ Ladbroke Grove. Daily 8am–8pm. Authentic and friendly Portu-guese *pastelaria*, with coffee and cakes including the best custard tarts this side of Lisbon. The *Oporto*, at 62a Golborne Rd, is a good fallback if this place is full.

North London

Café Delancey
Map 2, H3. 3 Delancey St, NW1 ☎020/7387 1985⊖ Camden Town

CAFÉS AND SNACKS | Kensington, Chelsea

or Mornington Crescent. Daily 9am–10.30pm. Still probably the best brasserie-style café in Camden, tucked away down a side road off Camden High Street – coffee, croissants, snacks and full meals.

Café Mozart

Map 2, H2. 17 Swains Lane, N6 ☎020/8348 1384 Gospel Oak train station. Mon–Fri 8am–10pm, Sat & Sun 9am–10pm. Conveniently located on the southeast side of Hampstead Heath, the best thing about this European-style café is the Viennese cake selection and the soothing classical music.

Louis Patisserie

Map 2, G2. 32 Heath St, NW3 ☎020/7435 9908⊖ Hampstead. Daily 9am–6pm. Popular Hungarian tearoom in Hampstead village serving sticky cakes to a mix of Heath-bound hordes and elderly locals.

Marine Ices

Map 2, G3. 8 Haverstock Hill, NW3 ☎020/7482 9003⊖ Chalk Farm. Mon–Sat 10.30am–11pm, Sun 11am–10pm. Situated halfway between Camden and Hampstead, this is a splendid and justly famous old-fashioned Italian ice cream parlour; pizza and pasta are served in the adjacent kid-friendly restaurant.

Ottolenghi

Map 2, I3. 287 Upper St, N1 ☎020/7288 1454⊖ Angel. Mon–Sat 8am–10.30pm, Sun 9am–10.30pm. An elegant, light space on fashionable Upper Street, with long white communal tables. There's a strong emphasis on imaginative and varied salads, with simple, delicious mains. It's fun for breakfast, with table-top toasters, and there's a tempting takeaway selection with exquisite, expensive cakes, tarts and pastries.

Greenwich

Goddard's

See p.154, B2. 45 Greenwich Church St, SE10 ☎020/8692 3601 Cutty Sark DLR or Greenwich DLR and train station from Charing Cross. Mon–Fri 10am–6.30pm, Sat & Sun 10am–7.30pm. Established in 1890, *Goddard's* serves traditional pies (including veggie ones), eels and mash in an emerald green-tiled interior, with crumble and custard for afters.

Tai Won Mein

See p.154, B2. 39 Greenwich Church St, SE10 ☎020/8858 1668 Cutty Sark DLR or Greenwich DLR and train station from Charing Cross. Daily 11.30am–11.30pm. Good-quality fast food noodle bar that gets very busy at weekends;

choose between rice, soup or various fried noodles, all for under a fiver. Décor is functional and minimalist.

Richmond

Maison Blanc
Map 2, C7. 27b The Quadrant, Richmond ☎020/8332 7041, ⓦwww .maisonblanc.co.uk⊖ Richmond. Mon–Sat 8am–7pm, Sun 9am–6pm. The cakes, croissants and bread at this French patisserie are absolutely fabulous, so either pop in on arrival in Richmond or take some away and eat them down by the river. Other branches in St John's Wood, Holland Park, Hampstead and Chelsea.

17

Restaurants

L ondon is an exciting – though often expensive – place in which to **eat out**, and, as it's home to people from all over the globe, you can sample pretty much any kind of cuisine here. The city boasts some of the best Cantonese restaurants in Europe, is a noted centre for Indian and Bangladeshi food, has great French, Greek, Italian, Japanese, Spanish and Thai restaurants and also offers more unusual options, from Georgian and Peruvian to Sudanese and Brazilian. Traditional and modern British food can be found all over town; some of the best venues are reviewed below.

The best of London's gastropubs, which provide high quality and affordable food, are reviewed in Chapter 18.

There are plenty of places to eat around the main tourist drags of the West End: **Soho** has long been renowned for its eclectic and fashionable restaurants, while **Chinatown**, on the other side of Shaftesbury Avenue, offers great value for money. Further west, upmarket areas like **Kensington** and **Chelsea** feature *haute cuisine* restaurants.

Many of the restaurants we've listed will be busy on most nights of the week, particularly from Thursday to Saturday, and you're best advised to **reserve a table**. With the most renowned places you'll probably be disappointed unless you plan at least a week ahead.

As for **prices**, you can pay an awful lot for a meal in London, and if you're used to North American portions you're not going to be particularly impressed by the volume in most places. In the listings, we've quoted the minimum you can get away with spending (on one main course and a drink) and the amount you can expect to pay for a full blowout. For really cheap eats, see the previous chapter.

At most places, **service** is discretionary, but restaurants tend to take no chances, emblazoning their bills with reminders that "Service is NOT included", or even including a ten to fifteen percent service charge on the bill (which they have to announce on the menu, by law). Normally you should, of course, pay service – it's how most of the staff make up their wages – but check to ensure you're not paying twice.

St James's, Mayfair and Marylebone

Fairuz
Map 3, E4. 3 Blandford St, W1
℡020/7486 8108 ⊖ Bond Street.
Mon–Sat noon–11.30pm, Sun
noon–10.30pm. £15–35. One of
London's more accessible Middle
Eastern restaurants, with an epic
list of mezze, a selection of char-
coal grills and one or two oven-
baked dishes. Get here early and
secure one of the nook-and-
crannyish, tent-like tables.

Mandalay
Map 3, D4. 444 Edgware Rd, W2
℡020/7258 3696, ⓦ www.bcity
.com/mandalay ⊖ Edgware
Road. Mon–Sat noon–2.30pm &
6–10.30pm. £6–16. Small non-
smoking restaurant that serves
pure, freshly cooked and unex-
purgated Burmese cuisine – a
melange of Thai, Malaysian, a
lot of Indian and a few things
that are unique. The portions are
huge, flavours hit the mark, the
service friendly and the prices
low. Booking essential in the
evening.

The Providores
Map 3, E3. 109 Marylebone
High St, W1 ℡020/7935
6175, ⓦ www.theprovidores
.co.uk ⊖ Baker Street or Bond
Street. Mon–Fri 9am–11pm, Sat
10am–11pm, Sun 10am–10pm.
£7–22. Outstanding fusion restaurant run by an amiable New

Zealander. It's split into two: a snacky tapas bar downstairs and full-on restaurant upstairs. At both the food, which may sound like an untidy assemblage on paper, is original and satisfying.

Truc Vert
Map 3, E4. 42 North Audley St, W1 ⓣ020/7491 9988⊖ Bond Street. Mon–Sat 7.30am–9.30pm, Sun 1–3pm. £15–40. Upmarket but friendly restaurant, offering quiche, salads, pâtés, cakes and pastries. The menu changes daily and begins early with breakfast; you can assemble your own charcuterie and cheese platter and pay by weight, and corkage is £4.50. Also a small deli.

The Wolseley
Map 4, C9. 160 Piccadilly, W1 ⓣ020/7499 6996⊖ Green Park. Mon–Fri 7am–midnight, Sat & Sun 11.30am–midnight. £10–40. The lofty and stylish 1920s interior of this brasserie/restaurant (built as the showroom for Wolseley cars) is a big draw, but the service – attentive and non-snooty – and the Viennese-inspired food also deliver, and given the glamour levels it is surprisingly affordable. A great place for breakfast or cream tea (£7.25).

Soho and Chinatown

Chowki
Map 4, E7. 2–3 Denman St, W1 ⓣ020/7439 1330⊖ Piccadilly Circus. Daily noon–11.30pm. £6–15. Large, cheap Indian restaurant serving authentic home-style food in stylish surroundings. The menu changes every month in order to feature three different regions of India – the regional feast for £10.95 is great value.

La Trouvaille
Map 4, D6. 12a Newburgh St, W1 ⓣ020/7287 8488 ⓦwww .latrouvaille.co.uk⊖ Oxford Circus. Mon–Sat noon–3pm & 6–11pm, Sat 6–11pm. £20–50. Here, they understand the English need for really French Frenchness – if you hanker after a "dangerously French" dish, try the tripe terrine.

Mildred's
Map 4, E6. 45 Lexington St, W1 ⓣ020/7494 1634 ⊖ Oxford Circus or Piccadilly Circus. Mon–Sat noon–11pm. £8–15. Mildred's, tucked away on a north Soho sidestreet, has a fresher and more stylish feel than many veggie restaurants. The stir-fries, pasta dishes and burgers are wholesome, delicious and inexpensive. No bookings or credit cards.

Mr Kong

Map 4, F7. 21 Lisle St, WC2
☎020/7437 7923 ⊖ Leicester
Square. Mon–Sat noon–2.45am, Sun
noon–1.45am. £8–22. Chinatown's
finest, with a chef-owner who
pioneered many of the modern
Cantonese dishes now on menus
all over town. You may have to
be firm if you want the more
unusual dishes – order from the
"Manager's Recommendations"
menu and don't miss the mus-
sels in black bean sauce. If you
want to avoid the rather grungy
basement, book ahead.

Spiga

Map 4, E6. 84–86 Wardour St,
W1 ☎020/7734 3444
⊖ Leicester Square. Tues noon–
midnight, Wed–Sat noon–3am, Sun
noon–10.30pm. £10–35. A pleasantly casual Italian affair, with
a lively atmosphere, a serious
wood-fired oven and a cool look
about it.

Thai Cottage

Map 4, E5. 34 D'Arblay St, W1
☎020/7439 7099 ⊖ Leicester
Square. Mon–Wed noon–4pm &
5.30–10.30pm, Thurs 5.30–10.30pm,
Fri noon–4pm & 5.30–11pm, Sat
5.30–11pm. £8–20. With many
cheap Soho favourites going out
of business, it's a relief to find
this tiny and resolutely unfashionable place. The welcome is

friendly and the décor simple,
with little lanterns hanging from
the low-beamed ceiling. Follow
the chicken satay with one of
their terrific fried-noodle dishes.

Covent Garden

Belgo Centraal

Map 4, H6. 50 Earlham St,
WC2 ☎020/7813 2233, Ⓦwww
.belgorestaurants.com ⊖ Covent
Garden. Mon–Thurs noon–11.30pm,
Fri & Sat noon–midnight, Sun noon–
10.30pm. £6–30. Massive metal-
minimalist cavern off Neal Street,
serving excellent kilo buckets of
moules marinières, with frites and
mayonnaise, a bewildering array
of Belgian beers, and waffles
for dessert. The £6 lunchtime
specials are a bargain for central
London.

J. Sheekey

Map 4, G7. 28–32 St Martin's Court,
WC2 ☎020/7240 2565, Ⓦwww
.caprice-holdings.co.uk ⊖ Leicester
Square. Mon–Sat noon–3pm &
5.30pm–midnight, Sun 6pm–midnight. £18–70. J. Sheekey's pedigree goes back to World War I,
but the place has been totally
redesigned and refurbished
since then. The menu is still
focused on fish, but in addition
to traditional fare such as Dover
sole, you're just as likely to find
contemporary dishes like braised

huss with polenta and gremolata. The weekend lunch menu, at £21.50, is the best value.

Mon Plaisir

Map 4, G5. 21 Monmouth St, WC2H ☎ 020/7836 7243 ⓦ www.monplaisir.co.uk ⊖ Covent Garden. Mon–Sat noon–3pm & 5.45pm–midnight. £15–65. Atmospheric and occasionally formidably French restaurant with an intimate tiled and wood-panelled interior. Deco posters and a glamorous mirrored bar give a vintage feel, while the classic French meat and fish dishes are excellent. The pre- and post-theatre menu is a bargain at £12.50 for two courses, £14.50 for three.

Bloomsbury and Fitzrovia

Cigala

Map 3, I3. 54 Lamb's Conduit St, WC1 ☎ 020/7405 1717, ⓦ www .cigala.co.uk ⊖ Russell Square. Daily 12.30–10.45pm. £18–60. Simple dishes, strong flavours, fresh ingredients and real passion are evident at this Iberian restaurant. The menu changes daily and is market-led, which makes for excellent seasonal dishes. There's also a tapas menu.

Ikkyu

Map 4, E2. 67a Tottenham Court Rd, W1 ☎ 020/7636 9280 ⊖ Goode

Street. Mon–Fri noon–2.30pm & 6–9.30pm, Sun 6–9.30pm. £10–40. Busy, basic basement Japanese restaurant, good enough for a quick lunch or a more elaborate dinner. Either way, prices are infinitely more reasonable than elsewhere in the capital, and the food is tasty and authentic.

Rasa Samudra

Map 4, E4. 5 Charlotte St, W1 ☎ 020/7637 0222 ⊖ Goodge Street. Mon–Sat noon–3pm & 6–11pm. £10–40. The exquisite food served at *Rasa Samudra* would be more at home in Madras than in London – the sophisticated southern Indian fish dishes are a million miles from the usual curry house staples.

Clerkenwell and Hoxton

Cicada

Map 3, K3. 132 St John St, EC1 ☎ 020/7608 1550, ⓦ www.cicada.nu ⊖ Farringdon. Mon–Fri noon–11pm, Sat 6–11pm. £17–40. Part bar, part restaurant, *Cicada* offers an unusual pan-Asian menu that allows you to mix and match from small, large and side dishes ranging from fishy tom yum to ginger noodles or sushi.

St John

Map 3, K3. 26 St John St, EC1 ☎ 020/7251 0848,

ⓦ www.stjohnrestaurant.co.uk
⊖ Farringdon. Mon–Fri noon–3pm
& 6–11pm, Sat 6–11pm. £20–60.
Genuinely English restaurant, a
stone's throw from Smithfield
meat market and specializing
in offal. All those strange and
unfashionable cuts of meat that
were once commonplace in rural
England – brains, bone marrow,
meat from a cow's sternum – are
cooked simply and beautifully at
this white-painted former smoke-
house.

Viet Hoa Café

Map 3, N2. 72–74 Kingsland
Rd, E2 ⓣ 020/7729 8293⊖ Old
Street. Mon–Fri noon–3.30pm &
5.30–11.30pm, Sat & Sun 12.30–
11.30pm. £8–18. Large, light and
airy Vietnamese café in a street
heaving with similar places. Try
one of the splendid "meals in
a bowl", or the noodle dishes
with everything from spring rolls
to tofu. Be sure, too, to sample
the pho soup, a Vietnamese
staple.

The City and the East End

Café Spice Namaste

Map 7, M5. 16 Prescot St, E1
ⓣ 020/7488 9242, ⓦ www.cafe
spice.co.uk⊖ Aldgate East or Tower
Hill. Mon–Fri noon–3pm & 6.15–
10.30pm, Sat 6.15–10.30pm. £20–
50. Very popular East End Indian,

where the menu is a touch more
varied than in many of its rivals
– Goan and Kashmiri dishes are
often included – and the tandoori
specials, in particular, are awesome. Weekday lunchtimes are
especially busy.

New Tayyab

Map 2, J4. 83 Fieldgate
St, E1 ⓣ 020/7247 9543,
ⓦ www.tayyabs.co.uk⊖ Aldgate
East or Whitechapel. Daily
noon–11.30pm. £4–15. Opened
in 1974, the *Tayyab* has been
spruced up lately but, miraculously, they still serve the same
straightforward Pakistani food:
good, freshly cooked and served
without pretension. Prices have
remained low, booking is essential, and service is speedy and
slick. Disabled access and kiddie
friendly.

1 Lombard Street

Map 7, F4. 1 Lombard St,
EC3 ⓣ 020/7929 6611,
ⓦ www.1lombardstreet.com
⊖ Bank. Mon–Fri noon–3pm & 6–
10pm. £30–80. This is a brasserie
in the City, of the City, by the
City and for the City. A long but
straightforward spread of dishes
delivers on pretty much every
front, and the buzzy circular bar
sits under the suitably imposing
glass dome of this former bank-
ing hall.

Fina Estampa

Map 7, I9. 150 Tooley St, SE1
☏020/7403 1342➌ London
Bridge. Mon–Fri noon–10.30pm, Sat
6.30–10.30pm. £15–30. One of
London's few Peruvian restaurants, which happens to be very
good, bringing a little of down-
town Lima to London Bridge.
The menu is traditional Peruvian;
you can kick things off with a
Pisco Sour cocktail.

Royal Festival Hall

Map 6, A3. South Bank Centre, SE1
☏0870/830 4300➌ Waterloo or
Embankment. Hours vary. £10–30.
The Festival Hall features a
welcome handful of upmarket
chain restaurants facing the river:
Wagamama (see p.196) dishes
up great noodles, *Giraffe* serves
family-friendly global cuisine, and
Strada has wood-fired pizzas
with fresh seasonal ingredients.

RSJ

Map 6, D3. 13a Coin St, SE1
☏020/7928 4554, ⓦwww.rsj.uk.com
➌ Waterloo. Mon–Fri noon–2pm
& 5.30–11pm, Sat 5.30–11pm.
£15–40. Regularly high standards
of Anglo-French cooking make
this a good spot for a meal after
or before an evening at the South
Bank. The set meals for around
£17 are particularly popular.

Tentazione

Map 2, J5. 2 Mill St, SE1
☏020/7237 1100, ⓦwww.tentazi
one.co.uk➌ Bermondsey or Tower
Hill. Mon & Sat 7–10.45pm, Tues–Fri
noon–2.30pm & 7–10.45pm. £10–
55. Smart, busy Italian restaurant serving high-quality peasant
dishes with strong, rich flavours;
try the splendid three-course
Tradizione Italiana (£28).

Bibendum Oyster House

Map 8, F8. Michelin House, 81
Fulham Rd, SW3 ☏020/7589
1480, ⓦwww.bibendum.co.uk
➌ South Kensington. Mon–Sat
noon–10.30pm, Sun noon–10pm.
£12–30. A glorious tiled affair built
in 1911, this former garage is
the best place to eat shellfish in
London. There are three types of
rock oysters, but if you're really
hungry, try the Plateau de Fruits
de Mer, which also has crab,
clams, langoustine, prawns,
shrimps, whelks and winkles.

Boisdale

Map 3, F7. 15 Eccleston St, SW1
☏020/7730 6922➌ Victoria. Mon–
Fri noon–1am, Sat 7.30pm–1am.
£15–50. Owned by Ranald Mac-
Donald, son of the Chief of Clan-
ranald, this restaurant offers the
best of Scottish – Orkney herring,
haggis and Cullen Skink tart – in

a very clubby and tartan atmosphere. Live jazz every evening.

Hunan
Map 3, E8. 51 Pimlico Rd, SW1
☎020/7730 5712☻ Sloane
Square. Mon–Sat noon–2.30pm
& 6–11.30pm. £32–60. Probably
England's only restaurant serving
Hunan food – related to Sichuan
cuisine with the same spicy kick
to most dishes, and a fair wallop
of pepper in those that aren't
actively riddled with chillis. Most
people opt for the £30.80 "leave-
it-to-us feast" which lets the chef,
Mr Peng, show what he can do.

Notting Hill

Alwaha
Map 3, A4. 75 Westbourne Grove,
W2 ☎020/7229 0806☻ Queensway
or Bayswater. Daily noon–midnight.
£12–35. Arguably London's best
Lebanese restaurant; mezze-
obsessed, but also painstaking
in its preparation of main course
dishes.

Galicia
Map 2, F4. 323 Portobello Rd, W10
☎020/8969 3539☻ Ladbroke
Grove or Westbourne Park. Tues–Sat
noon–3pm & 7–11.30pm, Sun noon–
3pm & 7–10.30pm. £14–35. A
pleasant unpretentious Spanish
restaurant that attracts a regular
Spanish clientele. For cheaper

eats, the tapas at the bar are
straightforward and good.

Osteria Basilico
Map 2, F4. 29 Kensington
Park Rd ☎020/7727 9372
☻ Ladbroke Grove. Mon–Fri 12.30–
3pm & 6.30–11pm, Sat 12.30–4pm
& 6.30–11pm, Sun 12.30–3.30pm &
6.30–10.30pm. £10–50. Pretty, traditional Italian restaurant on a picturesque street just off Portobello
Road; it offers pavement seating
in summer. It's a good place for
the full Italian monty – antipasto,
home-made pasta and then a fish
or meat dish – or just for a pizza.

Rodizio Rico
Map 3, A4. 111 Westbourne Grove,
W11 ☎020/7792 4035☻ Notting
Hill Gate or Queensway. Mon–Fri
6pm–midnight, Sat noon–4pm &
6pm–midnight, Sun 12.30–11pm.
£18–25. Eat as much as you like
for around £18 a head at this
Brazilian *churrascaria*. Carvers
come round and lop off chunks of
freshly grilled smoky meats from
whichever skewers they are holding, while you prime your plate
from the salad bar and hot buffet.

North London

Almeida
Map 2, I3. Almeida St, N1
☎020/7354 4777, ⓦ www.conran
-restaurants.co.uk☻ Angel or

Highbury & Islington. Mon–Sat noon–2.30pm & 6–11pm, Sun noon–3pm & 5.30–10pm. £18–80. A Conran restaurant, opposite the theatre of the same name, that is a distillation of all that is good about wonderful, old-fashioned, gently familiar French cooking.

Jin Kichi
Map 2, G2. 73 Heath St, NW3 ☎020/7794 6158⊖ Hampstead. Tues–Fri 6–11pm, Sat 12.30–2pm & 6–11pm, Sun 12.30–2pm & 6–10pm. £15–30. Eschewing the slick minimalism and sushi-led cuisine of most Japanese restaurants, *Jin Kichi* is cramped, homely and very busy (so book ahead), and specializes in skewers of grilled meat.

Manna
Map 2, G3. 4 Erskine Rd, NW3 ☎020/7722 8028, ⓦ www.manna -veg.com⊖ Chalk Farm. Mon–Sat 6.30–11pm, Sun 12.30–3pm & 6.30–11pm. £10–45. Old-fashioned, casual vegetarian restaurant with 1970s décor, serving large portions of very good food.

Chiswick to Richmond

Chez Lindsay
Map 2, C7. 11 Hill Rise, Richmond, Surrey ☎020/8948 7473⊖ Richmond. Mon–Sat 11am–11pm, Sun noon–10pm. £7–27. Small, bright, authentic Breton crêperie, with a loyal local following. The "Cider with Lindsay" fixed menu (£15.75) offers three courses plus a cup of Breton cider. Choose between galettes, crêpes or more formal French main courses, including lots of fresh fish and shellfish.

Fish Hoek
Map 2, E5. 6–8 Elliot St, W4 ☎020/8742 3374⊖ Turnham Green. Tues–Sat noon–2.30pm & 6.30–11pm, Sun noon–9pm. £15–60. Light and airy South African fish restaurant in leafy Chiswick with an impressive menu that changes daily. Most dishes are available in half or full portions.

The Gate
Map 2, F5. 51 Queen Caroline St, W4 ☎020/8748 6932, ⓦ www .gateveg.co.uk⊖ Hammersmith. Mon–Fri noon–3pm & 6–11pm, Sat 6–11pm. £10–40. Excellent and original vegetarian dishes with intense and satisfying tastes and textures. Located in a converted church with an outside courtyard that's lovely in summer.

18

Pubs and bars

L ondon's drinking establishments run the gamut from
traditional English alehouses to funky modern bars
with resident DJs catering to a pre-club crowd. **Pubs**
are one of England's most enduring social institutions, and have outlived the church and marketplace as the
focal points of communities, with London's fringe theatre,
alternative comedy and live music scenes still largely pub-
based. At their best, pubs can be as welcoming as their full
name, "public house", suggests, offering a fine range of
drinks and filling food. At their worst, they're dismal rooms
with surly bar staff and rotten snacks. One thing you can be
sure of, however, is that most pubs and bars remain smoke-
filled places where drinking alcohol is the prime activity.

London's great period of pub building took place in the
Victorian era, to which many pubs still pay homage; genuine Victorian interiors, however, are increasingly difficult to
find, as indeed are genuinely individual pubs. **Chain pubs**,
however, can be found all over the capital: branches of All
Bar One, Pitcher & Piano and Slug & Lettuce are the most
obvious, as they all share the chain name, whereas Fuller's,
Nicholson and J.D. Wetherspoon pubs do at least vary theirs.

Pub food, on the whole, is a lunchtime affair, although
"gastropubs", which put more effort into (and charge a lot
more for) their cooking, tend to offer meals in the evening,
too. The traditional image of London pub food is justifiably

dire – a pseudo "ploughman's lunch" of bread and cheese, or a murky-looking pie and chips – but the last couple of decades have seen plenty of improvements. You can get a palatable lunchtime meal at many of the pubs listed in this chapter, and at a few of them you're looking at cooking worthy of high restaurant-standard praise.

Though pubs may be constantly changing hands (and names), the quickest turnover is in **bars**, some of which

Beer

The classic English beer is **bitter**, a dark, uncarbonated drink that should be pumped by hand from the cellar. In the last three decades, however, the lighter, carbonated **lager** has overtaken bitter in popularity, and every pub will have at least two draught lagers on offer, plus a selection of foreign beers.

Those people that call themselves beer drinkers, however, go almost exclusively for bitter, and take the various brews extremely seriously. A moving force in this camp is **CAMRA** – the Campaign for Real Ale (Ⓦwww.camra.org.uk) – which worked hard to keep local beers from dying out amid the big brewery takeovers of the 1970s. Note that though even the big breweries distribute some very good beers, some of the beer touted as good English ale is nothing of the sort – if the stuff comes out of an electric pump, it isn't the real thing.

Smaller operations whose fine ales are available over a wide area include Young's and Fuller's – the two main London breweries – and Wadworth, Adnams, Greene King, Flowers and Samuel Smith's. Regional concoctions from other independent breweries are frequently available, too, at free houses, and London also has a number of brew-pubs, which produce their own peculiar brand on the premises.

Guinness, a very dark, creamy Irish stout, is also on sale virtually everywhere, and is an exception to the high-minded objection to electrically pumped beers – though purists will tell you that the stuff the English drink does not compare with the home variety.

go in and out of fashion with incredible speed. These can be very different places to your average pub, with some catering to a younger, trendy crowd and some playing to the more moneyed older set; many have designer interiors and drinks, and they also tend to be more expensive. We've included here a fair few **club-bars**, places which cater for a clubby crowd, and often have resident DJs, along with late opening hours.

For gay and lesbian pubs and bars, see Chapter 20.

After almost a century of draconian restrictions, the government has finally committed itself to liberalizing opening hours and England's **licensing laws** are changing. This will allow many more pubs and bars to stay open way beyond the standard 11pm last orders, so the times listed below may well have changed since this book went to press.

Whitehall and Westminster

ICA Bar
Map 4, F10. 94 The Mall, SW1
℡020/7930 3647, ⓦ www.ica.org
.uk⊖ Piccadilly Circus or Charing
Cross. Mon noon–11pm, Tues–Sat
noon–1am, Sun noon–10.30pm. You
have to be a member to drink
at the *ICA Bar* – but anyone can
join on the door (Mon–Fri £1.50,
Sat & Sun £2.50). It's a cool
drinking venue, with a *noir* dress
code observed by the arty crowd
and staff. Occasional club nights.

Westminster Arms
Map 4, F9. 9 Storey's Gate, SW1
℡020/7222 8520⊖ Westminster.

Mon–Fri 11am–11pm, Sat 11am–
6pm, Sun noon–5pm. A real parliamentary pub, with a division bell in the bar to call boozing MPs back to the Commons when it's time for a vote.

St James's, Mayfair and Marylebone

Dover Castle
Map 3, F3. 43 Weymouth Mews, W1
℡020/7580 4412⊖ Regent's Park.
Mon–Fri 11.30am–11pm, Sat 12.30–
11pm. A traditional, quiet boozer
hidden away down a labyrinthine
and picturesque Marylebone
mews. Green upholstery, dark
wood and a nicotine-stained

Lincrusta ceiling with ornate relief patterns add to the atmosphere.

O'Conor Don
Map 3, F4. 88 Marylebone Lane, W1 ⊤020/7935 9311⊖ Bond Street. Mon–Fri 11am–11pm. A stripped-bare, stout-loving pub that's a cut above the average, with excellent Guinness, a pleasantly measured pace and Irish food on offer.

Red Lion
Map 4, E10. 2 Duke of York St, SW1 ⊤020/7321 0782 ⊖ Piccadilly Circus. Mon–Sat 11.30am–11pm. Popular little gin palace that has preserved its classic Victorian décor of dark wood and mirrors. The clientele are more often than not besuited, as you'd expect in St James's, and the malt whisky selection is impressive.

Ye Grapes
Map 4, B10. 16 Shepherd Market, W1 (no phone)⊖ Green Park or Hyde Park Corner. Mon–Sat 11am–11pm, Sun noon–10.30pm. A great local in the heart of Mayfair, this busy Victorian free house has a good selection of real ales (including Young's and Fuller's) and an open fire.

Soho

Argyll Arms
Map 4, C5. 18 Argyll St, W1

⊤020/7734 6117⊖ Oxford Circus. Mon–Sat 11am–11pm, Sun noon–10.30pm. A stone's throw from Oxford Circus, this is a serious find: a great Victorian pub, which has preserved many of its original features and serves good real ales.

Atlantic
Map 4, E7. 20 Glasshouse St, W1 ⊤020/7734 4888⊖ Piccadilly Circus. Mon–Fri noon–3am, Sat 6pm–3am. The main downstairs bar is located in a wonderfully ornate and spacious Art Deco hall, built as the ballroom of the *Regent Palace Hotel*. A classy venue for a heady cocktail (from £8.50).

De Hems
Map 4, G6. 11 Macclesfield St, W1 ⊤020/7437 2494 ⊖ Leicester Square. Mon–Sat noon–midnight, Sun noon–10.30pm. Probably your best bet in Chinatown, this is London's official Dutch pub; it's a simple wood-panelled affair with Oranjeboom on tap and other Belgian beers in bottles.

Dog and Duck
Map 4, F5. 18 Bateman St, W1 ⊤020/7494 0697⊖ Leicester Square or Tottenham Court Road. Mon–Sat 11am–11pm, Sun 11am–10.30pm. Tiny Soho pub

that retains much of its old character, beautiful Victorian tiling and mosaics, a good range of real ales and a loyal clientele that often includes jazz musicians from nearby *Ronnie Scott's* club.

French House
Map 4, F6. 49 Dean St, W1 ☎020/7437 2799 ⊖ Leicester Square. Mon–Sat noon–11pm, Sun noon–10.30pm. This tiny French pub has been a Soho institution since before World War I. Free French and literary associations galore, and half-pints only at the bar (no real ale).

Two Floors
Map 4, D6. 3 Kingly St, W1 ☎020/7439 1007 ⊖ Oxford Circus. Mon–Sat noon–11pm. Laid-back, designer-style Soho bar, laid out, unsurprisingly, on two floors, attracting a mixed media crowd, and pumping out drum'n'bass in the evenings – quite a find in a part of Soho short of decent drinking holes.

Covent Garden

Bünker
Map 4, H5. 41 Earlham St, WC2 ☎020/7240 0606 ⊖ Covent Garden. Daily 11am–11pm. Busy, brick-vaulted basement bar with wrought iron pillars, lots of brushed steel and pricey lagers,

some made on the premises – in particular, there's a fine organic brew.

Detroit
Map 4, G6. 35 Earlham St, WC2 ☎020/7240 2662, ⓦ www .detroit-bar.com ⊖ Covent Garden. Mon–Sat 5pm–midnight. Cavernous underground venue with an open-plan bar area, secluded, Gaudíesque booths and a huge range of spirits. DJs take over at the weekends, with underground house on Saturdays.

Lamb & Flag
Map 4, H7. 33 Rose St, WC2 ☎020/7497 9504 ⊖ Leicester Square or Covent Garden. Mon–Thurs 11am–11pm, Fri & Sat 11am–10.45pm, Sun noon–10.30pm. Busy, tiny and highly atmospheric pub, well and truly hidden away down an alley between Garrick Street and Floral Street. John Dryden was attacked in this alley in 1679 after scurrilous verses had been written about one of Charles II's mistresses (by someone else, as it turned out).

Lowlander
Map 4, H5. 6 Drury Lane, WC2 ☎020/7379 7446 ⊖ Covent Garden. Mon–Sat noon–11pm, Sun noon–10pm. A lofty, busy bar specializing in hangover-inducing and wallet-bashing Belgian and

Dutch beers, many on tap. Table service and deli snacks from the Low Countries, including moules frites.

Punch & Judy
Map 4, H7. 40 The Market, WC2 ☎020/7379 0923⊖ Covent Garden. Mon–Sat 11am–11pm, Sun noon–10.30pm. It gets horribly mobbed and very loud, but this Covent Garden Market pub does boast an unbeatable location with a very popular balcony overlooking the Piazza – and a stone-flagged cellar.

Salisbury
Map 4, G7. 90 St Martin's Lane, WC2 ☎020/7836 5863 ⊖ Leicester Square. Mon–Fri 11am–midnight, Sat noon–11am, Sun noon–10.30pm. One of the most beautifully preserved Victorian pubs in the capital, with etched and engraved windows, bronze figures and a swirling lincrusta ceiling.

Bloomsbury and Fitzrovia

The Hope
Map 4, E2. 15 Tottenham St, W1 ☎020/7637 0896⊖ Goodge Street. Mon–Sat 11am–11pm, Sun 11.30am–6pm. Chiefly remarkable for its sausage (veggie ones included), beans and mash lunches, along with its real ales.

Lamb
Map 3, I3. 94 Lamb's Conduit St, WC1 ☎020/7405 0713⊖ Russell Square. Mon–Sat 11am–11pm, Sun 11am–4pm & 7–10.30pm. Pleasant Young's pub with a marvellously well-preserved Victorian interior of mirrors, old wood and "snob" screens to separate the upper classes from the lower orders.

Market Place
Map 4, D4. 11 Market Place, W1 ☎020/7079 2020, ⓦwww .marketplace-london.com⊖ Oxford Circus. Mon–Wed noon–midnight, Thurs–Sat noon–1am, Sun noon–10.30pm. Owned by the hip club *Cargo* (see p.231), *Market Place* may look more like a sauna than a thriving bar, but it has a varied music policy (with DJs tackling jazz funk, ska, hip-hop and breakbeat) that makes it well worth checking out. The food is above average too.

Museum Tavern
Map 3, H3. 49 Great Russell St, WC1 ☎020/7242 8987⊖ Tottenham Court Road or Russell Square. Mon–Sat 11am–11pm, Sun noon–10.30pm. Large and characterful old pub, the erstwhile drinking hole of Karl Marx, right opposite the main entrance to the British Museum.

The Social

🏃 **Map 4, D4.** 5 Little Portland St, W1 ☎020/7636 4992, ⓦwww.thesocial.com⊖ Oxford Circus. Mon–Fri noon–midnight, Sat 1pm–midnight. Industrial club-bar run by the Heavenly record label, with great DJs playing everything from rock to rap, a truly hedonistic-cum-alcoholic crowd and great snacks. Fab music on the upstairs jukebox, too.

Clerkenwell

Café Kick

🏃 **Map 3, J2.** 43 Exmouth Market, EC1 ☎020/7837 8077, ⓦwww.cafekick.co.uk⊖ Farringdon or Angel. Mon–Sat noon–11pm, Sun noon–10.30pm. Stylish take on a smoky, local French-style café/bar in the heart of fashionable Exmouth Market, with three busy table-football games to complete the retro theme.

Duke of York

Map 3, J3. 156 Clerkenwell Rd, EC1 ☎020/7837 8548⊖ Chancery Lane. Mon–Fri 11am–11pm, Sun noon–10.30pm. All the basics you need for a good pub – bare boards, table football, pool, TV sport, good mixed clientele and groovy tunes – and a lot less posey than much of Clerkenwell.

Dust

Map 3, K3. 27a Clerkenwell Rd, EC1 ☎020/7490 5120, ⓦwww.dustbar.co.uk⊖ Farringdon. Tues & Wed 5pm–midnight, Thurs 5pm–2am, Fri & Sat 5pm–4am. High-ceilinged bar in a former watchmaker's factory, with bare walls, great cocktails, and the bonus of a small dancefloor and a late licence at the weekends when quality DJs play house, soul, funk and hip-hop. £3–5 Fri & Sat.

Eagle

Map 3, J3. 159 Farringdon Rd, EC1 ☎020/7837 1353 ⊖ Farringdon. Mon–Sat noon–11pm, Sun noon–5pm. The first (and still one of the best) of London's pubs to go foody, this place is heaving at lunch and dinnertime, full of *Guardian* and *Observer* workers tucking into hearty Portuguese/Mediterranean dishes. You should be able to find a seat at other times.

Fox & Anchor

Map 3, K3. 115 Charterhouse St, EC1 ☎020/7253 5075 ⊖ Farringdon or Barbican. Mon–Fri 7am–9pm. Handsome Smithfield Market pub famous for its early opening hours and huge breakfasts (served 7–10am).

Jerusalem Tavern

Map 3, K3. 55 Britton St, EC1 ℡020/7490 4281 ⊖ Farringdon. Mon–Fri 11am–11pm. Cosy little converted Georgian coffee house, with bags of atmosphere, serving tasty food at lunchtimes, along with an excellent range of draught beers from St Peter's Brewery in Suffolk.

Bricklayer's Arms

Map 3, N2. 63 Charlotte Rd, EC2 ℡020/7739 5245⊖ Old Street. Mon–Fri 11am–11pm, Sat noon–11pm, Sun noon–10.30pm. An appealingly ramshackle Shoreditch pub (serving Thai food) that predates the area's trendification, and is therefore all the more popular with its arty residents.

Dragon

Map 3, M2. 5 Leonard St, EC2 ℡020/7490 7110 ⊖ Old Street. Mon noon–midnight, Tues–Thurs noon–1am, Fri & Sat noon–2am, Sun noon–midnight. Discreetly signed clubby pub with bare-brick walls and crumbling leather sofas. Nightly DJs avoid house and go for a more eclectic mix, covering everything from hip-hop to Sixties music.

Hoxton Square Bar and Kitchen

Map 3, N2. 2–4 Hoxton Square, N1 ℡020/7613 0709⊖ Old Street. Mon–Thurs & Sun 11am–midnight, Fri & Sat 11am–2am. This *Blade Runner*-esque concrete bar attracts trendy types with its mix of modern European food, kitsch-to-club soundtracks and yet more worn leather sofas.

Loungelover

Map 3, N2. 1 Whitby St, E1 ℡020/7012 1234, ⓦwww .loungelover.co.uk⊖ Liverpool Street. Mon–Thurs 6pm–midnight, Fri 6pm–1am, Sat 7pm–1am. Behind the unprepossessing facade of this former meat-packing factory lies a bizarre array of opulently camp bric-a-brac, expertly slung together to create a trendy and unique cocktail bar. Drinks are very well executed and deservedly expensive. Reservations (to be made Mon–Fri 10am–6pm, Sat noon–6pm) recommended for groups of more than two people.

Sosho

Map 3, M2. 2 Tabernacle St, EC2 ℡020/7920 0701, ⓦwww .matchbar.com⊖ Old Street. Mon 11.30am–10pm, Tues & Wed 11.30am–midnight, Thurs 11.30am–1am, Fri 11.30am–3am, Sat 7pm–3am. Very trendy club-bar with good cocktails and decent food; the ambience is chilled until the very popular DJs kick in at 8.30pm (Wed–Sat). There's a charge at the weekend.

The City: Fleet Street to St Paul's

Blackfriar
Map 5, G5. 174 Queen Victoria St, EC4 ☏020/7236 5474⊖ Blackfriars. Mon–Sat 11am–11pm, Sun noon–10.30pm. A gorgeous, utterly original pub, with Art Nouveau marble friezes of boozy monks and a wonderful highly decorated alcove – all original, dating from 1905. Non-smoking throughout.

Viaduct Tavern
Map 5, G2. 126 Newgate St, EC1 ☏020/7600 1863 ⊖ St Paul's. Mon–Fri noon–11pm. Glorious gin palace built in 1869 opposite what was then Newgate Prison and is now the Old Bailey. The walls are adorned with oils of faded ladies representing Commerce, Agriculture and the Arts. Ask staff to show you the old cells downstairs.

Ye Olde Cheshire Cheese
Map 5, E4. Wine Office Court, 145 Fleet St, EC4 ☏020/7353 6170⊖ Temple or Blackfriars. Mon–Sat 11am–11pm,

Sun noon–3.30pm. A famous seventeenth-century watering hole, with several snug, dark-panelled bars and real fires. Popular with tourists, but by no means exclusively so.

The City: Bank to Bishopsgate

The Counting House
Map 7, G4. 50 Cornhill, EC2 ☏020/7283 7123⊖ Bank. Mon–Fri 11am–11pm. A Fuller's bank con-version, with fantastic high ceil-ings, a glass dome, chandeliers and a central oval bar.

Lamb
Map 7, H4. Leadenhall Market, EC3 ☏020/7626 2454⊖ Monument. Mon–Fri 11am–9pm. A great pub right in the middle of Leadenhall Market, serving pricey (£5.50) but excellent roast beef sandwiches at lunchtime.

Vertigo 42
Map 7, G3. Tower 42, Old Broad St, EC2 ☏020/7877 7842⊖ Bank or Liverpool Street. Mon–Fri noon–3pm & 5–11pm. Rar-efied drinking in this champagne bar, 590ft above the City. Each seat looks out over an astound-ing view of London; prices are correspondingly high. Light meals are on offer. Smart jeans and trainers acceptable; booking essential.

18

PUBS AND BARS | The City

East End and Docklands

The Gun
Map 2, L5. 27 Cold Harbour,
E14 ☎020/7515 5222, ⊛www
.thegundocklands.com⊖ Canary
Wharf or South Quay or Blackwall
DLR. Mon–Sat 11am–11pm, Sun
noon–10.30pm; open Sat & Sun from
10.30am for brunch but no alcohol.
Old dockers' pub with a fresh lick
of paint and lots of maritime memorabilia, an unrivalled view of the
Millennium Dome from its outside
deck, and a classy dining area
serving modern European food.

Prospect of Whitby
Map 2, K4. 57 Wapping Wall, E1
☎020/7481 1095⊖ Wapping.
Mon–Fri 11am–11pm, Sat noon–
11pm, Sun noon–10.30pm. One
of London's most characterful
riverside pubs, with a flagstone
floor, a cobbled courtyard and
great views.

Ten Bells
Map 2, J4. 84 Commercial St, E1
☎020/7366 1721⊖ Liverpool
Street or Aldgate East. Mon–Sat
noon–11pm, Sun noon–10.30pm.
Plain and pleasantly ramshackle
pub that was a hub of nineteenth-
century Spitalfields when the area
was terrorized by Jack the Ripper
(one of his victims was known
to drink here). The interior has
some great Victorian tiling and

the crowd these days is a trendy,
relaxed bunch. DJs play electro,
rock, hip-hop and reggae Fri–Sun.

Town of Ramsgate
Map 2, K4. 62 Wapping High St,
E1 ☎020/7264 0001⊖ Wapping.
Mon–Sat noon–11pm, Sun noon–
10.30pm. Dark, narrow, medieval
pub located by Wapping Old
Stairs, which once led down
to Execution Dock. Captain
Blood was discovered here
with the Crown Jewels under his
cloak, "Hanging" Judge Jeffreys
was arrested here trying to flee,
and Admiral Bligh and Fletcher
Christian were regular drinking
partners in pre-mutiny days.

Lambeth and Southwark

Anchor Bankside
Map 7, C7. 34 Park St, SE1
☎020/7407 1577⊖ London Bridge,
Southwark or Blackfriars. Mon–Sat
11am–11pm, Sun noon–10.30pm.
While the rest of Bankside has
changed almost beyond recognition, this pub, near the Tate
Modern, still looks much as it
did when first built in 1770 (on
the inside, at least). Probably the
best – and most mobbed – spot
for alfresco drinking by the river.

George Inn
Map 7, E9. 77 Borough High St, SE1
☎020/7407 2056 ⊖ Borough

or London Bridge. Mon–Sat
11am–11pm, Sun noon–10.30pm.
Tucked away off Borough High
Street, this is London's only
surviving coaching inn, with a
rich historical pedigree stretching
back to the seventeenth century,
and now owned by the National
Trust. The food isn't great, service can be slow, but it serves a
good range of real ales.

Market Porter
Map 7, E9. 9 Stoney St, SE1
☎020/7407 2495➌ London Bridge.
Mon–Sat 6–8.30am & 11am–11pm,
Sun noon–10.30pm. Handsome
semicircular pub with early opening hours for workers at the
nearby Borough Market, and a
seriously huge range of real ales.

Royal Oak
Map 3, L6. 44 Tabard St, SE1
☎020/7357 7173➌ Borough.
Mon–Fri 11.30am–11pm. Beautiful,
lovingly restored Victorian pub
that eschews jukeboxes and
one-armed bandits and opts
simply for serving real ales from
Lewes in Sussex.

Kensington, Chelsea and Notting Hill

Cherry Jam
Map 2, F4. 52 Porchester Rd, W2
☎020/7727 9950, ⓦwww.cherryjam
.net➌ Royal Oak. Mon–Sat 6pm–

2am, Sun 4pm–midnight. Owned
by Ben Watt (house DJ and half
of 1980s pop group Everything
But The Girl), this smart intimate
basement spot mixes a decadent
cocktail bar with top-end West
London DJs from the broken beat
and deep house scenes.

The Cow
Map 3, A4. 89 Westbourne Park Rd,
W2 ☎020/7221 5400➌ Westbourne
Park or Royal Oak. Mon–Sat noon–
11pm, Sun noon–10.30pm. Vaguely
Irish-themed pub owned by Tom
Conran, son of gastro-magnate
Terence, which pulls in the beau-
tiful West London types thanks
to its spectacular seafoody food,
including a daily supply of fresh
oysters, and excellent Guinness.

Fox and Hounds
Map 3, E8. 29 Passmore St, SW1
☎020/7730 6367➌ Sloane Square.
Mon–Sat 11am–11pm, Sun noon–
10.30pm. On a quiet street near
Sloane Square, this Young's pub
provides a perfect snug winter
retreat. With an open fire, gleaming ranks of faux books and a
flagstone floor, as well as plenty
of hunting memorabilia, it feels as
if you've stumbled into a country
squire's manor.

The Nag's Head
Map 3, E6. 53 Kinnerton
St, SW1 ☎020/7235 1135

⊖ Hyde Park Corner or Knights-bridge. Mon–Sat 11am–11pm, Sun noon–10.30pm. A convivial, quirky and down-to-earth little pub tucked down a posh cobbled mews, with dark wood-panelling, nineteenth-century china handpumps and old prints on huntin', fishin' and military themes. The unusual sunken back room has a flagstone floor and fires in winter. Well-kept Adnams beers.

Prince Bonaparte

Map 3, A4. 80 Chepstow Rd, W2 ☎020/7313 9491 ⊖ Notting Hill Gate or Royal Oak. Mon–Sat noon–11pm, Sun noon–10.30pm. Very popular pared-down, trendy, minimalist pub, with acres of space for sitting and supping while enjoying the bar snacks or the excellent Brit or Med food in the restaurant area.

Windsor Castle

Map 2, E4. 114 Campden Hill Rd, W8 ☎020/7243 9551 ⊖ High Street Kensington or Notting Hill. Mon–Sat 11am–11pm, Sun noon–10.30pm. Pretty and popular traditional wood-panelled English pub with a great courtyard. You can easily imagine yourself out in the country rather than tucked away in the backstreets of one of London's poshest residential neighbourhoods.

St John's Wood and Maida Vale

Prince Alfred & Formosa Dining Rooms

Map 3, B3. 5a Formosa St, W9 ☎020/7286 3027 ⊖ Warwick Avenue. Mon–Sat 11am–11pm, Sun noon–10.30pm. A fantastic period-piece Victorian pub with all its original 1862 fittings intact, right down to the glazed snob screens that divide the bar into a series of "snugs", which are often reserved. Despite the heritage, the pub manages to pull in a young and funky crowd. The attached restaurant serves expensive modern European food.

Warrington Hotel

Map 3, B2. 93 Warrington Crescent, W9 ☎020/7286 2929 ⊖ Maida Vale. Mon–Sat 11am–11pm, Sun noon–10.30pm. Yet another architectural gem – this time flamboyant Edwardian Art Nouveau – in an area replete with them. The interior is rich and satisfying, as are the draught beers and the Thai restaurant upstairs. Understandably popular, with outside tables for the overspill.

Camden Town

Edinboro Castle

Map 2, H3. 57 Mornington Terrace,

NW1 ☎020/7255 9651 ⊖ Camden Town. Mon–Sat noon–11pm, Sun noon–10.30pm. Glammed up and slightly kitsch, this high-ceilinged pub is principally visited for its large, leafy beer garden which hosts summer weekend barbecues. Good selection of international lagers and a couple of bitter options.

The Engineer
Map 2, H3. 65 Gloucester Ave, NW1 ☎020/7722 0950, ⓦwww .the-engineer.com⊖ Chalk Farm. Mon–Sat 9am–11pm, Sun 9am–10.30pm. Smart Victorian pub and restaurant frequented by the trendy Primrose Hill posse. The food is excellent though pricey; get here early to eat in the pub, or book a table in the restaurant or lovely garden out back.

Lock Tavern
Map 2, H3. 35 Chalk Farm Rd, NW1 ☎020/7482 7163, ⓦwww.lock -tavern.co.uk⊖ Chalk Farm. Mon–Sat 11am–11pm, Sun 11am–10.30pm. Part-owned by DJ Jon Carter, this rambling refurbished pub has large battered wooden tables, comfy sofas, a leafy upstairs terrace and beer garden down below, as well as posh pub grub and DJs playing anything from punk funk and electro to rock. Effortlessly cool.

The Flask
Map 2, H2. 77 Highgate West Hill, N6 ☎020/8348 7346⊖ Highgate. Mon–Sat noon–11pm, Sun noon–10.30pm. Ideally situated at the heart of Highgate village green – with a rambling, low-ceilinged interior and a summer terrace – and as a result, very popular. Good food, too.

Holly Bush
Map 2, G3. 22 Holly Mount, off Holly Hill, NW3 ☎020/7435 2892 ⊖ Hampstead. Mon–Sat noon–11pm, Sun noon–10.30pm. A lovely old pub, with a real fire in winter, tucked away in the steep backstreets of Hampstead village. Delicious food served; it can get a bit too mobbed at weekends.

Islington

Duke of Cambridge
Map 2, I3. 30 St Peter's St, N1 ☎020/7359 3066, ⓦwww.singh boulton.co.uk⊖ Angel. Mon–Sat noon–11pm, Sun noon–10.30pm. Bright corner pub. The focus here is on the splendid organic food, accompanied by a range of great organic beers, wine and soft drinks. Restaurant seating at the back; book if you want to eat.

18

PUBS AND BARS | Hampstead, Highgate • Islington

223

Medicine

Map 2, I3. 181 Upper St, N1
℡ 020/7704 8056, ⓦ www.medicine
bar.net⊖ Highbury & Islington.
Mon–Thurs & Sun noon–midnight,
Fri & Sat noon–2am. Very nice if
you can get in, this former pub,
where comfy couches abound,
has DJs playing jazzy tunes as
well as rare groove, soul and
funk.

Dulwich and Greenwich

Crown & Greyhound

Map 2, J7. 73 Dulwich Village,
SE21 ℡ 020/8299 4976 North
Dulwich or West Dulwich train stations. Mon–Sat 11am–11pm, Sun
noon–10.30pm. Grand, spacious
Victorian pub with an ornate
plasterwork ceiling, good food
and beer, and a nice summer
beer garden. Convenient for the
Dulwich Picture Gallery, but be
prepared for crowds during Sunday lunchtimes.

Cutty Sark

Map 2, L5. Ballast Quay, off Lassell
St, SE10 ℡ 020/8858 3146 Cutty
Sark DLR or Maze Hill train station.
Mon–Sat 11am–11pm, Sun noon–
10.30pm. The nicest riverside pub
in Greenwich, spacious, more of
a local and much less touristy
than the more famous *Trafalgar
Tavern* (it's a couple of minutes
walk further east, following the

river). The views are great, as is
the draught beer.

Trafalgar Tavern

See map on p.154, E2. 5 Park Row,
SE10 ℡ 020/8858 2437 Cutty Sark
DLR or Maze Hill train station.
Mon–Sat 11.30am–11pm, Sun
noon–10.30pm. A great riverside
position and a mention in Dickens' *Our Mutual Friend* have
made this Regency-style inn a
firm tourist favourite, which is fair
enough, as it's a convivial period
piece, and serves good food
(including whitebait).

Chiswick to Richmond

The Dove

Map 2, E5. 19 Upper Mall, W6
℡ 020/8748 5405⊖ Raven-
scourt Park. Mon–Sat 11am–11pm,
Sun noon–10.30pm. A wonderful low-beamed old riverside
pub with literary associations:
Grahame Greene and Ernest
Hemmingway were regulars. It's
also distinguished by having the
smallest bar in the UK (4ft by 7ft),
and very popular Sunday roast
dinners.

White Cross Hotel

Map 2, C7. Water Lane, Richmond
℡ 020/8940 6844⊖ Richmond.
Mon–Sat 11am–11pm, Sun noon–
10.30pm. With a longer pedigree
and more character than its

clinical chain rivals nearby, the *White Cross* is also much closer to the river (its front garden regularly gets flooded), and serves Young's beer.

White Swan

Map 2, C7. Riverside, Twickenham
☎ 020/8892 2166 Twickenham train station. Mon–Sat 11am–11pm, Sun noon–10.30pm. Filling pub food, draught beer and a quiet riverside location – except on rugby match days – make this a good halt on any towpath ramble. The excellent summer Sunday BBQs are a big draw.

19

Live music and clubs

O ver the past decade London has established itself as the nightlife capital of not just Europe, but the world. The city's **live music** scene remains extremely diverse, encompassing all variations of rock, blues, roots and world music, and although London's jazz clubs aren't on a par with those in the big American cities, there's a highly individual scene of home-based artists, supplemented by top-name visiting players.

If you're looking for **dance music**, then welcome to Europe's party capital. After dark, London is thriving, with diverse scenes championing everything from hip-hop to house, techno to garage, samba to soca and drum'n'bass to R&B on virtually any night of the week. Venues once used exclusively by performing bands now pepper their weekly calendar with club nights, and you often find dance sessions starting as soon as a band has stopped playing. Bear in mind that there's sometimes an overlap between live music venues and clubs in the listings below; we've indicated which places serve a double function.

The dance and club scene is, of course, pretty much in constant flux, with the hottest nights constantly moving location, losing the plot or just cooling off. Weekly **listings magazines** such as *Time Out* give up-to-date details of prices and access, plus previews and reviews.

For club-bars and pre-club drinking dens, see Chapter 18; for lesbian and gay clubs and discos, see Chapter 20.

Live music

London is hard to beat for its musical mix: whether you're into **jazz**, **indie**, **rock**, **R&B**, **blues** or **world music**, you'll find something worth hearing on almost any night of the week. **Entry prices** for gigs run from a couple of pounds for an unknown band thrashing it out in a pub to up to £80 for the likes of U2, but you can reckon on around £10–15 for a good night out, not counting expenses at the bar. It's often cheaper to book tickets in advance with a credit card via the Internet, from sites such as ⓦ www.ticketweb.co.uk, ⓦ www.seetickets.com or ⓦ www.gigsandtours.com. We've listed websites for all venues that have them.

General venues

Astoria
Map 4, G5. 157 Charing Cross Rd, WC2 ☎ 020/7434 9592, ⓦ www .meanfiddler.com ⊖ Tottenham Court Road. One of London's best and most central medium-sized venues, this large, balconied one-time theatre hosts popular bands from a real variety of genres, usually from Mon–Thurs, with club nights on Friday and Saturday.

Brixton Academy
Map 2, I6. 211 Stockwell Rd, SW9 ☎ 0870/771 2000, ⓦ www.brixton-academy.co.uk ⊖ Brixton. This refurbished Victorian hall, complete with Classical décor, can hold 4000 but still manages to seem small and friendly, probably because most of the audience are standing,

dancing or waving their beers about.

Cargo

Map 3, N2. 83 Rivington St, EC2 ☎020/7749 7840, ⓦwww.cargo-london.com⊖ Old Street. Small, upmarket club/venue in what was once a railway arch, with an attached restaurant, and bar and garden areas. Hosts a wide variety of interesting live acts, including jazz, Latin, hip-hop, indie and folk, which are often part of their excellent lineup of club nights (see p.231).

Carling Academy Islington

Map 2, I3. N1 Centre, 16 Parkfield St, N1 ☎020/7288 4400, ⓦwww.islington-academy.co.uk⊖ Angel. Despite its awful location (in the midst of a modern shopping centre), the *Islington Academy* has some good up-and-coming and mid-level bands, as well as club nights in *Bar Academy* (in the same building).

Coronet

Map 3, L7. 28 New Kent Rd, SE1 ☎020/7701 1500, ⓦwww.coronet-london.co.uk⊖ Elephant and Castle. A theatre turned cinema turned music venue, with a gorgeous Deco interior. Live acts, DJ nights and talent shows.

Forum

Map 2, G3. 9–17 Highgate Rd, NW5 ☎020/7284 1001, ⓦwww.meanfiddler.com⊖ Kentish Town. This is one of the capital's best medium-sized venues – large enough to attract established bands, but also promoting less well known and interesting ones.

The Mean Fiddler

Map 4, G5. 165 Charing Cross Rd, W1 ☎020/7434 9592, ⓦwww.meanfiddler.com⊖ Tottenham Court Road. Next door to the *Astoria*, the *Mean Fiddler* has a good lineup of mainly rock and indie bands, with club nights on Friday and Saturday.

Spitz

Map 3, N3. Old Spitalfields Market, 109 Commercial St, E1 ☎020/7392 9032⊖ Liverpool Street. Friendly, small venue in the heart of Spitalfields Market, where you can catch a diverse range of music including jazz, world, indie, folk, blues and electronica. The downstairs bistro hosts free live music up to four nights a week.

Rock, blues and indie

The Garage

Map 2, I3. 20–22 Highbury Corner, N1 ☎020/7607 1818, ⓦwww.meanfiddler.com⊖ Highbury &

Islington. Modest, mainly indie place with a good reputation for up-and-coming talent which makes the occasional excursion into jazz and funk. Two doors down, *Upstairs at the Garage* is even smaller with more new acts. Both venues also have club nights.

Metro

Map 4, F4. 19–23 Oxford St, W1 ⓣ 020/7437 0964, ⓦ www .blowupmetro.com ⊖ Tottenham Court Road. An intimate venue with a forward-thinking booking policy – it's a good place to head if you're interested in seeing new bands just before they get big. Also club nights Mon–Sat till late.

Neighbourhood

Map 2, F5. 12 Acklam Rd, W10 ⓣ 020/8960 4590, ⓦ www .neighbourhoodclub.net ⊖ Ladbroke Grove. Formerly *Subterrania*, now run by Ben Watt of 1980s pop duo Everything But the Girl, this is a live-music/club crossover venue in an arch under a flyover, where the crowd is as trendy as the house-oriented music.

Shepherds Bush Empire

Map 2, E4. Shepherds Bush Green, W12 ⓣ 020/7771 2000, ⓦ www .shepherds-bush-empire.co.uk ⊖ Shepherds Bush. Yet another grand old theatre, the *Empire* now plays host to probably the finest cross-section of mid-league UK and US bands in the capital. Intimate, with a great atmosphere downstairs. Upstairs, balconies provide some of the best stage views around.

12 Bar Club

Map 4, G5. Denmark Street, WC2 ⓣ 020/7209 2248, ⓦ www.12barclub.com ⊖ Tottenham Court Road. Tiny, atmospheric blues, contemporary country and acoustic folk venue on London's Tin Pan Alley. It's also a bar and café.

Jazz, world music and folk

Bull's Head Barnes

Map 2, E5. 373 Lonsdale Rd, Barnes SW13 ⓣ 020/8876 5241 Bus #9 from Hammersmith, or Barnes Bridge train station from Waterloo. This riverside alehouse has been attracting Britain's finest jazz musicians for 45 years. Live music nightly and Sunday lunchtimes.

Cecil Sharp House

Map 2, H3. 2 Regent's Park Rd, NW1 ⓣ 020/7485 2206, ⓦ www.efdss.org ⊖ Camden Town. Headquarters of the English Folk Dance and Song Society, with singing and dancing performances as well as work-shops and classes.

Dover Street

Map 4, C9. 8–9 Dover St, W1
☎020/7629 9813 ⊖ Green Park.
London's largest jazz restaurant
has music and dancing every
night until 3am, plus Modern
British food. Attracts an older
crowd; dress smart.

Jazz Café

Map 2, H3. 5 Parkway, NW1
☎020/7916 6060, ⊛www
.meanfiddler.com ⊖ Camden Town.
Excellent, chilled-out venue with
an adventurous booking policy
exploring Latin, rap, funk, hip-
hop and musical fusions. The
restaurant upstairs has a few
prime tables overlooking the
small stage (book ahead if you
want one).

100 Club

Map 4, E5. 100 Oxford St, W1
☎020/7636 0933 ⊖ Tottenham
Court Road. An unpretentious,
inexpensive and fun jazz venue
with an incredible vintage – it's
been going strong for more than
sixty years.

Pizza Express

Map 4, F5. 10 Dean St, W1
☎020/7439 8722 ⊖ Oxford Circus.
Enjoy a good pizza, then listen
to the highly skilled guest players: recently these have included
Mose Allison and Andy Sheppard.

Ronnie Scott's

Map 4, F6. 47 Frith St, W1
☎020/7439 0747, ⊛www
.ronniescotts.co.uk ⊖ Leicester
Square. The most famous jazz
club in London: small, smoky
and still going strong. The place
for top-line names, who play
two sets – one at around 10pm,
the other after midnight. Book a
table, or you'll have to stand.

606 Club

Map 2, F6. 90 Lots Rd, SW10
☎020/7352 5953 ⊖ Fulham Broadway. A rare all-jazz venue, located
just off the less trendy end of the
King's Road. You can book a
table, and if you're a non-
member (that is, if you have visited fewer than three times) you
must eat if you want to drink.

Clubs

Roughly twenty years after acid house irreversibly shook up
the British club scene, London remains *the* place to come if
you want to party after dark. The sheer diversity of dance
music has enabled the city to maintain its status as **Europe's**

dance capital – and it's still a port of call for DJs from around the globe. The so-called super-clubs may be on the way out, but, in their place, there's more variety than ever, in music and the venues available. The relaxation of late-night licensing has encouraged many venues to keep serving alcohol until 6am or even later, and the resurgence of alcohol in clubland (much to the relief of the breweries) has been echoed by the meteoric rise of the club-bar (see chapter 18).

Nearly all of London's **dance clubs** open their doors between 10pm and midnight. Some are open six or seven nights a week, some keep irregular days, others just open at the weekend and very often a venue will host a different club on each night of the week. For up-to-the-minute details of these, and all the nights listed below, pop into one of Soho's many record shops (see p.288) to pick up flyers, or check magazines such as *Time Out* for details.

Admission charges vary enormously, with small midweek sessions starting at around £3–5 and large weekend events charging as much as £25; around £10–15 is the average for a Friday or Saturday night, but bear in mind that profit margins at the bar are even more outrageous than at live music venues.

Club venues

Bar Rumba
Map 4, F7. 36 Shaftesbury Ave, W1 ☏020/7287 6933, ⓦ www.barrumba .co.uk⊖ Piccadilly Circus. Fun, smallish West End venue with a mix of regular nights ranging from salsa through R&B and dance to drum'n'bass. Pop in during the early evening (when it's free) to sample happy hour cocktails.

Café de Paris
Map 4, F7. 3 Coventry St, W1

☏020/7734 7700⊖ Leicester Square. The elegant *Café* ballroom has been restored to its former glory and plays commercial house, garage and disco to a smartly dressed, trendy crowd of wannabes – no jeans or trainers.

Cargo
Map 3, N2. 83 Rivington St, EC2 ☏020/7739 5446, ⓦwww.cargo-london.com⊖ Old Street. *Cargo* plays host to a variety of excellent and often innovative club nights, from deep

house to jazz, and often features live bands alongside the DJs (see p.228).

The Cross

Map 3, I1. Arches 27–31, York Way, N1 ℡020/7837 0828, ⊛www .the-cross.co.uk⊖ King's Cross. Hidden underneath the arches, this renowned club favours hard house, house and garage. It's bigger than it looks from the outside, but is always packed full with chic clubby types – the cool garden is perfect for those chill-out moments.

EGG

Map 3, I1. 200 York Way, N7 ℡020/7609 8364, ⊛www .egglondon.net⊖ King's Cross. Two exposed-brick, medium-sized rooms, a loft-style bar and a small outdoor chill-out area make up this out-of-the-way club. All kinds of nights, including those that bring together techno, funky house and club classics, and electro, rock and industrial.

The End

Map 3, I3. 18 West Central St, WC1 ℡020/7419 9199, ⊛www.the-end.co.uk⊖ Tottenham Court Road or Holborn. Owned by Mr C (ex-Shamen MC), this club has been designed for clubbers by clubbers and has one of the best sound systems in the world.

Well known for its tech-house and drum'n'bass weekends, and worth checking out for monthly nights hosted by other clubs or record labels, along with Monday's anything-goes *Trash* with DJ Erol Alkan.

Fabric

Map 3, K3. 77a Charterhouse St, EC1 ℡020/7336 8898, ⊛www.fabriclondon.com⊖ Farringdon. Cavernous underground space with three rooms, holding 1600 people, as well as a devastating sound system. Fridays are *Fabric Live*, a mix of drum'n'bass and hip-hop with live acts. Saturdays concentrate on cutting-edge house, techno and electro, played by underground DJs from around the globe. Get there early to avoid a night of queuing.

Fridge

Map 2, I6. Town Hall Parade, Brixton Hill, SW2 ℡020/7326 5100, ⊛www .fridge.co.uk⊖ Brixton. Weekends alternate between pumping mixed/gay nights like Saturday's Love Muscle and trance favourites with a psychedelic vibe and plenty of lightstick-waving action.

Herbal

Map 3, N2. 10–14 Kingsland Rd, E2 ℡020/7613 4462, ⊛www.herbaluk .com⊖ Old Street or Liverpool Street. An intimate two-floored venue with a cool New York-style loft and sweaty ground-floor club. A great place to check out drum'n'bass and breaks.

KOKO

Map 2, H3. 1A Camden High St, NW1 ⓣ09062 100 200, ⓦwww.koko.uk.com⊖ Mornington Crescent. Gorgeously revamped theatre that famously hosted gigs as *The Music Machine* in the Seventies and *The Camden Palace* in the Eighties and Nineties. Indie club nights on Fridays, one-off promoter events and live music gigs see the club gaining popularity again.

Ministry of Sound

Map 3, L7. 103 Gaunt St, SE1 ⓣ020/7378 6528, ⓦwww.ministryofsound.co.uk⊖ Elephant & Castle. A vast, state-of-the-art enterprise based on New York's legendary *Paradise Garage*, with an exceptional sound system and the pick of visiting US and Italian DJs. This is corporate clubbing and full of tourists, but it still draws the top talent, especially on Saturdays. Look out for their excellent, hedonistic Bank Holiday parties – turn up early to ensure you get in.

93 Feet East

Map 7, M1. 150 Brick Lane, E2 ⓣ020/7247 5293, ⓦwww.93feeteast.co.uk⊖ Old Street. Weekends see this trendy club/venue (gigs during the week), set in part of the Truman Brewery, put on a varied programme of electro house, underground beats, hip-hop, breaks and funk. There's an excellent rooftop balcony and courtyard that's well worth a visit in the summer. Currently closes at 1am.

Notting Hill Arts Club

Map 3, A5. 21 Notting Hill Gate, W11 ⓣ020/7460 4459, ⓦwww.nottinghillartsclub.com ⊖ Notting Hill Gate. Basement club that's popular for everything from Latin-inspired funk, jazz and disco through to soul, house and garage. It's famed for its late afternoon/evening Sunday deep-house sessions.

Plan B

Map 2, I6. 418 Brixton Rd, SW9 ⓣ020/7733 0926, ⓦwww.plan-brixton.co.uk⊖ Brixton. Slicker and more style-conscious than the average Brixton club, with a good sound system, friendly staff and a great bar. House, hip-hop, funk, psychedelic soul and R&B.

Rhythm Factory

Map 2, J4. 16–18 Whitechapel Road ⓣ020/7375 3774, ⓦwww.rhythmfactory.co.uk⊖ Aldgate East or **Whitechapel**. This former textile factory-turned-club houses a bar area serving Thai food and two medium-sized rooms which usually see three live gigs during the week and a range of excellent monthly shenanigans at the weekends, including deep house night *Muak* and the funk and hip-hop *Breakin' Bread*.

Salsa!
Map 4, G5. 96 Charing Cross Rd, WC2 ☎020/7379 3277⊖ Leicester Square. Funky and fun salsa-based club-cum-restaurant that's a popular choice for group birthdays.

333
Map 3, N2. 333 Old St, EC1 ☎020/7739 5949, ⓦwww.333mother.com⊖ **Old Street.** One of London's best clubs for new dance music, in the heart of trendy-as-hell Hoxton. Three floors (including the *Mother* bar) of drum'n'bass, twisted disco and breakbeat madness.

Turnmills
Map 3, K3. 63b Clerkenwell Rd, EC1 ☎020/7250 3409, ⓦwww .turnmills.com⊖ Farringdon. The place to come if you want to sweat from dusk till dawn, with an alien invasion-style bar and funky split-level dancefloor in the main room. Friday's weekly *Gallery* night, where Tall Paul is resident, features trance, house and techno with top-name guest DJs.

20

Lesbian and gay London

L ondon's **lesbian and gay scene** is so huge, diverse and well established that it's easy to forget just how much - and how fast - it has grown over the last few years. Pink power has given rise to the pink pound, gay liberation to gay lifestyle, and the ever-expanding Soho - now firmly established as the homo heart of the city - is vibrant, self-assured and unashamedly commercial. As a result of all this high-profile activity, straight Londoners tend to be a fairly homo-savvy bunch and, on the whole, happy to embrace and even dip into the city's queer offerings.

Soho is the obvious place to start exploring London's gay and lesbian scene, and **Old Compton Street** is, so to speak, its main drag. Here, traditional gay pubs rub alongside café/bars selling expensive designer beers and lattes, while hairdressers, letting agencies, sex boutiques and spiritual health centres offer a range of gay-run services. There are clubs to cater for just about every musical, sartorial and sexual taste and, while the bigger ones increasingly congregate just south of the river in **Vauxhall**, there are equally well-established venues all over the city. Gay men still enjoy the best permanent facilities London-wide, but today's **lesbian scene** is bigger and more eclectic than ever, and the cruisey girl bars which took up prize pitches on the boys' Soho turf a few years ago look like they're there to stay.

You can also find pockets of queer activity away from the centre in the city's funkier residential areas, most notably Brixton in south London, Islington and (especially for dykes) Stoke Newington and Hackney. Bear in mind that although open anti-gay hostility is rare in London, it's probably wise not to hold hands or smooch too obviously in areas you don't know well.

The **outdoor event** of the year is **Pride London** in early July. Encompassing a rally in Trafalgar Square, a colourful, whistle-blowing march through the city streets and a live cabaret stage and Drag Idol contest in Leicester Square, Pride London is the somewhat trimmed-down but perhaps more focused successor to the highly commercialized events of recent years. For up-to-date details, festival plans, tickets and transport information, visit Ⓦ www.prideinthepark.com. Pride London is usually followed around the end of July by a ticket-only music festival, currently labouring under the name **Big Gay Out** (Ⓦ www.biggayout.com) and held in north London's Finsbury Park. It's generally judged to be an improvement on the patchy success of its immediate predecessors.

London also boasts several queer-oriented annual arts events: in March and April, the National Film Theatre, Odeon West End and Tate Modern host the annual **Lesbian and Gay Film Festival** (Ⓦ www.llgff.org.uk); while the **Pride Festival Fortnight**, staged at venues throughout London, leads the run-up to Pride itself.

Elsewhere, queer theatre and arts events take place all year round in the city's many fringe theatres, arts centres, galleries and clubs. If none of this is up your street, there are also a huge number of **gay groups and organizations** offering everything from ballroom dancing to spanking seminars.

LESBIAN AND GAY LONDON

For further details of lesbian and gay events, check out *Time Out* or the gay press – *The Pink Paper* (weekly, free), *Gay Times* (monthly), and lesbian magazine *Diva* (monthly) can be picked up from major newsagents, bookshops or cafés and bars in Soho. In addition, consumerist freesheets like *Boyz* and *qx* abound in clubs and bars and provide up-to-date club listings.

Websites

The following are the most useful **websites**, all of them offering more than just an online version of printed publications.

ⓦ www.fruitcamp.com

For a slice of London's lesbian and gay life online, *fruitcamp* provides useful info on flatshares, jobs, the scene and community events.

ⓦ www.gaydar.co.uk

The *gaydar* revolution has transformed the lives of gay men who prefer to cut to the chase and order a date like they'd order a pizza. If it works for you, it's not a bad place to meet up-for-it guys of all persuasions. ⓦ www.gaydargirls.com is the equivalent for queer girls nationwide.

ⓦ www.gaytoz.com

For a comprehensive online directory of gay, lesbian, bisexual and TV/TS-friendly organizations and businesses, you can't do better than GAY to Z. A print version is also available from Gay to Z Directories, 41 Cooks Rd, London SE17 3NG.

ⓦ www.gingerbeer.co.uk

Well-designed and regularly updated website for London dykes, offering listings and reviews of bars, clubs and events. *Gingerbeer* also holds regular women-only club nights - check the site for details.

ⓦ www.rainbownetwork .com

Lifestyle e-zine for boys and girls with masses of editorial content. Includes news on the latest events, interviews with scene faces, listings and message boards.

Useful, if in part rather medical
in tone, this transsexual and
transvestite site offers news plus
national club and venue listings.

Ⓦ www.uk.gay.com
British affiliate of the international
website for gay men, with regular
news stories, features, competitions and scene guide.

Cafés, bars and pubs

There are loads of lesbian and gay **cafés**, **bars and pubs** in
London, many of which have been around for years, while
some pop up and disappear within months – such is the
fickle nature of the scene. Our list is by no means exhaustive,
as every corner of London has its own gay local. Many cafés
and bars transform themselves into **drinking dens** at night
and, as some open beyond licensing hours, they can be a
cheap alternative to clubs. Bear in mind that, although more
and more lesbian bars admit gay men, "mixed" (as ever) tends
to mean mostly men.

Mixed cafés, bars and restaurants

The Admiral Duncan
Map 4, F6. 54 Old Compton St,
W1 ☏ 020/7437 5300 ⊖ Leicester
Square. Unpretentious, traditional-
style gay bar in the heart of Soho,
famous for having been bombed
in 1999, now always popular and
busy with a post-work crowd.

Balans Café
Map 4, F6. 34 Old Compton St,
W1 ☏ 020/7439 3309, Ⓦ www
.balans.co.uk ⊖ Tottenham Court

Road or Leicester Square.
This enduringly busy Soho
institution is open until the
early hours. Strong coffee and
a range of cakes and snacks
make it the obvious place to
head with mid- or post-party
wooziness.

Bar Aquda
Map 4, H7. 13–14 Maiden Lane,
WC2 ☏ 020/7557 9891 ⊖ Leicester
Square or Covent Garden. Bright,
modern and fashionable café/
bar with good food. Recently
refurbished. Mixed, but mostly
boys.

Helplines and information

All of the following services provide information, advice and counselling, but the **Lesbian & Gay Switchboard** is the one to turn to first: its volunteers have details on all the capital's resources and can point you in the direction of specific organizations and community or support groups.

Bisexual Helpline ℡08454/501263; Tues & Wed 7.30–9.30pm, Sat 10.30am–12.30pm. Advice, support and information for bisexuals.

London Friend ℡020/7837 3337, ⊛www.londonfriend.org.uk; daily 7.30–10pm. Confidential information and support for lesbians and gay men. The women-only service (℡020/7837 2782; 7.30–10pm) is Sun to Thurs.

London Lesbian & Gay Switchboard ℡020/7837 7324, ⊛www.queery.org.uk. Huge database on everything you might ever want to know, plus legal advice, good counselling skills and good humour. Lines are 24hr; do keep trying if you can't get through.

National AIDS Helpline ℡0800/567123, ⊛www.playingsafely.co.uk. Freephone 24hr service for anyone worried about HIV and AIDS-related issues and sexually transmitted infections.

Terrence Higgins Trust ℡0845/122 1200, ⊛www.tht.org.uk; Mon–Fri 11am–8pm. Information and advice on all HIV and AIDS-related issues. Service also available in French and Spanish. For self-referrals to the counselling unit, call ℡020/7835 1495.

The Black Cap
Map 2, H3. 171 Camden High St, NW1 ℡020/7428 2721 ⊖ Camden Town. Venerable north London institution offering cabaret of wildly varying quality almost every night. Laugh, sing and lip-synch along, and then dance to 1980s tunes until the early hours. The upstairs *Mrs Shufflewick's Bar* is quieter, and opens onto the Fong (after drag legend Regina) Terrace in the summer.

The Box
Map 4, G6. 32–34 Monmouth St, WC2 ℡020/7240 5828 ⊖ Covent Garden or Leicester Square. Popular, bright café/bar serving good food for a mixed gay/straight crowd during the day,

and getting queerer as the night draws in.

The Edge

Map 4, F5. 11 Soho Square, W1 ☏020/7439 1313, ⓦwww.edge.uk.com⊖ Tottenham Court Road. Busy, style-conscious and pricey Soho café/bar, which, though it's spread over several floors, doesn't seem to stop everyone ending up on the pavement, especially in summer. Food daily, good art exhibitions and DJs most nights.

Escape

Map 4, E6. 10a Brewer St, W1 ☏020/7734 2626⊖ Piccadilly Circus. Trendy DJ bar in the heart of Soho, attracting a young, mixed crowd and open until 3am most nights.

First Out

🏃 **Map 4, G5. 52 St Giles High St, WC2** ☏020/7240 8042, ⓦwww.firstoutcafebar.com ⊖ Tottenham Court Road. The West End's original gay café/bar, and still permanently packed, serving good veggie food at reasonable prices. Upstairs is airy and non-smoking, downstairs dark and foggy. *Girl Friday* is a busy pre-club Friday session for grrrls; gay men are welcome as guests.

Freedom

Map 4, F6. 60–66 Wardour St, W1 ☏020/7734 0071⊖ Leicester Square or Piccadilly. Hip, busy, late-opening café/bar, popular with a mixed straight/gay Soho crowd and recently given a glamorous makeover. The basement transforms itself into a funky, intimate club, complete with pink banquettes and masses of glitter balls.

G.A.Y Bar

Map 4, F6. 30 Old Compton St, W1 ☏020/7494 2756⊖ Tottenham Court Road or Leicester Square. Vast, pinky-purple video bar that attracts a young, fashionable, pre-G.A.Y crowd. The basement bar is for women and guests only in the evening.

The Green

🏃 **Map 3, K1. 74 Upper St, N1** ☏020/7226 8895⊖ Angel. Relaxed, stylish bar/restaurant fronting Islington Green, with interesting food, wine and beers and classic cocktails. It's open late Thurs–Sat and there's a distinctly brunchy vibe to Sunday.

Kudos

Map 4, H8. 10 Adelaide St, WC2 ☏020/7379 4573, ⓦwww.kudosgroup.com⊖ Leicester Square. Busy venue, popular amongst smart, besuited post-work boys and London's gay Chinese community, with a ground-floor café and a basement video bar.

Oak Bar

Map 2, I3. 79 Green Lanes, N16 ☏020/7354 2791 ⊖ Manor House then bus #341 or #141, or ⊖ Angel then bus #73 or #341. Friendly, spacious local pub with a dancefloor and pool table. Hosts a range of mixed and women-only special events and club nights, including the wildly popular mixed (but mostly women) *Lower The Tone* (see p.248).

Retro Bar

Map 4, H8. 2 George Court (off Strand), WC2 ☏020/7231 2811 ⊖ Charing Cross. Friendly, indie/retro gay bar playing 70s, 80s, goth and alternative sounds, and featuring regular DJs and karaoke.

The Royal Oak

Map 2, J4. 73 Columbia Rd, E2 ☏020/7739 8204 ⊖ Old Street or Shoreditch. In the heart of the famous Columbia Road flower market (see p.104), this old, comfortable market pub caters for a mixed gay/straight crowd, and offers Sunday breakfasts from 8am or Tex-Mex meals at the upstairs restaurant.

The Royal Vauxhall Tavern

Map 3, I9. 372 Kennington Lane, SE11 ☏020/7840 0596 ⊖ Vauxhall. A London institution with late opening hours, this huge, disreputable and divey drag and cabaret pub is home to legendary alternative club night, *Duckie* (Sat), with a staggeringly bonkers and queer range of appearances. Popular with an alt/indie crowd.

Shadow Lounge

Map 4, E6. 5 Brewer St, W1 ☏020/7287 7988, ⓦwww.the shadowlounge.co.uk ⊖ Covent Garden or Leicester Square. Glitzy gay members' bar which attracts an A to Z of celebrity punters. More fag hag than leather lez, and the boys rule the school.

Teds Place

Map 2, F5. 305a North End Rd, W14 ☏020/7385 9359 ⊖ West Kensington or West Brompton. Cruisey Fulham local, open weekdays only and men only, though there is a regular Thursday TV/TS night.

Trash Palace

Map 4, F7. 11 Wardour St, W1 ☏07956/549246 ⊖ Leicester Square or Piccadilly Circus. Alternative, indie/pop/electro bar on two floors, open until 3am Friday and Saturday, a popular spot pre-*Miss-Shapes* or *Popstarz*.

Village Soho

Map 4, F6. 81 Wardour St, W1
Ⓣ 020/7434 2124 ⊖ Leicester Square or Piccadilly Circus. Elegant three-floor café/bar with a relaxed atmosphere that attracts a young gay crowd – more pretty boyz than girlz. Serves food from 4pm.

The Yard

Map 4, F7. 57 Rupert St, W1
Ⓣ 020/7437 2652 ⊖ Piccadilly Circus. Attractive café/bar with courtyard and loft areas. One of the best in Soho for al fresco drinking. Occasional comedy weekday nights; regular changing artworks.

Lesbian bars and pubs

Blush

Map 2, J2. 8 Cazenove Rd, Stoke Newington N16 Ⓣ 020/7923 9202 ⊖ King's Cross or Angel then bus #73, or Stoke Newington railway station. This friendly local bar-club's two floors of fun – quiz nights, live music and a pool bar – make it a popular choice among lesbians north of the city centre.

Candy Bar

Map 4, F5. Carlisle St, WC2
Ⓣ 020/7494 4041, Ⓦ www .candybar.co.uk ⊖ Tottenham Court Road. The hottest girl bar in central London, with a crucial, cruisey vibe.

The Glass Bar

Map 3, H2. West Lodge, Euston Square Gardens, 190 Euston Rd, NW1 Ⓣ 020/7387 6184, Ⓦ www .southtopia.com/glassbar ⊖ Euston. Difficult to find (and hard to forget), this friendly, intimate late-opening women-only members' bar (membership is automatic once you're inside) is housed in a listed building and features a wrought-iron spiral staircase, which gets increasingly perilous as the night wears on. Knock on the door to get in. No admission after 12.30pm on Saturday.

Southtopia

Map 3, L7. 146-148 Newington Butts, SE11 Ⓣ 020/7735 6178, Ⓦ www.southtopia.com ⊖ Kennington or Elephant and Castle. New, stylish private members bar for women (men allowed in ground-floor bar as guests). Run by the same people as the *Glass Bar*, it has a friendly, grown-up atmosphere. Daily membership £2.

Star at Night

Map 4, E5. 22 Great Chapel St, W1 Ⓣ 020/7434 3749 ⊖ Tottenham Court Road. Comfortable new venue open from 6pm Tues–Sat, popular with a slightly older crowd who want somewhere to sit, a good glass of wine and good conversation.

Vespa Lounge

Map 4, G4. Upstairs at The Conservatory, Centrepoint House, 15 St Giles High St, WC1 ☏ 020/7836 8956, ⓔ evespalounge@aol.com ⊖ Tottenham Court Road. This centrally located girls' bar gets super-busy at weekends. Pool table, video screen, cute bar staff and a predominantly young crowd. Gay men welcome as guests.

Y Bar

Map 2, I3. 142 Essex Rd, N1 ☏ 020/7359 2661 ⊖ Angel. Run by Yolanda (formerly of the legendary *Due South* bar) and established as one of the cooler hangouts with the gorgeous girls. Mixed, but women-only on Thursday (4pm–midnight).

Gay men's cafés, bars and pubs

79CXR

Map 4, G6. 79 Charing Cross Rd, WC2 ☏ 020/7734 0769, ⓦ www.79cxr.co.uk ⊖ Leicester Square. Busy, cruisey men's den on two floors, with industrial décor, late licence and a no-messing atmosphere.

BarCode

Map 4, E7. 3–4 Archer St, W1 ☏ 020/7734 3342 ⊖ Piccadilly Circus. Busy, stylish cruise and dance bar on two floors, attracting a buff, masculine crowd. On Tues it hosts *Comedy Camp*, an award-winning gay comedy club.

Brief Encounter

Map 4, G7. 41–43 St Martin's Lane, WC2 ☏ 020/7379 8252 ⊖ Leicester Square. Now back with its original name, the West End's longest-running cruise bar is a popular pre-*Heaven* or post-opera hangout (it's next door to the Coliseum): the upper bar offers regular cabaret, while the lower bar is very, very dark.

Brompton's

Map 3, A8. 294 Old Brompton Rd, SW5 ☏ 020/7370 1344 ⊖ Earl's Court. Long-established, leathery and immensely popular late-opening bar-cum-club that's packed at weekends, and features regular cabarets and PAs.

Central Station

Map 3, I1. 37 Wharfdale Rd, N1 ☏ 020/7278 3294 ⊖ King's Cross. Award-winning, late-opening community pub on three floors, offering cabaret, cruisey club nights in the *Underground* basement area, and the UK's only gay sports bar. It's also the home of the long-running *Gummi* rubber fetish night. Not strictly men-only, but mostly so.

LESBIAN AND GAY LONDON | Cafés, bars, pubs

The Coleherne

Map 3, A8. 261 Old Brompton Rd, SW5 ☎020/7244 5951 ⊖ **Earl's Court.** Famous and permanently packed former leather bar, now popular with a wide range of the gay community and still bristling with history.

Comptons of Soho

Map 4, F6. 53 Old Compton St, W1 ☎020/7479 7961 ⊖ **Leicester Square or Piccadilly Circus.** This large, traditional-style pub is a Soho institution, always busy with a butch 25+ crowd, but still a relaxed place to cruise or just hang out. The upstairs *Club Lounge* is more chilled and attracts a younger crowd.

The Kings Arms

Map 4, E5. 23 Poland St, W1 ☎020/7734 5907 ⊖ **Oxford Circus.** London's best known and perennially popular bear bar, with a traditional London pub atmosphere, DJ on Saturday and karaoke night Sunday.

The Quebec

Map 3, E4. 12 Old Quebec St, W1 ☎020/7629 6159 ⊖ **Marble Arch.** Long-established and busy gay venue with downstairs disco and a late licence six days a week. Especially popular with an older crowd.

Tea dances

Somewhere between a café and a club is the institution of the **tea dance**, a fun and friendly place to try out old-fashioned partner dancing. Traditionally, tea dancing happens on a Sunday, which means you're unlikely ever to get a serious tea dance habit – although be warned, as it has happened. It's best to arrive early, especially if you need a class; ring in advance for details.

Original Sunday Tea Dance at BJs White Swan

Map 2, K4. 556 Commercial Rd, E14 ☎020/7780 9870 ⊖ **Aldgate East or Limehouse DLR. Sun 5.30pm–mid-night.** Hosted by popular local DJ Gary Malden, who plays ballroom, cheesy disco and everything in between. Tea and sandwiches served until 7pm.

Waltzing with Hilda at Jackson's Lane Community Centre

Map 2, H2. Jacksons Lane Community Centre, 269a Archway Rd, N6 ☎079390/72958 ⊖ Highgate. Second and last Sat of the month

7.45pm–midnight. Women-only Latin and ballroom dancing club – with a dash of country and western thrown in to keep you on your toes. Beer at pub prices and classes for beginners.

Clubs

London's **clubs** tend to open up and shut down with surreal frequency, only to pop up again a few months later in another part of town, or in the same place under a different name. It's a good idea, therefore, to check the gay press, listings magazines and club websites for up-to-date times and prices before you plan your night out. Our listings are by club night where that's best known, or by venue where there's a variety of changing theme nights.

- -

For a guaranteed harassment-free drive home, call Liberty Cars, 330 Old St, EC1 ☎020/7739 9080. They offer a reasonably priced, London-wide 24-hour gay-run cab service.

- -

Entry charges start at around £4–5, but are more often between £8 and £15, rising to around £35 or even £50 for special events like New Year's Eve extravaganzas. Some places offer concessions for students and those on benefits, and some extend **discounts** if you've managed to pick up the right flyer. Bear in mind also that clubs are usually significantly cheaper once you're out of the West End. Some clubs, especially the men's, stipulate **dress codes** – mainly leather, rubber, uniform and other fetish wear. We've specified such sartorial regulations, but it's best to check before setting out in your finery.

Mixed clubs

Beyond

Map 3, H9. Club Colosseum, 1 Nine Elms Lane, SW8 ☎07905/035682, ⓦwww.allthingsorange.com ⊖ Vauxhall. Sun 4.30am–late. London's biggest after-hours club kicks off each Sunday morning at 4.30am and parties on well into the morning. Two massive dance floors, four bars, chill-out areas and funky house music please an eclectic mix of up-for-it clubbers.

Bootylicious at Crash

Map 3, I8. 66 Goding St, SE11 (no phone), ⓦwww.bootylicioius-club .co.uk⊖ Vauxhall. Every second Fri from around midnight. London's only weekend club night devoted to urban dance music. Expect a full-on and sexy vibe at this hip-hop, R&B and ragga-tastic club night. For a hot'n'sweaty dance experience with a beautiful funky crowd, it doesn't get much better than this.

Club Kali at The Dome

Map 2, H3. 1 Dartmouth Park Hill, N19 (no phone)⊖ Tufnell Park. Third Fri of the month. *Kali* is a huge multi-ethnic extravaganza offering bhangra, Bollywood, Arabic, swing, Hindi and house flavours for a friendly, attitude-free crowd.

Crash

Map 3, I9. 66 Goding St, SE11 ☎020/7793 9262⊖ Vauxhall. Second and fourth Sat of the month. Four bars, two dancefloors, chill-out areas and hard bodies make this club busy, buzzy, sexy and mostly boyzy. First Sat of month is *Megawoof!* – a testosterone-fuelled mix of leathermen, bears and muscle boys; third Sat of month is Suzy Krueger's mixed fetish night, *Hard On* (ⓦwww .hardonclub.co.uk).

DTPM at Fabric

Map 3, K3. 77a Charterhouse St, EC1 ☎020/7749 1199, ⓦwww .blue-cube.net⊖ Farringdon. Sun weekly. This long-running Sunday-nighter can now be found in *Fabric*'s chic surroundings, with three dancefloors, the main floor offering the classic DTPM shirts-off experience plus great visuals, with harder electro sounds on the second floor and a mellow soul/oldies mix in the intimate upstairs R&B bar.

Duckie at the Royal Vauxhall Tavern

Map 3, I9. 372 Kennington Lane, SE11 ☎020/7737 4043, ⓦwww .duckie.co.uk⊖ Vauxhall. Sat weekly. *Duckie*'s modern, rock-based hurdy-gurdy provides a creative and cheerfully ridiculous antidote to the dreary forces of gay house domination. Cult DJs The Readers Wives are famed for playing *everything* from Kim Wilde to The Velvet Underground. Regular live art performances, plus occasional bouncy castles and theme nights.

Exilio
Map 5, A4. UCL, Houghton St, WC2 ☎07931/ 374 391 ⊖ **Holborn. Sat weekly.** Every Saturday night, *Exilio* erupts in a lesbian and gay Latin frenzy, spinning salsa, cumbias and merengue, and also featuring live acts.

Fiction at The Cross
Map 3, I1. King's Cross Freight Depot, Arches 27–31, off York Way, N1 ☎020/7749 1199 ⓦwww.blue-cube.net⊖ **King's Cross. Fri weekly.** Brought to you by Blue Cube promotions of *Fabric* fame, *Fiction* is a mellow but funky Friday night dancefest in a series of brick railway arches, which manages to be both big and intimate at the same time. If it gets too sweaty, there are two garden areas in which to chill. Stylish.

G.A.Y. at The Astoria
Map 4, F4. 157 Charing Cross Rd, W1 ☎020/7734 6963, ⓦwww.g-a-y.co.uk⊖ **Tottenham Court Road. Mon, Thurs & Sat.** Widely considered to be *the* launch pad

for new (and ailing) boy and girl bands, this huge, unpretentious and fun-loving dance night is where the young crowd gathers. There are lots of cheap entry deals to be had at the *G.A.Y. Pink Pounder* trash bash (Mon) - just £1 for a night on the tiles.

The Ghetto
Map 4, F4. Falconberg Court, W1 ☎07090/421 940 ⊖ **Tottenham Court Road. Sun–Thurs 10.30pm–3am, Fri until 4am, Sat until 5am.** Late-night, cruisey club behind the *Astoria* (see above) with a range of nights catering to every taste (mainly male) from goth/indie to funk, including Wednesday's *Nag, Nag, Nag*, Friday's *The Cock*, and Saturday night's *Wig Out* – a very, very trashy disco.

Heaven
Map 4, H9. Under the Arches, Villiers St, WC2 ☎020/7930 2020, ⓦwww.heaven-london.com⊖ **Charing Cross or Embankment. Mon, Wed, Fri & Sat 10.30pm till late.** Probably the UK's most popular gay club, this legendary, 2000-capacity venue continues to reign supreme. Big nights are Mondays (*Popcorn*), Wednesdays (*Fruit Machine*) and Saturdays (just *Heaven*), all with big-name DJs, PAs and shows. More Muscle Mary than Diesel Doris.

Horse Meat Disco

Map 3, J9. South Central, 349 Kennington Lane, SE11 ☏ 07090/422 304 ⓦ www.horsemeatdisco.co.uk ⊖ Vauxhall. Sun 4pm–1am. Freaky, underground disco & electrofunk club for a diverse gay/hetero crowd.

Lower The Tone at Oak Bar

Map 2, I3. 79 Green Lanes, N16 ☏ 020/7354 2791 ⊖ Manor House then bus #341 or #141, or ⊖ Angel then bus #73 or #341. Last Fri of the month. This hugely popular monthly cult club night is the brainchild of painter Sadie Lee and rock-star pals Lea Andrews and Jonathan Kemp. Billed as a club for people who don't like clubbing, *LTT* is a cocktail of sugar-coated hip-hop, classic 1970s pop, sleazy foreign disco and bizarre theme tunes. Mixed, but especially popular with girls.

Miss-Shapes at The Ghetto

Map 4, F4. Falconberg Court, W1 ☏ 07956/549 246, ⓦ www .miss-shapes.co.uk ⊖ Tottenham Court Road. Thurs weekly. Popular with indie girlz, this Thursday-nighter is the sister club to *Popstarz*, and plays trash and indie to entice a bevvied and up-for-it, grunge-cool crowd. Now with a sister club in New York.

Popstarz at the Scala

Map 3, I1. 275 Pentonville Rd, N1 ☏ 020/7738 2336, ⓦ www.popstarz .co.uk ⊖ King's Cross. Fri weekly. A ground-breaking indie club, *Popstarz* has had to enforce a gay and lesbian majority door policy as its winning formula of alternative toons, 1970s and 1980s trash, cheap beer and no attitude continues to attract a growing straight, studenty crowd.

Queer Nation at Substation South

Map 2, I6. 9 Brighton Terrace, SW9 ☏ 020/7732 2095 ⊖ Brixton. Sat weekly. Long-running and popular New York-style soulful house and garage club for funksters. Chilled, multi-racial and attitude free.

Salvation

Map 4, F7. Café de Paris, Leicester Square, W1 (no phone), ⓦ www .salvation-london.com ⊖ Leicester Square. First Sun of every month. Expect a surfeit of muscled beauties at this glamorous central venue. The fun starts at 5pm and keeps pumping till midnight, ensuring that even the hardest of clubbers gets a good night's kip.

WayOut Club at Charlie's

Map 7, K5. 9 Crosswall, off Minories, EC3 ☏ 07958/473599, ⓦ www .thewayout.com ⊖ Aldgate or Tower

Hill. **Sat weekly.** Long-established Saturday night for gays, straights, cross-dressers, drag queens, TVs, TSs and friends, which offers a warm welcome, changing rooms, video screen and regular cabaret.

Lesbian clubs

Curves at Agenda
Map 7, I5. Minster Court, 3 Mincing Lane EC3 ☎ 07947/310967, ⓦ www.curvesclub.net. ⊖ Tower Hill or Aldgate. **First Sat of the month.** Recently relaunched dance club in sophisticated surroundings – a plush lounge environment for a sexy, sassy crowd.

Dolly Mixtures at Candy Bar
Map 4, F2. 4 Carlisle St, WC2 ☎ 07090/422339, ⓦ www.candybar.easynet.co.uk ⊖ Tottenham Court Road. **Sun–Thurs noon–11pm, Fri & Sat noon–3am.** DJ Slamma plays house and soul while Crystal gets busy on the mic every Saturday. Friday nights see *Grind* with R&B and hip hop.

Girl Friday at First Out
Map 4, G5. 52 St Giles High St, WC2 ☎ 020/7240 8042, ⓦ www.firstoutcafebar.com ⊖ Tottenham Court Road. **Fri weekly.** This long-standing night is the place to meet girl pals at the end of a busy working week. Expect a packed basement for mingling and pre-club drinking.

Liberté at G Lounge
Map 2, H3. 18 Kentish Town Rd, NW1 ☎ 020/7354 2791 ⊖ Camden Town. **Last Sat of the month.** Great late-night women-only watering hole offering the hugely popular *Liberté*, with soulful grooves, reggae and garage for girls who like to smile when they're swinging.

Lyrical Lounge
Map 3, G9. Battersea Barge, Nine Elms Lane, SW8 (no phone), ⓦ www.gingerbeer.co.uk ⊖ Vauxhall. **Quarterly.** Live music night showcasing girl talent and organized by the women behind the *Gingerbeer* website (see p.237); the venue is a candlelit barge on the Thames. The same venue hosts the monthly Sunday club *Diva Night*.

Rumours at Minories
Map 7, K5. 64–73 Minories, EC3 ☎ 07961/158 375, ⓦ www.girl-rumours.co.uk ⊖ Tower Hill or Aldgate. **Biweekly Sat 8pm–2am.** There's room for 500 grrrls at this popular and cheap club night, which offers two bars, quiet lounges and two dancefloors.

Gay Men's Clubs

Action at the Renaissance Rooms
Map 3, I9. Miles St, SW8 ☎ 07973/233377, ⓦ www.actionclub.net ⊖ Vauxhall. **Sat**

11pm–6am. Big circuit-party-style dance night with mucho muscle, lavish production values and an Ibiza-style outdoor terrace.

Backstreet
Map 2, K4. Wentworth Mews, off Burdett Rd, E3 ☎020/8980 8557 or 8980 7880 (outside club hours), ⓦ www.thebackstreet.com ⊖ Mile End. Thurs–Sun. Long-running, traditional leather and rubber club with a strict, *very* butch dress code.

The Fort
Map 3, 7N. 131 Grange Rd, SE1 ☎020/8549 4339 ⊖ Bermondsey or London Bridge. Mon–Sat 7–11pm, Sun 2–10.30pm. There's no set dress code at this sleazy, sexy cruise bar, but check the free press or phone for details about special themed nights (boots, perhaps, or underwear).

The Hoist
Map 3, I9. Railway Arch, 47b-c South Lambeth Rd, SW8 ☎020/7735 9972, ⓦ www.thehoist.co.uk ⊖ Vauxhall. Thurs 8.30pm–midnight, Fri 10pm–3am, Sat 10pm–4am, Sun 10pm–2am. Weekend men's cruise bar with a leather/rubber/ industrial/uniform dress code. Hosts *SM Gays* every third Thursday.

XXL at the London Bridge Arches
Map 7, C9. 53 Southwark St, SE1 ☎07812/048574, ⓦ www.xxl -london.com ⊖ London Bridge. Wed & Sat. Massively popular dance club for big, burly men and their fans, attracting a very diverse crowd with its two dance floors, two bars and outside chill-out area.

21

Classical music, opera and dance

With the South Bank, the Barbican and the Wigmore Hall offering year-round appearances by generally first-rate musicians, and numerous smaller venues providing a stage for less established or more specialized performers, the capital should satisfy most devotees of **classical music**. What's more, in the annual Promenade Concerts at the Royal Albert Hall, London has one of the world's greatest, most democratic music festivals (see p.252).

Despite its elitist image, **opera** in the capital has an enthusiastic following. While the Royal Opera House (ROH) can attract top international stars to perform there, the downside is the high price of most of the tickets. The nearby English National Opera (ENO) is better value, and rather more adventurous in its repertoire and productions.

The more modest economic demands of **dance** mean that you'll often find a broad spectrum of ambitious work on offer, with some of the world's outstanding companies appearing on a regular basis at Sadler's Wells. Meanwhile, fans of classicism can revel in the **Royal Ballet** – a company with some of the most accomplished dancers in Europe.

Classical music

London is spoilt for choice when it comes to **orchestras**. On most days you'll be able to catch a concert by either the London Symphony Orchestra, the London Philharmonic, the Royal Philharmonic, the Philharmonia or the BBC Symphony Orchestra, or a smaller-scale performance from the English Chamber Orchestra or the Academy of St Martin-in-the-Fields. There are also more specialized ensembles, like the Orchestra of the Age of Enlightenment, who perform a pre-twentieth century repertoire on period

The Proms

The Royal Albert Hall's **BBC Henry Wood Promenade Concerts** – known as the "Proms" – tend to be associated with the raucous "Last Night", when the flag-waving audience sings its patriotic heart out. This jingoistic knees-up is untypical of the season as a whole, however, which from July to September features at least one concert daily in an exhilarating melange of favourites and new or recondite works. You can book a seat as you would for any other concert, but for many the essence of the Proms is the fact that all the stalls seats are removed to create hundreds of standing places costing around £4 and bought on the day. The upper gallery is similarly packed with people sitting on the floor or standing. The acoustics aren't the world's best – OK for orchestral blockbusters, less so for small-scale works – but the performers are usually outstanding, the atmosphere is great, and the hall is so vast that the likelihood of being turned away if you turn up on the night is slim. A recent innovation is the **Proms Chamber Series**, a handful of lunchtime concerts (£8, with some £4 gallery tickets available on the day) held in the recently reopened Cadogan Hall, just off Sloane Square.

The annual *Proms Guide*, available at most bookshops from May, gives information on every concert. You can also call the Albert Hall direct on ☏020/7589 8212, or visit the BBC Proms website at ⊛www.bbc.co.uk/proms/.

CLASSICAL MUSIC, OPERA AND DANCE

instruments, and the London Sinfonietta, one of the world's finest contemporary music groups. Full houses are a rarity, so even at the biggest concert halls you should be able to pick up a ticket for around £12 (the usual range is about £5–30), and it's always worth asking about concessions.

As well as the "Proms" (see opposite), there are a number of other superb **music festivals**, notably the month-long City of London Festival in July; the Spitalfields Festival which is held in June in the magnificent Baroque church of Christchurch; and the South Bank's challenging Meltdown Festival (also June), which is programmed by a different leading musician each year.

During the week there are also many **free concerts**, often during lunchtimes, by students or professionals in several London churches, particularly in the City; performances in the Royal College of Music and Royal Academy of Music are of an amazingly high standard, and the choice of work is often a lot riskier than in commercial venues.

Barbican Centre

Map 7, D1. Silk St, EC2 ☎020/7638 8891, ⓦwww.barbican.org.uk ⊖ Barbican or Moorgate. With the excellent resident London Symphony Orchestra, and with top foreign orchestras and big-name soloists in regular attendance, the Barbican is one of the capital's best arenas for classical music. Programming is much more adventurous than it was, and free music in the foyer is often very good. Unfortunately, it's a difficult place to find your way around.

Cadogan Hall

Map 3, E8. Sloane Terrace, SW1 ☎020/7730 4500⊖ Sloane Square. This handsome neo-Byzantine building, built in 1901 as a Christian Scientist church, has recently been converted into a 900-seat concert hall with a superlative acoustic. The London Royal Philharmonic are its resident orchestra and it is also the venue for the Proms chamber concerts (see opposite).

Royal Academy of Music

Map 3, F3. Marylebone Rd, NW1 ☎020/7873 7373, ⓦwww.ram .ac.uk⊖ Regent's Park or Baker Street. During term time, you can catch at least one lunchtime concert each week (1pm; Fri) and an early-evening recital, for which there is usually an entry charge.

Royal College of Music

Map 3, C7. Prince Consort Rd, SW7 ☎020/7591 4314, ⌨www.rcm .ac.uk⊖ South Kensington. During term time, free lunchtime (1pm) concerts are staged at London's top music college on Tuesday, Wednesday and Thursday, and at nearby St Mary Abbots Church, Kensington High Street, on Friday. There are also occasional evening concerts, for which you need to book, and opera performance, for which there is an entry charge.

St James

Map 4, E8. Piccadilly, W1 ☎020/7381 0441, ⌨www.st-james -piccadilly.org⊖ Piccadilly Circus. As well as free lunchtime concerts on Monday, Wednesday and Friday, this heavily restored Wren church also hosts fee-paying evening concerts, and has the London Festival Orchestra as its resident orchestra. The restaurant in the crypt is good for before or after.

St John

Map 3, H7. Smith Square, SW1 ☎020/7222 1061, ⌨www.sjss.org.uk⊖ Westminster. This striking Baroque church, situated behind Westminster

Abbey, was gutted in 1941 and later turned into a concert hall with a fine acoustic. Its varied musical menu includes orchestral and choral concerts, chamber music and solo recitals, with the Academy of Ancient Music its current resident orchestra. There's a good restaurant in the crypt.

St Martin-in-the-Fields

Map 4, H8. Trafalgar Square, WC2 ☎020/7839 8362, ⌨www.stmartin -in-the-fields.org⊖ Charing Cross or Leicester Square. Free lunchtime recitals Monday, Tuesday and Friday (1pm), plus fee-charging concerts in the evenings, sometimes featuring the top-notch orchestra of the Academy of St Martin-in-the-Fields.

South Bank Centre

Map 6, B3. South Bank, SE1 ☎0870 4242, ⌨www.rfh.org.uk⊖ Waterloo or Embankment. The SBC has three concert venues, none of which is exclusively used for classical music. The Royal Festival Hall (RFH) is closed until 2007 for major refurbishment and acoustical enhancement. A gargantuan space, it's tailor-made for large-scale choral and orchestral works, and plays host to some big-name soloists, though only a few can fill it. The Queen Elizabeth Hall

(QEH) is the prime location for chamber concerts, solo recitals and contemporary work; while the Purcell Room is the most intimate venue, excellent for chamber music and recitals by up-and-coming instrumentalists and singers.

The Warehouse
Map 6, D4. 13 Theed St, SE1 ⊤020/7928 9251⊖ Waterloo. The home of the London Festival Orchestra, this multi-purpose commercial space has become one of the best and most exciting venues for contemporary music, with many concerts promoted by the Society for the Promotion of New Music (SPNM).

Wigmore Hall
Map 4, A4. 36 Wigmore St, W1 ⊤020/7935 2141, ⓦwww.wigmore-hall.org.uk⊖ Bond Street or Oxford Circus. With its near-perfect acoustics, this small hall is a favourite with artists and audiences alike; concerts are best booked well in advance. An exceptional venue for chamber music, it is also well known for its song recitals by some of the world's greatest singers. It stages very popular, fee-paying mid-morning concerts on a Sunday.

Opera

Of London's two main companies, the **Royal Opera House** is undergoing a new lease of life since the appointment of a new music director. Meanwhile, **English National Opera** has completely renovated its Edwardian theatre, the vast London Coliseum, while continuing to show what can be achieved with largely home-grown talent and lively, radical productions.

English National Opera
Map 4, H8. Coliseum, St Martin's Lane, WC2 ⊤020/7632 8300, ⓦwww.eno.org⊖ Leicester Square or Charing Cross. English National Opera differs from its Royal Opera House counterpart in that all its operas are sung in English, productions tend to be more experimental, and the cost is far lower. Ticket prices start at as little as £8, rising to just over £80; day seats are also available to personal callers after 10am on

the day of the performance, with balcony seats going for just £5. It is also worth checking out standbys which go on sale three hours before a performance (£12.50 students, £18 senior citizens and unemployed). Major restoration work has now been completed and, despite suffering the resignation of its music director, the company continues to produce challenging and often outstanding work.

21 Royal Opera House

Map 4, I6. Bow St, WC2 ☏020/7304 4000, ⓦwww.royaloperahouse.org ⊖ Covent Garden. Though the ROH still has a deserved reputation for snobbery, and is ludicrously overpriced (over £150 for the very best seats), it does make some concessions nowadays to being more accessible. The Floral Hall foyer is open to the public during the day, there are regular free lunchtime recitals, and more modestly priced – and often more innovative – productions in the small Linbury Theatre. As well as this, its dynamic music director, Antonio Pappano, seems keen to rid the company of its conservatism, although the repertoire continues to be pretty standard. A small number of day seats (£30 or under) are put on sale from 10am on the day of a performance – these are restricted to one per person, and you need to get there by 8am for popular shows. Four hours before performances, standbys (subject to availability) can be bought for around £15 by students, senior citizens and the unemployed. In summer, some performances are occasionally relayed live to a large screen in Covent Garden Piazza. All operas are performed in the original language but are discreetly subtitled.

Dance

For classical ballet lovers, the **Royal Ballet** possesses a number of truly outstanding soloists, while those interested in more cutting-edge work can chose between the intimacy of **The Place** or the larger **Sadler's Wells**. London also has a good reputation for international dance festivals showcasing a wide range of companies. The biggest of the annual events is the **Dance Umbrella** (☏020/8741 5881,

@www.danceumbrella.co.uk), a six-week season (Sept–Nov) of often ground-breaking new work at various venues across town.

Note that in addition to the places reviewed below, the three venues in the **South Bank Centre** (see p.115) all stage dance performances, often as part of Dance Umbrella. The SBC is also the main venue for Asian dance in the capital, and the Royal Festival Hall is occasionally home to English National Ballet.

Barbican Centre

Map 7, D1. Silk St, EC2 ☎020/7638 8891, @www.barbican.org.uk ⊖ Barbican or Moorgate. As part of its mixed programming the Barbican regularly stages contemporary dance by top international companies. It's also used as a venue for Dance Umbrella events.

Laban

Map 2, L6. Creekside, SE8 ☎020/8691 8600, @www.laban.org ⊖ Charing Cross then Deptford station. Named after one of the founding figures of European contemporary dance, Laban has a brand new building designed by Herzog and de Meuron (architects of Tate Modern) which includes the 300-seater Bonnie Bird Theatre. The venue showcases many leading names in contemporary dance as well as work by Laban students.

London Coliseum

Map 4, H8. St Martin's Lane, WC2 ☎020/7632 8300, @www.eno.org ⊖ Leicester Square or Charing Cross. The Coliseum (home to English National Opera) is often used for dance between breaks in the opera season, most regularly by English National Ballet (ENB). This touring company's frequent performances in London include a regular Christmas slot at the Coliseum, and occasional visits to the Royal Festival Hall and the Royal Albert Hall.

The Place

Map 3, H2. 17 Duke's Rd, WC1 ☎020/7387 0031, @www.theplace .org.uk ⊖ Euston. The Place is the base of the Richard Alston Dance Company and home to the London Contemporary Dance School. Its small Robin Howard Dance Theatre presents the work of new choreographers and student performers, and hosts some of the finest

CLASSICAL MUSIC, OPERA AND DANCE

small-scale contemporary dance from across the globe.

Royal Ballet

Map 4, I6. Royal Opera House, Bow St, WC2 ☎ 020/7304 4000, ⓦ www .royaloperahouse.org ⊖ Covent Garden. The Royal Ballet is one of the most renowned classical companies in the world, whose extraordinary principals include Darcey Bussell, Sylvie Guillem and Carlos Acosta. There are two small performing spaces, the Linbury Theatre and the Clore Studio, where more experimental work can be seen. Prices are almost half of those for the opera, and you should be able to get decent seats for around £25 if you act quickly, though sellouts are frequent (see Royal Opera House, p.256, for details of day tickets and standbys).

Sadler's Wells Theatre

Map 3, K2. Rosebery Ave, EC1 ☎ 0870 737 7737, ⓦ www.sadlers-wells.com ⊖ Angel. Sadler's Wells Theatre in Islington is home to Britain's best contemporary dance companies, including the Rambert, and many of the finest international companies are also regular visitors. The Lillian Baylis Theatre, tucked around the back, puts on smaller-scale shows, while the Peacock Theatre in the West End is where Sadler's Wells stages more populist dance, including flamenco and tango.

22

Theatre, comedy and cinema

London has enjoyed a reputation for quality **theatre** since the time of Shakespeare and, despite the continuing prevalence of blockbuster musicals and revenue-spinning star vehicles, the city still provides a platform for innovation. The **comedy** scene in London goes from strength to strength, so much so that the capital now boasts more comedy venues than any other city in the world. **Cinema** is rather less healthy, with arthouse cinemas a dying breed, edged out by the generally more mainstream multiscreen complexes. A few excellent independent cinemas still exist, though, including the National Film Theatre, which is the focus of the richly varied **London Film Festival** in November.

Current details of **what's on** can be found in a number of publications, the most comprehensive being the weekly *Time Out*. Saturday's *Guardian* and Friday's *Evening Standard* are other good sources.

Theatre

Few cities in the world can match the variety of the London theatre scene. The **West End** is the domain of big-budget musicals, while the government-subsidized **Royal Shakespeare Company** and the **National Theatre** stage extremely original productions of mainstream masterpieces. Some of the most exciting work is performed in the **Off West End** theatres; further still down the financial ladder are the **Fringe** theatres, more often than not pub venues, where ticket prices are low, and quality variable.

Unfortunately, most theatre-going doesn't come cheap. **Tickets** under £10 are restricted to the Fringe; the box office average is closer to £15–25, with £30–40 the usual top whack. Tickets for the durable musicals and well-reviewed plays are like gold dust. Agencies such as Ticketmaster (☎020/7344 4444, ⓦwww.ticketmaster.co.uk) or First Call (☎020/7420 0000, ⓦwww.firstcalltickets.com) can get seats for most West End shows, but add up to ten percent on the price. You're also likely to be charged a booking fee if you book over the phone; the cheapest way to buy is to go to the theatre box office in person. Students, senior citizens and the unemployed can get **concessionary rates** for many shows, and many theatres offer reductions on standby tickets to these groups. Whatever you do, avoid the touts and the suspicious-looking ticket agencies that abound in the West End – there's no guarantee that the tickets are genuine.

The Society of London Theatre (ⓦwww.official londontheatre.co.uk) runs **tkts**, the **half price ticket booth** in Leicester Square (Mon–Sat 10am–7pm, Sun noon–3.30pm; ⓦwww.tkts.co.uk), which sells on-the-day tickets for all the West End shows at discounts of up to fifty percent, though they tend to be in the top end of the price range, are limited to four per person, and carry a service charge of £2.50 per ticket.

What follows is a list of those West End theatres that offer a changing roster of good plays, along with the most consistent of the Off West End and Fringe venues. This by no means represents the full tally of London's stages, as there are scores of Fringe places that present work on an intermittent basis – *Time Out* provides the most comprehensive and detailed up-to-the-minute survey.

Almeida

Map 2, I3. Almeida St, N1 ⓣ020/7359 4404, ⓦwww .almeida.co.uk⊖ Angel or Highbury & Islington. Popular Off West End venue in Islington that premieres excellent new plays and excitingly reworked classics, and has attracted some big Hollywood names.

Barbican Centre

Map 7, D1. Silk St, EC2 ⓣ020/7638 8891, ⓦwww.barbican.org.uk ⊖ Barbican or Moorgate. The Barbican's two venues – the excellently designed Barbican Theatre and the much smaller Pit – put on a wide variety of theatrical spectacles from puppetry and musicals to new drama works, and of course Shakespeare, courtesy of the Royal Shakespeare Company who perform here (and elsewhere in London) on and off from autumn to spring each year.

Battersea Arts Centre

Map 2, H6. 176 Lavender Hill, SW11 ⓣ020/7223 2223, ⓦwww.bac.org. uk Clapham Junction station, from Victoria or Waterloo. The BAC is a triple-stage building, housed in an old town hall in south London, and has acquired a reputation for excellent Fringe productions from straight theatre to comedy and cabaret.

Bush

Map 2, F5. Shepherd's Bush Green, W12 ⓣ020/7610 4224, ⓦwww .bushtheatre.co.uk⊖ Goldhawk Road or Shepherd's Bush. This minuscule above-pub theatre is London's most reliable venue for new writing after the Royal Court, and it has turned out some great stuff.

Donmar Warehouse

Map 4, H5. Thomas Neal's, Earlham St, WC2 ⓣ0870/060 6624, ⓦwww .donmar-warehouse.com⊖ Covent Garden. A performance space that's noted for new plays and top-quality reappraisals of the classics, and whose former artistic director, Sam Mendes, managed to entice several Hollywood stars to take to the stage.

Drill Hall

Map 4, F2. 16 Chenies St, WC1 ⓣ020/7307 5060, ⓦwww.drillhall .co.uk⊖ Goodge Street. This

THEATRE, COMEDY AND CINEMA | Theatre

studio-style venue specializes in gay, lesbian, feminist and all-round politically correct new work.

Hampstead Theatre

Map 2, G3. Eton Avenue, NW3 ☎020/7722 9301, ⓦwww.hampsteadtheatre.co.uk⊖ Swiss Cottage. A spanking new zinc-and-glass-fronted theatre in Swiss Cottage (not in Hampstead proper) whose productions often move on to the West End. Such is its prestige that the likes of John Malkovich have been seduced into performing here.

ICA

Map 4, F10. Nash House, The Mall, SW1 ☎020/7930 3647, ⓦwww.ica.org.uk⊖ Charing Cross. The Institute of Contemporary Arts attracts the most innovative practitioners in all areas of performance. It also attracts a fair quantity of modish junk, but the hits generally outweigh the misses.

King's Head

Map 2, I3. 115 Upper St, N1 ☎020/7226 1916, ⓦwww.kingsheadtheatre.org⊖ Angel or Highbury & Islington. The oldest and probably most famous of London's thriving pub-theatres (with a useful late licence). Adventurous lunchtime and evening performances in a pint-sized room.

Menier Chocolate Factory

Map 2, C9. 51–53 Southwark St, SE1 ☎020/7907 7060, ⓦwww.menierchocolatefactory.com⊖ London Bridge. Great new fringe venue in an old Victorian factory; consistently good shows and a nice bar and restaurant attached.

National Theatre

Map 6, C2. South Bank Centre, South Bank, SE1 ☎020/7452 3000, ⓦwww.nationaltheatre.org.uk ⊖ Waterloo. The Royal National Theatre, as it's now officially known, consists of three separate theatres: the 1100-seater Olivier, the proscenium-arched Lyttelton and the experimental Cottesloe. Standards set by the late Laurence Olivier, founding artistic director, are maintained by the country's top actors and directors in a programme ranging from Greek tragedies to Broadway musicals. Some productions sell out months in advance, but twenty to thirty of the cheapest tickets go on sale on the morning of each performance – get there by 8am for the popular shows.

Open Air Theatre

Map 3, E2. Regent's Park, Inner Circle, NW1 ☎0870/060 1811, ⓦwww.open-air-theatre.org.uk⊖ Regent's Park or Baker Street. If the weather's good, there's nothing quite like a dose of alfresco drama. This beautiful space in Regent's Park hosts a tourist-friendly summer programme of Shakespeare, musicals, plays and concerts.

Royal Court
Map 3, E8. Sloane Square, SW1 ☎020/7565 5000, Ⓦwww.royalcourttheatre.com⊖ Sloane Square. One of the best places in London to catch radical new writing, either in the proscenium-arch Theatre Downstairs, or the smaller-scale Theatre Upstairs studio space.

Shakespeare's Globe
Map 7, B7. New Globe Walk, SE1 ☎020/7401 9919, Ⓦwww.shakespeares-globe.org ⊖ London Bridge, Blackfriars or Southwark. This thatch-roofed replica Elizabethan theatre uses only natural light and the minimum of scenery, and currently puts on solid, fun Shakespearean shows from mid-May to mid-September, with "groundling" tickets (standing-room only) for around a fiver.

Tricycle
Map 2, F3. 269 Kilburn High Rd, NW6 ☎020/7328 1000, Ⓦwww.tricycle.co.uk⊖ Kilburn. One of London's most dynamic fringe venues, showcasing a mixed bag of new plays, often aimed at the neighbourhood's multicultural community, and often with a sharp political focus.

Young Vic
Map 6, E5. 66 The Cut, SE1 ☎020/7928 6363, Ⓦwww.youngvic.org⊖ Waterloo. The Young Vic was built in 1969 as a temporary structure with a five-year lifespan. Now, 36 years later, it has finally been rebuilt from scratch and will open in 2006. Big names have appeared at the main stage over the years and its productions are often very good indeed.

Comedy and cabaret

London's **comedy scene** continues to live up to its media-coined status as the new rock'n'roll with its leading funnypersons catapulted to unlikely stardom on both stage and screen. The Comedy Store is the best-known and most central venue on the circuit, but just about every London suburb has a venue giving a platform to young hopefuls (full listings appear on Ⓦwww.chortle.co.uk, and in *Time Out*).

Note that many venues operate only on Friday and Saturday nights, and that August, when much of London's talent heads north for the Edinburgh Festival, is a lean month. Tickets at smaller venues can be had for around £5, but in the more established places you're looking at £10 or more.

Backyard Comedy Club

Map 2, J4. 231 Cambridge Heath Rd, E2 ☏020/7739 3122, ⓦwww.leehurst.com✺ Bethnal Green. **Thurs–Sat.** Purpose-built club established by comedian Lee Hurst, who has successfully managed to attract a consistently strong lineup.

Canal Café Theatre

Map 3, B3. The Bridge House, Delamere Terrace, W2 ☏020/7289 6054, ⓦwww.canalcafetheatre.com✺ Warwick Avenue. **Thurs–Sun.** Perched on the water's edge in Little Venice, this venue hosts good improvisation acts and is home to the *Newsrevue* team of topical gagsters.

Comedy Café

Map 3, N2. 66 Rivington St, EC2 ☏020/7739 5706, ⓦwww.comedycafe.co.uk✺ Old Street. **Wed–Sat.** Long-established, purpose-built club in Shoreditch/Hoxton, often with impressive lineups, and free admission for the new acts slot on Wednesday nights.

Comedy Store

Map 4, F8. Haymarket House, 1a Oxendon St, SW1 ☏020/7344 0234, ⓦwww.thecomedystore.co.uk✺ Piccadilly Circus. **Nightly.** Widely regarded to be the birthplace of alternative comedy, though no longer in its original venue, the Comedy Store has catapulted many a stand-up onto primetime TV. Improvisation by in-house comics on Wednesdays and Sundays, in addition to a stand-up bill; Friday and Saturday are the busiest nights, with two shows, at 8pm and midnight – book ahead.

Jongleurs Camden Lock

Map 2, H3. Dingwalls Building, 36 Camden Lock Place, Chalk Farm Rd, NW1 ☏020/7564 2500, ⓦwww.jongleurs.com✺ Camden Town. **Fri & Sat.** Jongleurs is the chain store of comedy, with sixteen branches nationwide, three of them in London. This central venue doles out high-quality stand-up and post-revelry disco dancing on Fridays. Book well in advance. Also branches in Battersea and Bow.

Cinema

There are an awful lot of **cinemas** in the West End, but very few places committed to independent films, and even fewer repertory cinemas programming serious movies from the back catalogue. November's **London Film Festival** (ⓦwww.lff.org.uk), which occupies half a dozen West End cinemas, is now a key event, and so popular that many of the films sell out soon after publication of the festival's programme.

Tickets at the major screens in the West End cost £8 and upwards, although afternoon shows are usually discounted. The suburban screens run by the big companies (see *Time Out* for full listings) tend to be a couple of pounds cheaper, as do independent cinemas. Students, senior citizens and the unemployed can get **concessionary rates** for some shows at virtually all cinemas, usually all day Monday or at other off-peak times on weekdays.

Below is a selection of the cinemas that put on the most interesting programmes.

BFI London Imax Centre
Map 6, C4. South Bank, SE1 ☏020/7902 1234, ⓦwww.bfi.org .uk/showing/imax❖ Waterloo. The British Film Institute's remarkable glazed drum houses Europe's largest screen. It's stunning, state-of-the-art stuff, showing 2D and 3D films on a massive screen, but like all IMAX cinemas, it suffers from the paucity of good material that's been shot in the format.

Electric
Map 2, F4. 191 Portobello Rd, W11 ☏020/7299 8688,
ⓦwww.the-electric.co.uk❖ Notting Hill Gate or Ladbroke Grove. One of the oldest cinemas in the country (opened 1910), the Electric is a hip place to watch independent and offbeat movies, filled out with luxury leather armchairs, footstools and sofas. Most seats cost £12.50.

Everyman
Map 2, G2. Hollybush Vale, NW3 ☏020/7431 1777, ⓦwww .everymancinema.com❖ Hampstead. The city's oldest rep cinema, and still one of its best, with strong programmes of classics,

cultish crowd-magnets and directors' seasons. Two screens and very plush seating.

ICA Cinema

Map 4, E10. Nash House, The Mall, SW1 ☎020/7930 3647, ⓦwww.ica.org.uk⊖ Piccadilly Circus or Charing Cross. Vintage and underground movies shown on one of two tiny screens in the avant-garde HQ of the Institute of Contemporary Arts.

National Film Theatre

Map 6, B2. South Bank, SE1 ☎020/7928 3232, ⓦwww.bfi.org.uk/showing/nft⊖ Waterloo. Known for its attentive audiences and an exhaustive, eclectic programme that includes directors' seasons and thematic series. Around six films daily are shown in the sizeable NFT1 and the smaller NFTs2 and 3.

Prince Charles

Map 4, G7. 2–7 Leicester Place, WC2 ☎020/7494 3654, ⓦwww.princecharlescinema.com⊖ Leicester Square or Piccadilly Circus. The bargain basement of London's cinemas (entry for most shows is just £4), with a programme of new movies, classics and cult favourites – the regular *Sing-Along-A-Sound-of-Music* (as well as other participatory romps) is a favourite.

Galleries

The vast collections of the **National Gallery**, the two **Tates** and **Victoria and Albert Museum**, along with the select holdings of such institutions as the **Courtauld** and the **Wallace Collection**, make London one of the world's great repositories of Western art. However, the city is also a dynamic creative centre, with the Young British Artists (YBAs) such as Tracey Emin and Gary Hume maintaining the momentum established by the likes of Frank Auerbach, Anthony Caro and Lucien Freud.

While there are hundreds of **small commercial galleries** and **artist-run spaces** scattered across the city, pockets of concentrated activity make it easy to visit several in an afternoon. Mayfair's **Cork Street** and the surrounding area continues to be the upmarket home of historical and traditional fine arts and antiquities dealers, but the recent growth of spaces exhibiting and trading in contemporary art has dramatically expanded the art map of London, pushing it north and eastwards, to **Shoreditch**, **Hoxton**, **Bethnal Green** and beyond.

An increasing number of art prizes offer the chance to see what's hot in any given year. These include the **Turner Prize** at Tate Britain in the autumn, which recognizes artists under forty working in the UK; **Becks Futures Award** at the ICA in winter, which showcases up-and-coming artists; and the international **Photography Prize** at the Photographers' Gallery each spring. Other annual fixtures include, at one end of the scale, the **Royal Academy's Summer Exhibition**, when amateur artists enter their efforts for sale, and at the other, the **Frieze Art Fair** in Regents Park (October) when the cream of the international art market descends on London to buy, sell, network and party.

Art school **degree shows** at the Royal College, Royal Academy, Slade, St Martin's and Goldsmiths', usually in May and June, offer opportunities to spot future stars and collect while their prices are still low. Another option for buying original art is at the **Affordable Art Fair**, held twice yearly in Battersea Park, where all prices are under £3000.

As for **admission prices**, unlike most other countries, the national collections of Great Britain, many of which are in London, are free to visit. Some private collections also offer free entry. For special exhibitions, however, expect to pay around £8–10 at the major art spaces. Students, senior citizens and the unemployed are eligible for reductions.

Many spaces hold weekly and monthly late nights with special events, talks and debates. It's always best to check the website or ring the gallery before setting off. For a rundown of the latest exhibitions, with opening times, check *Time Out* or look at Ⓦ www.newexhibitions.com, which lists more than 200 galleries in London alone.

Permanent collections

British Museum
Map 4, G3. Great Russell St, WC1 Ⓣ020/7323 8000, Ⓦwww.british -museum.ac.uk↔ Russell Square or Tottenham Court Road. See p.61. As well as its world-class collection of antiquities, the BM has outstanding drawings and prints and interesting one-off exhibitions.

Courtauld Institute
Map 5, A6. Strand, WC2 Ⓣ020/7845 4600, Ⓦwww.somerset-house.org .uk↔ Covent Garden or Temple. See p.75. An excellent collection of Impressionists and Post-Impressionists.

Dalí Universe
Map 6, A6. Riverside Building,

County Hall, SE1 ☎0870/744 7485, ⓦwww.daliuniverse.com ⊖ Westminster or Waterloo. See p.117. Permanent collection of works by Dalí, mostly little-known bronzes and illustrated books.

Dulwich Picture Gallery
Map 2, J7. College Rd, SE21 ☎020/8693 5254, ⓦwww.dulwich picturegallery.org.uk West Dulwich station from Victoria. See p.152. London's oldest public art gallery houses a small but high-quality selection of work ranging from Poussin and Gainsborough to Rembrandt.

Estorick Collection
Map 2, I3. 39a Canonbury Square, N1 ☎020/7704 9522, ⓦwww.estorickcollection.com ⊖ Highbury & Islington. Georgian mansion with a small but interesting collection of twentieth-century Italian art, including Modigliani, di Chirico and the Futurists.

Geffrye Museum
Map 3, N1. Kingsland Rd, E2 ☎020/7739 9893, ⓦwww .geffrye-museum.org.uk ⊖ Old Street. Furniture, textiles, paintings and decorative arts, displayed in a series of period rooms from 1600 to the present day.

Guildhall Art Gallery
Map 7, D3. Gresham St, EC2 ☎020/7323 3700, ⓦwww.cityof london.gov.uk ⊖ Bank or St Paul's. See p.96. Gallery housing the Corporation of London's collection, which contains one or two exceptional Pre-Raphaelite works by the likes of Rossetti and Holman Hunt.

Leighton House
Map 2, F5. 12 Holland Park Rd, W14 ☎020/7602 3316, ⓦwww.rbkc.gov .uk ⊖ High Street Kensington. See p.137. The house itself is a work of art, but it also contains several works by Lord Leighton himself and his Pre-Raphaelite chums.

National Gallery
Map 4, G8. Trafalgar Square, WC2 ☎020/7747 2885, ⓦwww.national gallery.org.uk ⊖ Charing Cross or Leicester Square. See p.29. The country's premier collection; it's difficult to think of a major artist born between 1300 and 1850 whose work isn't on show here.

National Portrait Gallery
Map 4, G8. 2 St Martin's Place, WC2 ☎020/7312 2463, ⓦwww .npg.org.uk ⊖ Leicester Square or Charing Cross. See p.31. The collection, ranging from paintings of historical figures to exceptional photographic portraits of contemporary celebrities, is

23

GALLERIES | Permanent collections

supplemented with excellent thematic exhibitions.

Queen's Gallery

Map 4, C13. Buckingham Palace, Buckingham Palace Rd, SW1 ℡020/7321 2233, ⊛www.royal.gov .uk⊖ St James's Park or Victoria. See p.44. Changing exhibitions from the wide-ranging collection of art and treasures held in trust by The Queen for the Nation.

Saatchi Gallery

Map 6, A6. County Hall, SE1 ℡020/7823 2363, ⊛www.saatchi -gallery.co.uk⊖ Westminster or Waterloo. See p.117. Charles Saatchi is a major private collector of international contemporary art and his space at County Hall exhibits a selection of his current favourites.

Sir John Soane's Museum

Map 5, A2. 12-14 Lincoln's Inn Fields WC2 ℡020/7405 2107, ⊛www.soane.org⊖ Holborn. See p.81. This eighteenth century collector rebuilt two neighbouring houses for his ever expanding collection of art and antiquities. The quirky museum is crammed with gems, displayed in an eccentric and distinctive manner.

Tate Britain

Map 6, H/I2. Millbank, SW1 ℡020/ 7887 8008, ⊛www.tate.org.uk ⊖ Pimlico. See p.39. The original Tate is now devoted to British art from the sixteenth century onwards. Several galleries display a selection from Turner's immense bequest to the nation.

Tate Modern

Map 6, H2. Bankside, SE1 ℡020/7887 8008, ⊛www.tate.org.uk⊖ Southwark. See p.121. Housed in a spectacularly converted power station on the South Bank, the new Tate displays the nation's finest international modern art collection.

Victoria and Albert Museum

Map 8, E7. Cromwell Rd, SW7 ℡020/7942 2000, ⊛www.vam .ac.uk⊖ South Kensington. See p.133. The city's principal applied arts museum boasts a scattering of European painting and sculpture, a fine collection of English statuary, two remarkable rooms of casts and much more.

Wallace Collection

Map 3, E4. Hertford House, Manchester Square, W1 ℡020/7563 9500, ⊛www.wallacecollection .org⊖ Bond Street. See p.52. A country mansion just off Oxford Street, with a small, eclectic collection: fine paintings by Rembrandt, Velázquez, Hals, Gainsborough and Delacroix.

Major galleries and exhibition spaces

Barbican Art Gallery
Map 7, D1. Level 1 & 3, Barbican Centre, Silk St, EC2 ☎020/7638 8891, ⓦ www.barbican.org.uk ⊖ Barbican or Moorgate. The newly refurbished Barbican Gallery shows major exhibitions of modern and historical art, photography and design. The Curve, the Barbican's free exhibition space, is dedicated to site responsive commissioned works by contemporary artists. Open until 8pm most nights.

Camden Arts Centre
Map 2,3G. Cnr Arkwright and Finchley Rds, NW3 ☎020/7472 5500, ⓦ www.camdenartscentre.org ⊖ Finchley Road. Well known for its artists-in-residence programmes, and for its consistently interesting exhibitions of new work by acclaimed and lesser-known artists. The garden is a great place for lazing on a sunny afternoon, and there's a nice café.

Hayward Gallery
Map 6, B3. South Bank Centre, Belvedere Rd, SE1 ☎020/7960 5226, ⓦ www.hayward-gallery.org.uk ⊖ Waterloo. Part of the huge concrete 1960s South Bank arts complex, the Hayward is one of London's most prestigious venues for major touring exhibitions, staging broad-ranging thematic exhibitions and solo shows of major figures.

ICA Gallery
Map 4, F10. The Mall, SW1 ☎020/7930 3647, ⓦ www.ica.org.uk ⊖ Piccadilly Circus or Charing Cross. The Institute of Contemporary Arts is housed in an elegant Regency building opposite St James' Park. The multipurpose venue benefits also from an in-house cinema and trendy café/bar. A day's membership costs £1.50 (Mon–Fri) or £2.50 (Sat & Sun).

Royal Academy of Arts
Map 4, D8. Burlington House, Piccadilly, W1 ☎020/7300 8000, ⓦ www.royalacademy.org.uk ⊖ Green Park or Piccadilly Circus. See p.48. Alongside extensive non-western surveys such as the Aztecs and Turks, the Royal Academy is well known for its blockbuster one-off art exhibitions. For the most popular shows, you're advised to pre-book.

Serpentine Gallery
Map 8, D2. Kensington Gardens, Hyde Park, W2 ☎020/7298 1501, ⓦ www.serpentinegallery.org ⊖ Lancaster Gate.

23

GALLERIES | Major galleries

Free. Free exhibitions of dynamic work by new and established artists, as well as a high profile architecture commission each summer which doubles as a café and space for film screenings, talks and music events.

South London Gallery
Map 2, J6. 65 Peckham Rd, SE5
℡ 020/7703 6120, Ⓦ www.south londongallery.org ⊖ Oval then bus #36 or #436. **Free.** Purpose-built gallery, established in Camberwell back in 1891 on socialist principles, the South London Gallery is devoted to contemporary art, with an outstanding A–Z of exhibited artists.

Whitechapel Gallery
Map 7, M2. 80–82
Whitechapel High St, E1
℡ 020/7522 7888, Ⓦ www .whitechapel.org ⊖ Aldgate East. See p.106. Dubbed by the press as "the gallery that taught Britain to love Modern Art", the Whitechapel has a critically acclaimed national and international programme of exhibitions. Its biennial summer survey, East End Academy, showcases the work of artists living in the area. Excellent café/bar and late night events including films, music and poetry, high-profile talks and lectures.

Commercial galleries

Though London's commercial galleries might seem intimidating, they welcome casual visitors and all are free. Note that many galleries are closed in August.

Central

Frith Street
Map 4, F5. 59–60 Frith St, W1
℡ 020/7494 1550, Ⓦ www.frith streetgallery.com ⊖ Tottenham Court Road. A particularly strong list of women artists are exhibited in the domestic-scale rooms of this fine, if creaky, old Soho building.

Gagosian
Map 3, I2. 6–24 Brittannia St, WC1
℡ 020/7841 9960, Ⓦ www.gagosian .com ⊖ Kings Cross. The Gagosian empire recently opened a new space in a vast warehouse near Kings Cross, and produces museum-quality exhibitions with a portfolio of artists to match.

Haunch of Venison
Map 4, B6. 6 Haunch of Venison

Yard, W1 ☎020/7495 5050
ⓦ www.haunchofvenison.com
🚇 Bond Street In the corner of
this wonderfully named yard
tucked behind Bond Street
are three floors of galleries in
an eighteenth-century town
house once occupied by
Admiral Lord Nelson. Contemporary British talent such as
Keith Tyson and Ian Monroe
nuzzle between its line up of
international stars including Dan
Flavin, Robert Ryman and Bill
Viola.

Hauser and Wirth
Map 4, E8. 196A Picca-
dilly, W1 ☎020/7287 2300,
ⓦ www.hauserwirth.com
🚇 Piccadilly Circus. Housed in
a magnificent 1920s Edwin
Lutyens-designed former bank
and maintaining some original
spaces, the London branch of
the Swiss gallery brings major
figures such as Eva Hesse,
Louise Bourgeois and Paul
McCarthy together with relative
newcomers.

Lisson
Map 3, C3. 29 & 52–54 Bell St, NW1
☎020/7724 2739, ⓦ www.lisson
.co.uk🚇 Marylebone or Edgware
Road. Two spaces showing
international artists, among them
Carl Andre, Anish Kapoor and
Rodney Graham.

Sadie Coles HQ
Map 4, D7. 35 Heddon St, W1
☎020/7434 2227, ⓦ www
.sadiecoles.com🚇 Piccadilly Circus.
Tucked upstairs in an alley off
Regent St, Sadie Coles consistently exhibits some of the most
interesting contemporary artists
including Sarah Lucas, Jim Lam-
bie and Elizabeth Peyton.

Spruth Magers Lee
Map 4, C9. 12 Berkeley St, W1
☎020/7491 0100, ⓦ www.spruth
magerslee.com🚇 Green Park. Slick
Mayfair gallery with an impressive line up of international artists
including Jenny Holtzer, Barbara
Kruger and Cindy Sherman.

Hoxton and the East End

The Approach
Map 2, J3. 1st floor, 47 Approach Rd,
E2 ☎020/8983 3878, ⓦ www
.theapproach.co.uk🚇 Bethnal
Green. With a reputation for
launching the careers of many
young and emerging artists, this
single storey space is situated
above a welcoming Victorian pub
frequented by artists.

Chisenhale Gallery
Map 2, K3. 64 Chisenhale Rd, E3
☎020/8981 4518, ⓦ www.chisen
hale.org.uk🚇 Mile End. Non-profit
exhibition space in a converted
East End factory dedicated to

one-person shows by up-and-coming contemporary artists.

Maureen Paley
Map 2, J4. 21 Herald St, E2
☏020/7729 4112, ⓦwww.interimart
.net↔ Bethnal Green. One of the first galleries to set up in East London, Maureen Paley shows intelligent contemporary artists such as Paul Noble, Wolfgang Tillmans and Gillian Wearing.

Victoria Miro
Map 3, L1. 16 Wharf Rd, N1
☏020/7336 8109, ⓦwww
.victoria-miro.com↔ Angel or Old

Street. This large former factory is one of the most impressive galleries in London. Victoria Miro has helped promote the likes of Doug Aiken, William Egglestone and Chris Ofili.

White Cube
Map 3, N2. 48 Hoxton Square, N1 ☏020/7930 5373, ⓦwww
.whitecube.com↔ Old Street. Major art dealer Jay Jopling has advanced the careers of many of the most collectable YBAs. His popular gallery produces high quality solo and group exhibitions.

Photography

Many of the galleries detailed above have fine temporary photography exhibitions; for permanent collections, check especially the **V&A** (see p.133) and the **National Portrait Gallery** (see p.31), which also has an annual photographic portrait award.

Photofusion
Map 2, I6. 17a Electric Lane, SW9 ☏020/7738 5774, ⓦwww
.photofusion.org↔ Brixton. Community-based photo co-op, situated in the heart of Brixton, that concentrates on social documentary.

Photographers' Gallery
Map 4, G7. 5 & 8 Great Newport St, WC2 ☏020/7831 1772, ⓦwww
.photonet.org.uk↔ Leicester Square. London's premier photography gallery shows work by new and established British and international photographers and has a print sale gallery. Excellent programme of talks and events and a nice little café.

Architecture and design

As well as the specialist museums reviewed below, check the **V&A** (see p.133), which has recently joined forces with the RIBA to show their extraordinary collection of architectural drawings, models and manuscripts. For the finest contemporary international crafts, **Chelsea Crafts Fair**, held in Chelsea Town Hall each autumn is a fantastic showcase.

Crafts Council
Map 3, J1. 44 Pentonville Rd, N1
℡020/7278 7700, ⓦwww.crafts
council.org.uk⊖ Angel. Britain's largest crafts gallery and resource for craftspeople.

Design Museum
Map 7, L9. Butlers Wharf, Shad Thames, SE1
℡0870/8339 955, ⓦwww.design
museum.org⊖ Tower Hill. See p.128. In an old brick warehouse, the Design Museum shows several exhibitions concurrently, enabling you to contemplate the best in design, fashion and architecture. The shop sells an eclectic range of well-designed gifts.

Royal Institute of British Architects (RIBA)
Map 4, B2. 66 Portland Place, W1 ℡020/7580 5533, ⓦwww.architecture.com⊖ Regents Park. See p.53. Regular architectural exhibitions by the leading lights, housed in a beautiful 1930s building, with an excellent café.

24

Shops and markets

W hether it's time or money you've got to burn, London is one big shopper's playground. And, although chains and superstores predominate along the high streets, you're still never too far from the kind of oddball, one-off establishment that makes shopping an adventure rather than a chore. From the *folie de grandeur* that is Harrods to the frantic street markets of the East End, there's nothing you can't find in some corner of the capital.

In the centre of town, **Oxford Street** is the city's most frantic chain-store strip, and together with **Regent Street**, which crosses it halfway along, offers pretty much every mainstream clothing label you could wish for. Just off Oxford Street, high-end designer outlets line **St Christopher's Place** and **South Molton Street**, and you'll find even pricier designers and jewellers along swish **Bond Street**.

Tottenham Court Road, which heads north from the east end of Oxford Street, is the place to go for electrical goods and, further along, furniture and design shops. **Charing**

Opening hours

Opening hours for central London shops are generally Monday to Saturday 9.30am to 6pm, although some stay open later, especially on Thursdays. Many are now open on Sundays, although hours tend to be shorter, typically from around noon to 5pm. The cheapest time to shop is during one of the two annual **sale seasons**, centred on January and July, when prices can be slashed by up to seventy percent. **Credit cards** are almost universally accepted by shops. Always keep your receipts: whatever the shop may tell you, the law allows a full refund or replacement on purchases which turn out to be faulty.

Cross Road, heading south, is the centre of London's book trade, both new and secondhand. At its north end, and particularly on **Denmark Street**, you can find music shops selling everything from instruments to sound equipment and sheet music. **Soho** offers an offbeat mix of sex boutiques, specialist record shops and fabric stores, while the streets surrounding **Covent Garden** yield art and design shops, mainstream fashion stores and designer wear.

Just off Piccadilly, **St James's** is the natural habitat of the quintessential English gentleman, with **Jermyn Street** in particular harbouring shops dedicated to his grooming. **Knightsbridge**, further west, is home to Harrods and Harvey Nichols, and the big-name fashion stores of **Sloane Street** and **Brompton Road**.

Department stores

Although all of London's **department stores** offer a huge range of high-quality goods under one roof, most specialize in fashion and food. Many of them are worth visiting if only to admire the scale, architecture and interior design, and most have cafés or restaurants.

Fortnum & Mason

Map 4, D9. 181 Piccadilly, W1 ☎020/7734 8040, ⓦwww.fortnum andmason.com⊖ Green Park or Piccadilly Circus. Beautiful and eccentric store featuring heavenly ceiling murals, gilded cherubs, chandeliers and fountains as a backdrop to its perfectly English offerings. Justly famed for its fabulous, gorgeously presented and pricey food, plus upmarket clothes, furniture and stationery.

Harrods

Map 3, D7. 87–135 Brompton Rd, Knightsbridge, SW1 ☎020/7730 1234, ⓦwww.harrods.com ⊖ Knightsbridge. Put an afternoon aside to visit this enduring landmark of quirks and pretensions, most notable for its fantastic Art Nouveau tiled food hall, obscenely huge toy department, and supremely tasteless memorial to Diana and Dodi in the basement. Wear shorts and you may fail the rigorous dress code. (See also p.137.)

Harvey Nichols

Map 3, E6. 109–125 Knightsbridge, SW1 ☎020/7235 5000, ⓦwww .harveynichols.com⊖ Knights-bridge. All the latest designer collections on the scarily fashionable first floor, where even the shop assistants look like catwalk models. The cosmetics department is equally essential, while the food hall offers famously frivolous and pricey luxuries.

John Lewis

Map 4, B5. 278–306 Oxford St, W1 ☎020/7629 7711, ⓦwww .johnlewis.com⊖ Oxford Circus. Famous for being "never knowingly undersold", this reliable institution can't be beaten for basics, from buttons to stockings to rugs, along with reasonably priced and well-made clothes, furniture, fabric and household goods. The staff are knowledgeable and friendly, too.

Liberty

Map 4, D6. 210–220 Regent St, W1 ☎020/7734 1234, ⓦwww .liberty-of-london.com⊖ Oxford Circus. This fabulous and rather regal emporium of luxury is most famous for its fabrics and accessories, but is also building an excellent reputation for both mainstream and new fashion. The perfume, cosmetics and household departments are good, too.

Marks & Spencer

Map 3, E4. 458 Oxford St, W1 ☎020/7935 7954, ⓦwww.marks andspencer.com⊖ Marble Arch. London's largest branch of this British institution offers a huge range of well-made own-brand clothes (the lingerie selection is fancier than in local branches), food, homeware and furnishings.

Selfridges
Map 3, F4. 400 Oxford St, W1 ℡08708/377 377, ⓦwww .selfridges.com⊖ Bond Street.

This huge, airy compound of fine clothes, food and furnishings was London's first great department store, and remains its best, with a fashionable menswear department and a solid womenswear floor. The food hall is impressive, too.

Clothes and accessories

The listings below concentrate on the home-grown rather than the ubiquitous international names, but if you're after **designer wear** bear in mind that nearly all of the department stores listed on these pages stock lines from both major and up-and-coming designers. For designer-style fashion at lower prices, try the more upmarket high-street **chain stores** such as Jigsaw, French Connection and Whistles. Mango, Zara and Top Shop are good bets for even cheaper versions of the same styles, while H&M does funky at incredibly low prices. For street, clubwear, secondhand and vintage gear, London's **markets** (see p.290) also have plenty to offer.

Designer

Browns
Map 4, B6. 23–27 South Molton St, W1 ℡020/7514 0000, ⓦwww .brownsfashion.com⊖ Bond Street. Huge range of designer wear for men and women, with big international names under the same roof as the hip young things. Browns' Labels for Less, across the way at 50 South Molton St, W1 (℡020/7514

0052), could save you precious pennies.

Burberry
Map 4, C7. 21–23 New Bond St, W1 ℡020/7839 5222, ⓦwww.burberry .com⊖ Bond Street or Oxford Circus. The quintessential British outdoors label has relaunched itself as a fashion essential. Get the traditional stock at a huge discount from Burberry's Factory Shop, 29–53 Chatham Place,

E9 (☎020/8985 3344; Hackney Central train).

Ghost

Map 2, F5. 36 Ledbury Rd, W11 ☎020/7229 1057, ⓦwww.ghost .co.uk⊖ Notting Hill Gate. Romantic bias-cut clothes with a 1930's influence, made from soft, wearable fabric that will emerge from a packed suitcase looking pristine.

Joseph

Map 4, C7. 23 Old Bond St, W1 ☎020/7629 3713 (and many other branches), ⓦwww.joseph.co.uk ⊖ Bond Street. Offering classic cuts in imaginative styles, Joseph is the last word in luxury fashion for men as well as women. The Joseph Sale Shop at 53 King's Rd, SW3 (☎020/7730 7562;⊖ Sloane Square), offers good discounts on womenswear.

Koh Samui

🏃 **Map 4, G6. 65 Monmouth St, WC2** ☎020/7240 4280 ⊖ Leicester Square or Covent Garden. The leading promoter of young British designers, stocking a highly selective, and very expensive, range of womenswear with an elegant, eclectic and feminine feel, along with some gorgeous vintage pieces.

Nicole Farhi

Map 4, C7. 158 New Bond St, W1 ☎020/7499 8368 (and other branches)⊖ Bond Street. Classic designs and cuts for men and women, invariably in the shades of a chameleon resting on a sandy rock, but no less elegant and popular for that.

Paul Smith

Map 4, H6 & Map 4, B6. Westbourne House, 122 Kensington Park Rd, W11 ☎020/7727 3553 (⊖ Notting Hill Gate) and 40–44 Floral St, WC2 ☎020/7379 7133 (⊖ Covent Garden), ⓦwww.paulsmith.co.uk Both stores are worth a visit in their own right, selling Smith's whole range of well-tailored, very English clothes for men, women and children. The Smith Sale Shop, 23 Avery Row, W1 (☎020/7493 1287;⊖ Bond Street), offers huge discounts.

Souvenir

Map 4, E6. 47 Lexington St, W1 ☎020/7287 9877 ⊖ Piccadilly Circus. A cute north Soho boutique with a Japan-meets-Cannes feel. Offerings include Anna Sui's delicate and covetable designs and quirky Marc Jacobs shoes.

Vivienne Westwood

Map 4, A6. 6 Davies St, W1 ☎020/7629 3757 (and other

branches)⊖ **Bond Street.** Somewhat eccentric but revered by the international fashion pack, this quintessentially English maverick is still going strong.

Mid-range and high street

Agnès B
Map 4, H6. 35–36 Floral St, WC2 ⊕020/7379 1992 (and other branches), ⓦ www.agnesb.com ⊖ **Covent Garden.** Sitting with one foot in the designer camp, this French fashion house brings understated Parisian chic to the high street.

Dispensary
Map 4, D6. 8–9 Newburgh St, ⊕020/7287 8145⊖ **Oxford Circus.** Located on a small road, parallel to Carnaby Street, that's great for original fashion, Dispensary has friendly, helpful staff and offers effervescent dressy womenswear with a street edge.

French Connection
Map 3, F4. 396 Oxford St, W1 ⊕020/7629 7766 (and many other branches), ⓦ www.frenchconnection .com⊖ **Bond Street.** Their tongue-in-cheek FCUK advertising campaign saw French Connection relaunch itself for a younger, funkier market. Top-quality fabrics and cuts don't come cheap, but for your money you get catwalk styling at a fraction of the cost.

H&M
Map 4, C5. 261–271 Regent St, W1 ⊕020/7493 4004 (and many other branches), ⓦ www.hm.com ⊖ **Piccadilly Circus or Oxford Circus.** Fashion basics for men and women for very little outlay – pick up a sparkly party top for under a tenner. Men's clothes, especially shirts, are well cut and amazingly cheap.

Joy
Map 2, I6. 432 Coldharbour Lane, ⊕020/7787 9616, ⓦ www.joy thestore.com⊖ **Brixton.** A joy indeed, and one of the places to be in Brixton, this lively store features fantastic imported designer fashion at high-street prices, from well-cut sassy streetwear to ballgowns. There's a good range of more subdued men's clothes, including Chunk T-shirts.

The Laden Showroom
Map 7, M1. 103 Brick Lane, E1 ⊕020/7247 2431, ⓦ www.laden .co.uk⊖ **Aldgate East.** A showcase for more than forty independent designers, and great for exuberant dressers on a budget. You can pick up Indian tunics, handmade customized T-shirts, batik bags and stripey bias-cut frocks.

Primark

Map 2, J3. Kings Mall, 365–371 Mare St, E8 ☏ 020/8748 7119, ⓦ www.primark.co.uk **Hackney Central station.** The shop of choice for poorly paid magazine fashion assistants, Primark provides astonishingly cheap and stylish garments, often "inspired" by more established high street stores. Wide selection of swimming costumes, underwear and nighties, plus cheap, fun handbags.

Top Shop

Map 4, C5. 214 Oxford St, W1 ☏ 020/7636 7700 (and many other branches), ⓦ www.tops .co.uk ⊖ **Oxford Circus.** Proving a big hit with the celebs as well as mere mortals, Top Shop's flagship store is *the* place to go for this season's must-have item at a snip of the designer prices. One floor is entirely given over to accessories, another to Top Shop's own-brand stuff and a third to independent labels.

Street and clubwear

AdHoc/Boy

Map 3, D8. 153 King's Rd, SW3 ☏ 020/7376 8829 ⊖ **Sloane Square.** Party gear for exhibitionists: plenty of PVC, Lycra, feathers and spangles, with fairy wings and magic wands to match your outfit, and a body-piercing studio downstairs.

Burro

Map 4, H6. 29a Floral St, WC2 ☏ 020/7240 5120 ⊖ **Covent Garden.** Funky but with an air of studied nonchalance, this is for boys who want to look cool without looking like they want to look cool.

Diesel

Map 4, H6. 43 Earlham St, WC2 ☏ 020/7497 5543, ⓦ www.diesel .com ⊖ **Covent Garden.** Still cool despite the hype, this industrial-looking store for label-conscious men and women continues to offer that retro-denim look in a dazzling variety of colours and styles.

Duffer of St George

Map 4, H5. 29 Shorts Gardens, WC2 ☏ 020/7379 4660, ⓦ www.duffer ofstgeorge.com ⊖ **Covent Garden.** Covetable own-label boys' casuals and streetwear, plus a range of other hip labels in the land of jeans, shoes, jackets and so on.

Home

Map 4, D7. 39 Beak St, W1 ☏ 020/7287 3708 ⊖ **Covent Garden.** The cheeky monkey featured on some of the capital's cooler streetwear accessories originated here. Jeans, shirts, trainers, shoes, bags, wallets and hats all serve to produce a one-stop, Paul Frank-style combo.

Mambo
Map 4, H5. 39 Shelton St, WC2
☎020/7438 9800, 🌐www.mambo .com.au⊖ Covent Garden. Surf, skate and graffiti gear, including a range of books, mugs and hats.

Miss Sixty
Map 4, H5. 39 Neal St, WC2
☎020/7836 3789, 🌐www.misssixty .com⊖ Covent Garden. A day-glo store selling skinny girls' clothes with a psychedelic feel.

Urban Outfitters
Map 4, H6. 2–56 Earlham St, WC2 ☎020/7759 6390, 🌐www .urbanoutfitters.com⊖ Covent Garden. Bedraggled boho style meets streetwear in this large Covent Garden cornerstore. Blokes' clothes include own-brand T-shirts and Levi's.

Vintage, retro and secondhand

Annie's Vintage Costume and Textiles
Map 2, I3. 10 Camden Passage, N1 ☎020/7359 0796 ⊖ Angel. A tiny and well-stocked shop, draped in shimmering fabrics and specializing in fabulous 1920s and 1930s glamour, from party dresses and embroidered

Chinese jackets to handmade shoes and suitcases.

The Antiques Clothing Shop
Map 2, F4. 282 Portobello Rd, W10 ☎020/8946 4830 ⊖ Ladbroke Grove. Lots of treasures in this store, with affordable Victoriana and vintage menswear a speciality.

The Emporium
See map on p.154. 330–332 Creek Rd, SE10 ☎020/8305 1670 ⊖ Greenwich or Greenwich station. Elegant retro store specializing in 1940s to 1960s clothes for men and women, and featuring kitsch displays in its beautiful glass-fronted cases. Well-kept bargains start at a tenner.

Laurence Corner
Map 2, H4. 62–64 Hampstead Rd, NW1 ☎020/7813 1010⊖ Warren Street. London's oldest and most eccentric army-surplus shop, with lots of bargains and an extensive theatrical and fancy-dress hire section.

Rokit
Map 7, M1. 105–107 Brick Lane E1, ☎020/7375 3864, 🌐www .rokit.co.uk⊖ Aldgate East. Stylishly presented vintage clothes, with no fusty second-hand smells – you'll find sparkly knits, jeans, legwarmers and 1970s shades the size of

dinnerplates, plus baseball caps for the boys.

Shoes

Aldo
Map 4, H6. 3–7 Neal St, WC2 ☎020/7836 7692, ⓦwww .aldoshoes.com➔ Covent Garden. A Canadian store providing high-fashion, high-quality and really rather sexy shoes for men and women at very reasonable prices.

Birkenstock
Map 4, H5. 37 Neal St, WC2 ☎020/7240 2783, ⓦwww.Birken stock.co.uk➔ Covent Garden. Comfortable, classic sandals and shoes in leather, suede and nubuck, with vegetarian options too.

Buffalo Boots
Map 4, H5. 47–49 Neal St, WC2 ☎020/7379 1051, ⓦwww .buffalo-boots.com➔ Covent Garden. Everything from the practical to the clubby via spike-heeled boots and enormous platform shoes.

L.K. Bennett
Map 4, H6. 130 Long Acre, WC2 ☎020/7379 1710 (and other branches), ⓦwww.lk bennett.com➔ Covent Garden.

Girlie shoes galore: glamorous kitten heels, sharp boots and strappy sandals. Well made, very stylish and with a price tag to match.

Natural Shoe Store
Map 4, H5. 21 Neal St, WC2 ☎020/7836 5254 (and other branches)➔ Covent Garden. Well-made, stylish, comfortable and sometimes strange shoes. Good value, although not cheap.

Office
Map 4, H5. 57 Neal St, WC2 ☎020/7379 1896 (and many other branches), ⓦwww.officelondon .co.uk➔ Covent Garden. Good, broad range of basics, including many own-label creations, at reasonable prices, plus some more frivolous fashion moments, too.

Shellys
Map 4, C5. 266–270 Regent St, W1 ☎020/7287 0939 (and many other branches), ⓦwww.shellys.co.uk ➔ Oxford Circus. Offering pretty much everything from the sensible to the silly and with a good deal in between, this always madly busy store has a huge range, over several floors and at every price, for both men and women.

Books

As well as the big-name **chain bookstores**, most of which have branches throughout the city, London is blessed with a wealth of **local, independent and specialist bookshops**. Charing Cross Road has the highest concentration of the latter and, though these may not have as extensive a stock as the chains, they will almost certainly be more interesting to browse around, and you may well find some hidden jewels on their shelves.

Secondhand books are also sold at the
Riverside Walk stalls, under Waterloo Bridge
on the South Bank, SE1 (Sat & Sun 10am–5pm,
and occasionally midweek);⊖ Waterloo or Waterloo station.

Any Amount of Books
Map 4, G7. 62 Charing Cross Rd, WC2 ☎020/7240 8140, ⓦwww. anyamountofbooks.com⊖ Leicester Square. Sprawling secondhand bookshop stocking everything from obscure 50p bargains to rare and expensive first editions. Especially strong on fiction, the arts and literary biography.

Arthur Probsthain Oriental & African Bookseller
Map 4, G3. 41 Great Russell St, WC1 ☎020/7636 1096, ⓦwww.oriental -african-books.com⊖ Tottenham Court Road. Connected to the School of Oriental and African Studies, this impressive academic store covers all relevant aspects of art, history, science and culture.

Atlantis Bookshop
Map 4, H4. 49a Museum St, WC1 ☎020/7405 2120, ⓦwww.theatlan tisbookshop.com⊖ Tottenham Court Road. Splendid occult-oriented place with the perfect ambience for browsing through books and magazines covering spirituality, psychic phenomena, witchcraft and so on.

Blackwell's
Map 4, G5. 100 Charing Cross Rd, WC2 ☎020/7292 5100 (and many other branches), ⓦwww.bookshop .blackwell.co.uk⊖ Tottenham Court Road or Leicester Square. The London flagship of Oxford's best

academic bookshop has a wider range than you might expect; academic stock is unsurprisingly excellent, but so is the range of computing, travel and fiction titles.

Bookmarks
Map 4, G4. 1 Bloomsbury St, WC1 ☏020/7637 1848, ⊛www.book marks.uk.com⊖ **Tottenham Court Road.** Leftist and radical fare in the heart of Bloomsbury, with a wide range of political biography, history, theory and assorted political ephemera. There's even a children's section.

Books Etc
Map 5, B1. 264 High Holborn, WC1 ☏020/7404 0261 (and many other branches), ⊛www.booksetc.co.uk ⊖ **Holborn.** Large, laid-back and user-friendly, with an on-site coffee shop and a wide and well-stocked range of mainstream and specialist titles, and especially good on contemporary fiction. This branch is closed on Saturdays; most others are not.

Books for Cooks
Map 2, F5. 4 Blenheim Crescent, W11 ☏020/7221 1992, ⊛www .booksforcooks.com⊖ **Ladbroke Grove.** Anything and everything to do with food can be found on the shelves of this wonderful new and secondhand bookshop,

which also has a tiny café (see p.199) offering cookery demonstrations, coffee for browsers, and lunch.

Borders Books & Music
Map 4, D5. 203 Oxford St, W1 ☏020/7292 1600 (and many other branches), ⊛www.borders.co.uk ⊖ **Oxford Circus or Tottenham Court Road.** Enormous London flagship of the American import, boasting four floors of books alongside a huge range of CDs and magazines. Good range of titles, with staff recommendations and reviews, and a solid children's section.

Daunt Books
Map 3, E3. 83–84 Marylebone High St, W1 ☏020/7224 2295 (and other branches)⊖ **Bond Street or Baker Street.** Wide and varied range of travel literature as well as the usual guidebooks, presented by expert staff in the beautiful, galleried interior of this famous shop.

Forbidden Planet
Map 4, G5. 179 Shaftesbury Ave, WC2 ☏020/7420 3666, ⊛www.forbiddenplanet.com ⊖ **Tottenham Court Road.** All things science-fiction and fantasy-related, ranging from books and graphic novels to games and ephemera.

Foyles

Map 4, G5. 113–119 Charing Cross Rd, WC2 ☎ 020/7437 5660, ⓦ www .foyles.co.uk⊖ Tottenham Court Road. Long-established, huge and famous London bookshop with a big feminist section and Ray's Jazz Shop and café on the first floor.

Gay's the Word

Map 3, H3. 66 Marchmont St, WC1 ☎ 020/7278 7654, ⓦ www.gays theword.co.uk⊖ Russell Square. Extensive collection of lesbian and gay classics, pulps, contemporary fiction and non-fiction, plus cards, calendars, magazines and more. Weekly lesbian discussion groups and readings held in the back.

Gosh!

Map 4, G3. 39 Great Russell St, WC1 ☎ 020/7636 1011 ⊖ Tottenham Court Road. All kinds of comics for all kinds of readers, whether you're the casually curious or the serious collector. Check out the Cartoon Gallery in the basement.

Offstage Theatre & Cinema Bookshop

Map 2, H3. 37 Chalk Farm Rd, NW1 ☎ 020/7485 4996⊖ Camden Town or Chalk Farm. Excellent, well-stocked shop covering all aspects of stage and screen craft, plus theory, criticism, scripts and biographies.

Persephone Books

Map 3, I3. 59 Lamb's Conduit St, WC1 ☎ 020/7242 9292, ⓦ www.persephonebooks.co.uk ⊖ Russell Square. A true one-off – the attractive bookshop of a publishing house which specializes in neglected early twentieth-century work, mostly by women. The books are beautifully produced, all with endpapers in a textile from the relevant period (£10 each or £27 for 3).

Politico's

Map 3, G7. 8 Artillery Row, SW1 ☎ 020/7828 0010, ⓦ www.politicos .co.uk⊖ St James's Park. Mainstream political fare, new and secondhand, with plenty of big biographies. A cosy café, board games and irreverent window displays give it a more frivolous edge.

Stanford's Map and Travel Bookshop

Map 4, H6. 12–14 Long Acre, WC2 ☎ 020/7836 1321, ⓦ www .stanfords.co.uk⊖ Leicester Square or Charing Cross. The world's largest specialist travel bookshop, this features pretty much any map of anywhere, plus a huge range of travel books and guides.

Unsworths Booksellers

Map 4, G4. 12 Bloomsbury St, WC1 ℡020/7436 9836◉ Tottenham Court Road. Good for bargains, including recent and just-out-of-print novels and academic titles. Specializes in the humanities, and features an interesting antiquarian selection.

Waterstone's

Map 4, E8. 203–206 Piccadilly, W1 ℡020/7851 2400 (and many other branches), ⓦwww.waterstones.co.uk ◉ Piccadilly Circus or Green Park. This flagship bookshop – Europe's largest – occupies the former Simpson's department store building and boasts a café, bar, gallery and events rooms, as well as five floors of books.

Zwemmer Arts & Architecture

Map 4, G6. 24 Litchfield St, WC2 ℡020/7240 4158, ⓦwww.zwemmer.com◉ Leicester Square. Specialist art bookshop with a fantastic and expert selection. Zwemmer Media Arts, nearby (80 Charing Cross Rd, WC2 ℡020/7240 4157;◉ Leicester Square), specializes in film, design and photography.

Music

There are hundreds of mainstream, independent and specialist **music shops** in London, catering equally well for the CD bulk-buyer and the obsessive rare-vinyl collector. This is a selection of the best and best known. Bear in mind that London's markets, especially Camden, are also good sources of vinyl (see "Markets", p.290).

Megastores

FOPP

Map 4, G6. 1 Earlham St, WC2 ℡020/7379 0883, ⓦwww.fopp.co.uk◉ Covent Garden. Three floors of music, at prices that generally undercut its competitors. Lots of DVDs and classic albums for under a fiver, and new releases for as little as £10.

HMV

Map 4, D4. 150 Oxford St, W1 ℡020/7631 3423, ⓦwww.hmv.co.uk◉ Oxford Circus. All the latest releases, as you'd expect, but also an impressive backlist, a reassuring amount of vinyl, and a good classical section downstairs. Dance music is also a strength.

Virgin Megastore
Map 4, F4. 14–16 Oxford St, W1 ☎020/7631 1234, ⊛www.virgin.com⊖ Tottenham Court Road. The mainstream floor here is better stocked than the specialist sections: the bias is rock-heavy, but there's a little of everything else, and plenty of books, magazines, T-shirts and assorted music ephemera.

Independent stores

Eukatech
Map 4, H5. 49 Endell St, WC2 ☎020/7240 8060, ⊛www.ucmguk.com⊖ Covent Garden. House, techno and trance on two floors, both vinyl and CD.

Gramex
Map 6, C7. 25 Lower Marsh, SE1 ☎020/7401 3830⊖ Waterloo or Waterloo station. A splendid find for classical music lovers, this new and secondhand record store features CDs and vinyl, and offers comfy leather armchairs to sample or discuss your finds at leisure.

Honest Jon's
Map 2, F5. 276 & 278 Portobello Rd, W10 ☎020/8969 9822, ⊛www.honestjohns.co.uk⊖ Ladbroke Grove.

Jazz, soul, funk, R&B, rare groove, dance and plenty more make this place a browser's delight, with current releases, secondhand finds and reissues on vinyl and CD.

MDC Classic Music
Map 4, H8. 437 Strand, WC2 ☎020/7240 2157 (and many other branches), ⊛www.mdcmusic.co.uk ⊖ Charing Cross or Embankment. Big and brassy, this central chain store has an impressive range of stock, but specializes in special offers and cut-price CDs.

Mr Bongo
Map 4, D3. 44 Poland St, WC1 ☎020/7287 1887, ⊛www.mrbongo.com⊖ Oxford Circus. Good on 12-inch singles, and equally reliable for hip-hop, jazz, Latin American and Brazilian sounds.

Sister Ray
Map 4, E6. 94 Berwick St, W1 ☎020/7287 8385, ⊛www.sisterray.co.uk⊖ Oxford Circus or Piccadilly Circus. Up-to-the-minute indie sounds, with lots of electronica and some forays into the current dance scene, most on vinyl as well as CD.

Stern's African Record Centre
Map 3, G2. 293 Euston Rd, NW1 ☎020/7387 5550, ⊛www.sternsmusic.com⊖ Euston

Square. World-famous for its global specialisms, this knowledgeable store has an unrivalled stock of African music and excellent selections from pretty much everywhere else in the world.

Steve's Sounds
Map 4, G7. 20–20a Newport Court, WC2 ⊕020/7437 4638⊖ Leicester Square. Quick-moving stock of CDs and vinyl, from rock and pop to dance, jazz, world and classical music. Irresistible prices.

Markets

London's **markets** are more than just a cheap alternative to high-street shopping: many of them are significant remnants of communities endangered by the heedless expansion of the city. You haven't really got to grips with London unless you've rummaged through the junk at Brick Lane on a Sunday morning, or haggled over a leather jacket at Camden. Do keep an eye out for **pickpockets**: the weekend markets provide them with easy pickings.

The East End markets of Brick Lane, Columbia Road, Petticoat Lane and Spitalfields are reviewed on p.104.

Bermondsey (New Caledonian) Market
Map 3, N6. Bermondsey Square, SE1⊖ Borough or London Bridge. Fri 5am–2pm. Huge, unglamorous but highly regarded antique market offering everything from obscure nautical instruments to attractive but pricey furniture. The real collectors arrive at dawn to pick up the bargains, and you need to get here by noon at the latest to ensure you don't go home empty-handed.

Borough Market
Map 7, E8. 8 Southwark St ⊕020/7401 7300, ⓦwww .boroughmarket.org⊖ London Bridge or Borough. Fri noon–6pm, Sat 9am–4pm. Fine-food heaven – suppliers from all over the UK converge here to sell piles of organic veg, venison, fish, wines and home-baked goodies. The

Victorian structure itself, with its slender grass-green wrought-iron columns, is well worth a look.

Brixton Market

Map 2, J6. Electric Avenue, Pope's, Brixton Station and Atlantic roads, SW9 ⊖ Brixton. Mon–Thurs & Sat 8am–3pm. Based in the arcades just off Atlantic Road, but spilling out along nearly all of the neighbouring streets, this huge, energetic market is the centre of Brixton life, offering a vast range of African and Caribbean foods, hair and beauty products, records, clothes, a dazzling range of African fabrics and even triple-fast-action spiritual cleanser-cum-floor-wash.

Camden Market

Map 2, H3. Camden High St to Chalk Farm Rd, NW1 ⊖ Camden Town. Mainly Thurs–Sun 9am–5.30pm. Camden Market (Camden High Street, on the junction of Buck Street; Thurs–Sun 9am–5.30pm) offers a good mix of new, secondhand, retro and young designer clothes, as well as records and ephemera, while the Electric Market (Camden High Street, just before the junction of Dewsbury Terrace; Sat & Sun 10am–5.30pm) and Camden Canal Market (just over Camden Lock bridge; Fri–Sun 9am–6pm) offer cheap fashion, hippiewear, smoking paraphernalia and souvenir knick-knacks. Camden Lock (Camden Lock Place, off Chalk Farm Road; daily 9.30am–5.30pm; outdoor stalls Sat & Sun 10am–6pm) offers mainly arts, crafts and clothes stalls, with the shops adding a few hip designers, antique dealers and booksellers to the mix. The Stables Yard (leading off from Camden Lock or from Chalk Farm Road; Sat & Sun 8am–6pm) is a sprawling adventure of clubwear, more young designers, furniture, retro design, trinkets and antiques.

Covent Garden Market

Map 4, I7. Apple Market, The Piazza, and Jubilee Market, off Southampton St, WC2 ⊖ Covent Garden. Daily 9am–5pm. The Apple Market offers handmade, rather twee craft stalls most days, while Jubilee Market offers endless cheap T-shirts, jewellery, souvenirs and so on. On Mondays, Jubilee is taken over by an antiques market, which has some more enjoyable stalls (closes 3pm). Whichever day you visit, there are street performers to distract you in the Piazza, and it's an amiable area in which to wander about.

Greenwich Market

See map on p.154. Greenwich High Rd, Stockwell St and

College Approach, SE10 ⊖ North Greenwich or Greenwich train, or Cutty Sark DLR. Mainly Thurs–Sun 9.30am–5pm. The covered Crafts Market on College Approach sells mostly twentieth-century antiques on Thursday (7.30am–5pm) and handmade goods, clothes and gifts from Friday to Sunday (9.30am–5.30pm), while the Central Market, off Stockwell Street (indoor Fri & Sat 10am–5pm, Sun 10am–6pm; outdoor Sat 7am–6pm, Sun 7am–5pm), hosts funky secondhand clothes, bric-a-brac and furniture. The surrounding streets, and the shops inside the covered market, offer obscure maritime devices, new and old, plus lots of secondhand books and retro clothes.

Portobello Road Market

Map 2, F5. Portobello Rd, W10, and Golborne Rd, W10/W11, ⓦwww .portobelloroad.co.uk (antiques) ⊖ Ladbroke Grove or Notting Hill Gate. Antique market Sat 4am–6pm; general market Mon–Wed 8am–6pm, Thurs 9am–1pm, Fri & Sat 7am–7pm; organic market Thurs 11am–6pm; Golborne Road market Mon–Sat 9am–5pm. Start at the Notting Hill end and make your way through the antiques and bric-a-brac down to the fruit and veg stalls, and then under the Westway to the seriously hip new and secondhand clothes stalls and shops around which local style vultures circle and swoop. The Golborne Road market is cheaper and less crowded, with some very attractive antiques and retro furniture.

Miscellaneous

The listings below represent a small selection of shops which don't really fit into any particular category, or which are just interesting to visit.

Contemporary Ceramics

Map 4, D6. William Blake House, 7 Marshall St, W1 ☎020/7437 7605⊖ Oxford Circus. You can get anything and everything by and for ceramicists at this fascinating gallery-cum-shop, which is also the showcase and retail outlet for the Craft Potters' Association.

Davenport's Magic Shop

Map 4, H9. 7 Charing Cross Tube Arcade, Strand, WC2 ☎020/7836 0408⊖ Charing Cross or Embankment. The world's oldest family-run magic business, stocking marvellous tricks for both amateurs and professionals.

G. Smith & Sons
Map 4, G6. 74 Charing Cross Rd, WC2 ☎020/7836 7422 ⊖ Leicester Square. Exactly what an old English tobacconist's ought to look and smell like. Every variety of tobacco, including some of the shop's own creations, plus a huge range of snuff and a walk-in humidor featuring some very classy cigars.

James Smith & Sons
Map 4, G4. 53 New Oxford St, WC1 ☎020/7836 4731 ⊖ Tottenham Court Road. A survivor from an earlier time (it was established in 1830), this venerable shop purveys hip-flasks, portable seats and canes, but its main trade is in umbrellas. The most enduringly popular is the man's classic city umbrella (£47).

Neal's Yard Dairy
Map 4, G5. 17 Shorts Gardens, WC2 ☎020/7240 5700 ⊖ Covent Garden. Quality cheeses from around the British Isles, with a few exceptionally good choices from further afield. A huge selection, and you can taste before you buy.

Radio Days
Map 6, C7. 87 Lower Marsh, SE1 ☎020/7928 0800 ⊖ Waterloo or Waterloo station. A fantastic collection of memorabilia and accessories from the 1930s to the 1970s, including shoes, shot glasses, cosmetics and vintage magazines, plus a huge stock of well-kept ladies' and menswear from the same period.

Story
Map 2, J4. 4 Wilkes St, E1 ☎020/7377 0313 ⊖ Liverpool Street. Exquisitely tasteful and eclectic shop located in a modern industrial space on a street of Huguenot houses. Practically everything here – art, textiles, furniture, clothing – is in shades of white or cream. There's a delicious whiff of Miss Haversham about the fading lace and Venetian mirrors, and you can pick up useful items such as cheap white towels.

25

Sport

As the quickest of glances at the national press will tell you, **sport** in Britain is a serious matter, with each international defeat (or victory) taken as an index of the country's slide down (or up) the scale of world powers. Many of the crucial international fixtures of the **football**, **rugby and cricket** seasons take place in the capital, as does one of the world's greatest tennis tournaments, the **Wimbledon** championships, and London is also set to host the **2012 Olympic Games**.

Paradoxically, those wishing to participate in sports, will find London poorly served by sport facilities. However, it's to be hoped that this problem will be addressed as the capital gears up for the Olympics. Obviously, several of the existing stadiums – Wembley, Wimbledon, Lord's and the Dome – will be used for the Games, but there'll also be a number of new purpose-built arenas (including an athletics stadium, an aquatic centre and a velodrome) in the Olympic Park in East London.

For up-to-the-minute details of sporting events in London, check *Time Out* or the *Evening Standard*, or contact the London Sportsline (☎08458/508 508, ⓦ www.sportengland .org).

Football

English **football** (or soccer) is passionate and, if you have the slightest interest in the game, then catching a league or FA Cup fixture is a must. The season runs from mid-August to early May, when the **FA Cup Final** rounds things off. There are four league divisions: at the top is the twenty-club Premiership, followed by the Championship and leagues one and two. There are London clubs in every division, with around five or six in the Premiership at any one time.

The battle between Manchester United and **Arsenal**, London's most successful club, provided high drama at the top of the Premiership over the last decade. However, another

---

Major football stadiums and clubs

Arsenal 2005–06: Highbury Stadium, Avenell Rd, N5 ⊖ Arsenal. **2006–07:** Emirates Stadium, Ashburton Grove, N7 ☎020/7704 4040, ⓦwww.arsenal.com ⊖ Arsenal.

Charlton Athletic The Valley, Floyd Rd, SE7 ☎020/8333 4010, ⓦwww.charlton-athletic.co.uk Charlton train station from Charing Cross.

Chelsea Stamford Bridge, Fulham Rd, SW6 ☎0870/300 1212, ⓦwww.chelseafc.com ⊖ Fulham Broadway.

Fulham Craven Cottage, Stevenage Rd, SW6 ☎0870/442 1222, ⓦwww.fulhamfc.com ⊖ Putney Bridge

Tottenham Hotspur White Hart Lane Stadium, High St, N15 ☎0870/420 5000, ⓦwww.spurs.co.uk White Hart Lane station from Liverpool Street.

Wembley Stadium Wembley Way, Middlesex ⓦwww.wembley stadium.com ⊖ Wembley Park or Wembley Central. Rebuilt in 2006 at enormous expense, Wembley is the traditional venue for the FA Cup and England's home internationals.

West Ham United Upton Park, Green St, E13 ☎0870/112 2700, ⓦwww.whufc.co.uk ⊖ Upton Park or Stratford train station from Liverpool Street, then bus #104.

London club, **Chelsea**, lifted the title for the first time in fifty years in the 2004–05 season. With countless millions at their disposal thanks to the new owner, Russian oil tycoon Roman Abramovich, and the tactical acumen of manager Jose Mourinho, Chelsea look set to dominate for the foreseeable future.

Football **matches** traditionally kick off at 3pm on Saturday – the highlights of the day's best Premiership games are shown on BBC 1 TV on Saturday and Sunday nights. However, there are usually one or two games each Saturday (kick-off around noon & 5pm), Sunday (kick-off between 2pm & 4pm) and Monday (kick-off around 8pm), broadcast live on Sky TV.

Tickets for most Premiership games start at £20–25 and are virtually impossible to get hold of on a casual basis: you need to book in advance, or try and see one of the European or knock-out cup fixtures.

Cricket

In the days of the Empire, the English took **cricket** to the colonies as a means of instilling the gentlemanly values of fair play while administering a sound thrashing to the natives. It hasn't always quite gone according to plan, although the current England side is one of the more successful of recent times. To see the game at its best you should try to get tickets for one of the **Test matches** between England and the summer's touring team. These international fixtures are played in the middle of the cricket season, which runs from April to September.

Two of the matches are played in London: one at **Lord's** (☎020/7432 1000, 🌐www.lords.org), the home of English cricket, in St John's Wood (⊖St John's Wood), the other at **The Oval** (☎020/7582 6660, 🌐www.surreycricket.com), in Kennington (⊖Oval). In tandem with the full-blown five-day Tests, there's also a series of **one-day internationals**, two of which are usually held in London.

Getting to see England play one of the big teams can be difficult unless you book months in advance. If you can't wangle your way into a Test, you could settle down instead to an inter-county match, either in the **county championship** (these are four-day games) or in one of the fast and furious **one-day competitions** – tickets cost around £10. An even more frenetic innovation, which is a great introduction to cricket, is the **Twenty20 Cup**, in which each team gets to bowl just twenty over each in the course of just three hours. Two county teams are based in London – **Middlesex**, who play at Lord's, and **Surrey**, who play at The Oval.

Rugby

Rugby gets its name from Rugby public school, where the game mutated from football (soccer) in the nineteenth century. A rugby match may at times look like a bunch of weightlifters grappling each other in the mud – as they say, rugby is a hooligan's game played by gentlemen, while football is a gentleman's game played by hooligans – but it is in reality a highly tactical and athletic game. England's rugby team tends to enjoy more success than many of the national teams, winning the World Cup in Rugby Union as recently as 2003.

There are two types of rugby played in Britain. Thirteen-a-side **Rugby League** is a professional game played almost exclusively in the north of England. The Super League features the big-name northern clubs and one London club, the former London Broncos, now known as the **Harlequins**, who play at the Stoop Memorial Ground in Twickenham (☎020/8410 6000, ⓦwww.quins.co.uk; Twickenham train station from Waterloo). The season runs from March to September, and games traditionally take place on Sundays at 3pm, but there are also matches on Friday and Saturday nights.

In London, however, virtually all rugby clubs play fifteen-a-side **Rugby Union**, which has upper-class associations (though the game is also very strong in working-class Wales) and only became a professional sport in 1995. Two Premiership teams play in London – **Harlequins**, who play at the same stadium as their Rugby League namesake (see above), and the more successful of the two, **Wasps**, who play in Acton (℡020/8993 8298, Ⓦwww.wasps.co.uk; ⊖ Ealing Common). The season runs from September until May, finishing off with the Challenge cup final. The cup final and international matches are played at **Twickenham Stadium**, Whitton Road (℡020/8831 6666, Ⓦwww.rfu .com). Unless you are affiliated to one of the two thousand clubs of the Rugby Union, or willing to pay well over the odds at a ticket agency, it is tough to get a ticket for one of these big Twickenham games. A better bet is to go and see a Harlequins league game, where there's bound to be an international player or two on display – you can usually get in for around £10–15.

Tennis

Tennis in England is synonymous with **Wimbledon** (℡020/8971 2473, Ⓦwww.wimbledon.com), the only Grand Slam tournament in the world to be played on grass, and for many players the ultimate goal of their careers. The Wimbledon championships last a fortnight, and are always held during the last week of June and the first week of July. Most of the **tickets**, especially seats for the main show courts (Centre and No. 1), are allocated in advance to the Wimbledon tennis club's members, other clubs and corporate "sponsors" – as well as by public ballot – and once these have taken their slice there's not a lot left for the general public.

On weekdays, **queues** start to form around dawn – if you arrive by around 7am, you have a reasonable chance of securing one of the limited number of Centre and No. 1 court tickets held back for sale on the day. If you're there by around 9am, you should get admission to the outside courts (where you'll catch some top players in the first week of the tournament). Either way, you then have a long wait until play commences at noon. Avoid the middle Saturday, when thousands of people camp overnight – so many, in fact, numbers have now been restricted. For the unlucky, there's the consolation of TV coverage, which is pretty all-consuming.

If you want to see big-name players in London, an easier opportunity is the Stella Artois men's championship at **Queen's Club** (℡020/7385 3421, Ⓦwww.queensclub .co.uk) in Hammersmith, which finishes a week before Wimbledon. Many of the male tennis stars use this tournament to acclimatize themselves to British grass-court conditions. As with Wimbledon, you have to apply for tickets in advance, although there is a limited number of returns on sale at 10am each day.

If you want to play tennis, there are **public courts** in most of London's parks, including Hyde Park (℡020/7262 3474) and Regent's Park (℡020/7486 4216); again, you'll need to book in advance.

Horse racing

There are five **horse racecourses** within easy reach of London: **Kempton Park** (℡01932/782292, Ⓦwww.kempton .co.uk), near Sunbury-on-Thames; **Sandown Park** (℡01372/463072, Ⓦwww.sandown.co.uk), near Esher in Surrey; and **Windsor** (℡01753/498400, Ⓦwww.windsor -racecourse.co.uk), all of which hold top-quality races on the flat (April–Sept) and over jumps (Aug–March). There's also **Ascot** (℡01344/876876, ⓦwww.ascot.co.uk), in Berkshire, and **Epsom** (℡01372/726311, ⓦwww.epsomderby .co.uk) in Surrey, which are the real glamour courses, hosting major races of the flat-racing season every June.

Thousands of Londoners have a day out at Epsom on Derby Day, which takes place on the first or second Saturday in June. **The Derby**, a mile-and-a-half race for three-year-old thoroughbreds, is the most prestigious of the five classics of the April to September English flat season, and is preceded by another classic, **the Oaks**, which is for fillies only. The three-day Derby meeting is as much a social ritual as a sporting event, but for sheer snobbery nothing can match the **Royal Ascot** week in mid-June, when the Queen and selected members of the royal family are in attendance, along with half the nation's blue bloods. The best seats are the preserve of the gentry, who get dressed up to the nines for the day; but, as is the case at most racecourses, the rabble are allowed into the public enclosure for around a fiver.

Greyhound racing

Greyhound racing is an inexpensive, often boozy spectacle: a grandstand seat costs less than £5, and all the London stadiums have one or more restaurants, some of which are surprisingly good. Indeed, the sport has become so popular that you should book in advance if you want to watch the races from a restaurant table, particularly around Christmas. Meetings usually start around 7.30pm and finish at 10.30pm, and generally include around a dozen races. The easiest stadium to get to is **Wimbledon** (℡0870/880 1000, ⓦwww.wimbledonstadium.co.uk; Wimbledon Park or Haydons Road train station from Blackfriars), though **Walthamstow** (℡020/8498 3300, ⓦwww.wsgreyhound .co.uk; ⊖ Walthamstow then bus #97), in the northeast, is probably the most famous.

Ice skating

From October to March, there's the Broadgate **outdoor ice rink** (see below), supplemented in the Christmas and New Year period with outdoor rinks at Somerset House (Ⓦ www.somerset-house.org.uk) and numerous other locations around London, such as Marble Arch, the Tower of London and Hampton Court Palace. Prices for these rinks tend to be pretty high (£10 or more for a one-hour session) and advance booking absolutely essential. Otherwise, London has just one centrally located **indoor ice rink**, in Bayswater.

Broadgate Ice Rink
Map 7, H1. Broadgate Circus, Eldon St, EC2 ℡ 020/7505 4068, Ⓦ www .broadgateice.co.uk ⊖ Liverpool Street. A little circle of ice open from Oct–March. It's fun (in fine weather), but can get crowded during the weekend. Mon–Wed evenings are for "broomball" matches.

Leisurebox
Map 3, A5. 17 Queensway, W2 ℡ 020/7229 0172 ⊖ Queensway or Bayswater. The whole family can skate at this rink, which has ice-discos on Fri and Sat evenings. Session times tend to vary, but generally last for around two to three hours and cost between £5 and £7.

Swimming, gyms and fitness centres

Below is a selection of the best-equipped, most central of London's multipurpose **fitness centres**. We haven't given the addresses of the city's many council-run swimming pools, virtually all of which now have fitness classes and gyms. Wherever you go, however, a swim will usually cost you around £3.

If you fancy an alfresco dip, then the Serpentine Lido in Hyde Park (see p.130) or the **open-air pools** on Hampstead Heath are your best bet.

Hampstead Ponds

Map 2, G2. Hampstead Heath NW3 ⊤020/7485 5757, ⓦwww.city oflondon.gov.uk⊖ Hampstead. Daily 7/8am–9pm or dusk. Hampstead Heath has three natural ponds: the Women's and Men's ponds are on the Highgate side of the heath, while the Mixed Bathing Pond is nearer Hampstead.

Ironmonger Row Baths

Map 3, M2. Ironmonger Row, EC1 ⊤020/7253 4011⊖ Old Street. Men: Tues, Thurs & Sat 9am–6.30pm. Women: Wed, Fri & Sun 10am–6.30pm. An old-fashioned kind of place that attracts all shapes and sizes, with a steam room, sauna, small plunge pool, masseurs, a lounge area with beds, and a large pool. Admission for a three-hour weekday morning session is a bargain at around £7 (Mon–Fri) or £11.50 (weekends).

Oasis Sports Centre

Map 4, H5. 32 Endell St, WC2 ⊤020/7831 1804⊖ Covent Garden. Pools: Mon–Fri 6.30am–9.30pm, Sat & Sun 9.30am–5pm. Oasis has two pools, one of which is the only heated outdoor pool in central London, open in all weather. Other facilities include a gym, a health suite with sauna and sunbed, massage and squash courts.

Parliament Hill Fields Lido

Map 2, H3. Gordon House Rd NW5 ⊤020/7485 3873 Gospel Oak train station. Daily 7am–6pm. Beautifully refurbished 200ft x 90ft open-air pool with notoriously chilly water but lovely Art Deco trimmings.

Porchester Spa

Map 3, A4. 225 Queensway, W2 ⊤020/7792 3980⊖ Bayswater or Queensway. Men: Mon, Wed & Sat 10am–10pm. Women: Tues, Thurs & Fri 10am–10pm, Sun 10am–4pm. Mixed couples: Sun 4–10pm. Built in 1926, the Porchester is one of only two Turkish baths in Central London, and is well worth a visit for the Art Deco tiling alone. Admission is around £20, and entitles you to use the saunas, steam rooms, plunge pool, Jacuzzi and swimming pool.

The Sanctuary

Map 4, H6. 12 Floral St, WC2 ⊤0870/770 3350, ⓦwww .thesanctuary.co.uk⊖ Covent Garden. Mon, Tues, Sat & Sun 9.30am–6pm, Wed–Fri 9.30am–10pm. For a day of self-indulgence, this women-only club in Covent Garden is the place to go: the interior is filled with lush tropical plants and you can swim naked. It's a major investment at £40–75 for day/eve membership, but your money gets you unlimited use of the swimming pools, Jacuzzi, plunge pool, sauna and steam room, as well as free beauty products to play with and lots of relaxation areas to doze in.

Serpentine Lido
Map 3, C6. Hyde Park W2

℡ 020/7706 3422, ⓦ www .serpentinelido.com ⊖ Knightsbridge or Lancaster Gate. Mid-June to mid-Sept daily 10am–6pm. More then 100yds of straight swimming in Hyde Park's lake, plus a paddling pool. Deck chairs and sun loungers for hire.

26

Festivals and events

This chapter gives a rundown of the principal **festivals** and **annual events** in the capital, ranging from the rituals of Royal Ascot to the sassy street party of the Notting Hill Carnival, with a few oddities like Horseman's Sunday thrown in. Our listings cover a pretty wide spread of interests, but they are by no means exhaustive; London has an almost endless roll call of ceremonials and special shows, and for daily information, it's well worth checking *Time Out* or the *Evening Standard*.

January 1

London Parade
To kick off the new year, a procession of floats, marching bands, clowns, American cheerleaders and classic cars wends its way from Parliament Square at noon, through the centre of London, to Berkeley Square, collecting money for charity from around one million spectators en route. Admission charge for grandstand seats in Piccadilly, otherwise free. ☏020/8566 8586, ⓦwww.londonparade.co.uk

Late January

London International Mime Festival
Annual mime festival which takes place in the last two

weeks of January on the South Bank, and in other funky venues throughout London. It pulls in some very big names in mime, animation and puppetry. ☎020/7637 5661, ⓦwww.mimefest.co.uk

Chinese New Year Celebrations

Soho's Chinatown explodes in a riot of dancing dragons and firecrackers on the night of this vibrant annual celebration, and the streets and restaurants are packed to capacity. ⓦwww.chinatown-on-line.org.uk

March

Head of the River Race

Less well-known than the Oxford and Cambridge Boat Race, but much more fun; more than four hundred crews set off at ten-second intervals and chase each other from Mortlake to Putney. ⓦwww.horr.co.uk

Late March/early April

Oxford and Cambridge Boat Race

Since 1845, the rowing teams of Oxford and Cambridge universities have battled it out on a four-mile, upstream course on the Thames from Putney to Mortlake. It's as much a social as sporting event, and the pubs at prime vantage points pack out early. You can also catch it on TV. ⓦwww.theboatrace.org.uk

Third Sunday in April

London Marathon

The world's most popular marathon, with more than forty thousand masochists sweating the 26.2 miles from Greenwich Park to Westminster Bridge. Only a handful of world-class athletes enter each year; most of the competitors are club runners and obsessive flab-fighters. There's always someone dressed up as a gorilla, and you can generally spot a fundraising celebrity or two. ☎020/7902 0189, ⓦwww.london-marathon.co.uk

May Bank Holiday weekend

IWA Canal Cavalcade

Lively celebration of the city's inland waterways held at Little Venice (near Warwick Avenue), with scores of decorated narrowboats, Morris dancers and lots of children's activities. ⓦwww.waterways.org.uk

26

FESTIVALS AND EVENTS | February–May

305

Sunday nearest to May 9

May Fayre and Puppet Festival

The garden of St Paul's church in Covent Garden is taken over by puppet booths to commemorate the first recorded sighting of a Punch and Judy show, by diarist Samuel Pepys in 1662. ☎020/7375 0441, ⓦwww.alternativearts.com

Third or fourth week in May

Chelsea Flower Show

Run by the Royal Horticultural Society, the world's finest horticultural event transforms the normally tranquil grounds of the Royal Hospital in Chelsea for four days, with a daily inundation of up to fifty thousand gardening gurus and amateurs. It's a solidly bourgeois event, with the general public admitted on the last two days only, and charged an exorbitant fee for the privilege. Tickets must be bought in advance: ☎0870/906 3781, ⓦwww.rhs.org.uk

May 29

Oak Apple Day

The Chelsea Pensioners of the Royal Hospital honour their founder, Charles II, by wearing their posh uniforms and decorating his statue with oak leaves, in memory of the oak tree in which the king hid after the Battle of Worcester in 1651. ☎020/7730 5282.

Late May/early June

Beating Retreat

This annual display takes place on Horse Guards' Parade over three evenings, and marks the old military custom of drumming and piping the troops back to base at dusk. Soldiers on foot and horseback provide a colourful, very British ceremony which precedes a floodlit performance by the Massed Bands of the Queen's Household Cavalry. ☎020/7414 2271, ⓦwww.army.mod.uk/ceremonialandheritage.

First or second Saturday in June

Derby Day

Run at the Epsom racecourse in Surrey, the Derby is the country's premier flat race: the beast that gets its snout over the line first is instantly worth millions. Admission prices reflect proximity to the horses and to the watching nobility. The race is always shown live on TV. ☎01372/726311, ⓦwww.epsomderby.co.uk

Early June to mid-August

Royal Academy Summer Exhibition

Thousands of prints, paintings, sculptures and sketches, most by amateurs and nearly all of them for sale, are displayed at one of the city's finest galleries. See p.48. ☎020/7300 8000, Ⓦwww.royalacademy.org.uk

June

Spitalfields Festival

Classical music recitals in Hawksmoor's Christ Church, the parish church of Spitalfields, and other events in and around the old Spitalfields Market (see p.104) for a fortnight or so. ☎020/7377 1362, Ⓦwww.spitalfieldsfestival.org.uk

Second Saturday in June

Trooping the Colour

This celebration of the Queen's official birthday (her real one is on April 21) features massed bands, gun salutes, fly-pasts and crowds of tourists and patriotic Britons paying homage. Tickets for the ceremony itself (limited to two per person, allocated by ballot) must be applied for before the end of February; send an SAE to the Brigade Major, HQ Household Division, Horse Guards, Whitehall, London SW1A 2AX, ☎020/7839 5323. Otherwise, the royal procession along the Mall lets you glimpse the nobility for free, and there are rehearsals (minus Her Majesty) on the two preceding Saturdays.

Mid-June

Royal Ascot

A highlight of the society year, held at the Ascot racecourse in Berkshire, this high-profile meeting has the Queen and sundry royals completing a crowd-pleasing lap of the track in open carriages prior to the opening races. The event is otherwise famed for its fashion statements, especially on Ladies' Day, and there's TV coverage of both the races and the more extravagant headgear of the female racegoers. ☎01344/622211, Ⓦwww.ascot.co.uk

Last week of June and first week of July

Wimbledon Lawn Tennis Championships

This Grand Slam tournament attracts the cream of the world's professionals and is one of the highlights of the sporting and social calendar. For information on how to get

hold of tickets, see p.298.
☎020/8946 2244, ⓦwww
.wimbledon.org

Late June to mid-July

City of London Festival
For nearly a month,
churches (including St Paul's
Cathedral), livery halls and corporate buildings around the City
play host to classical and jazz
musicians, theatre companies
and other guest performers.
☎020/7377 0540, ⓦwww
.colf.org

July

Pride London
A gay pride rally in Trafalgar
Square, a colourful, whistle-
blowing march through the city
streets, a live cabaret stage and
a Drag Idol contest in Leicester
Square. See p.236. ⓦ www
.pridelondon.org

Mid-July

Greenwich & Docklands
Festival
Ten-day festival of fireworks,
music, dance, theatre, art and
spectacles at venues on both
sides of the river, plus a village
fayre in nearby Blackheath.
☎020/8858 7755, ⓦwww
.festival.org

Mid-July to mid-September

BBC Henry Wood
Promenade Concerts
Commonly known as the Proms,
this series of nightly classical
concerts at the Royal Albert Hall
is a well-loved British institution.
See p.132. ☎020/7589 8212,
ⓦwww.bbc.co.uk/proms

Mid-July

Doggett's Coat and Badge
Race
The world's oldest rowing race,
from London Bridge to Chelsea,
established by Thomas Dog-
gett, an eighteenth-century Irish
comedian, to commemorate
George I's accession to the
throne. The winner receives a
Hanoverian costume and silver badge. ☎020/7361 2826,
ⓦwww.watermenshall.org
/doggett_race.htm

Third week of July

Swan-Upping
Five-day scramble up the
Thames, from Sunbury to
Pangbourne, during which liv-
eried rowers search for swans,
marking them (on the bill) as
belonging to either the Queen or
the Dyers' or the Vintners' City
liveries. At Windsor, all the oars-
men stand to attention in their

boats and salute the Queen.
☎01628/523030, ⓦwww.royal
.gov.uk

Last bank holiday weekend in August

Notting Hill Carnival
The two-day free festival in Notting Hill is the longest-running and best-known street party in Europe. Dating back forty years, Carnival is a tumult of imaginatively decorated floats, eye-catching costumes, thumping sound systems, live bands, irresistible food and huge crowds. See p.140.

Saturday in early September

Great River Race
Hundreds of boats are rowed or paddled from Ham House, Richmond, down to Island Gardens on the Isle of Dogs. Starts are staggered and there's any number of weird and wonderful vessels taking part. ⓦwww .greatriverrace.co.uk

Third Sunday in September

Horseman's Sunday
In an eccentric 11.30am ceremony at the Hyde Park church of St John & St Michael, a vicar on horseback blesses a hundred or so horses; the newly consecrated

beasts then parade around the neighbourhood before galloping off through the park, and later taking part in showjumping.
☎020/7262 1732

Third weekend in September

Open House
A once-a-year opportunity to peek inside more than 400 buildings around London, many of which don't normally open their doors to the public. You'll need to book in advance for some of the more popular places.
ⓦwww.londonopenhouse.org

First Sunday in October

Costermongers' Pearly Harvest Festival Service
Cockney fruit and vegetable festival at St Paul's Church, Covent Garden. Of most interest to the onlooker are the Pearly Kings and Queens who turn up in their traditional pearl-button-studded outfits. ☎020/8778 8670, ⓦwww.pearlysociety.co.uk

Late October/early November

State Opening of Parliament
The Queen arrives by coach at the Houses of Parliament at 11am accompanied by the Household Cavalry and gun salutes. The ceremony itself

takes place inside the House of Lords and is televised; it also takes place whenever a new government is sworn in. ☎020/7219 3000, 🌐www.parliament.uk

Late October/November

London Film Festival
A three-week cinematic season with scores of new international films screened at the National Film Theatre and some West End venues. ☎020/7928 3232, 🌐www.bfi.org.uk or (nearer the time) 🌐www.lff.org.uk

Early November

London Jazz Festival
Big ten-day international jazz-fest held in all London's jazz venues, large and small, in association with BBC Radio 3. ☎020/7405 9900, 🌐www.bbc.co.uk/radio3

First Sunday in November

London to Brighton Veteran Car Run
In 1896 Parliament abolished the Act that required all cars to crawl along at 2mph behind someone waving a red flag. Such was the euphoria in the motoring community that a rally was promptly set up to mark the occasion, and a century later it's still going

strong. Classic cars built before 1905 set off from Hyde Park at 7.30am and travel the 58 miles to Brighton along the A23 at the heady maximum speed of 20mph. 🌐www.vccofgb.co.uk/lontobri

November 5

Bonfire Night
In memory of Guy Fawkes – executed for his role in the 1605 Gunpowder Plot to blow up King James I and the Houses of Parliament – effigies of the hapless Mr Fawkes are burned on bonfires all over Britain. There are also council-run fires and firework displays right across the capital – Alexandra Palace provides a good vantage point from which to take in several displays at once. ☎020/8365 2121

Second Saturday in November

Lord Mayor's Show
The newly appointed Lord Mayor begins his or her day of investiture at Westminster, leaving there at around 9am for Guildhall. At 11.10am, the vast ceremonial procession, headed by the 1756 State Coach, begins its journey from Guildhall to the Law Courts in the Strand, where the oath of office is taken at 11.50am. From there the coach and its train of

140-odd floats make their way back towards Guildhall, arriving at 2.20pm. Later in the day there's a firework display from a barge tethered between Waterloo and Blackfriars bridges, and a small funfair on Paternoster Square, by St Paul's Cathedral. ⓦwww.cityoflondon.gov.uk

Remembrance Sunday

A day of nationwide commemorative ceremonies for the dead and wounded of the two world wars and other conflicts. The principal ceremony, attended by the Queen, various other royals and the Prime Minister, takes place at the Cenotaph in Whitehall, beginning with a march-past of veterans and building to a one-minute silence at the stroke of 11am.

Christmas

Each year since the end of World War II, Norway has acknowledged its gratitude to the country that helped liberate it from the Nazis with the gift of a mighty spruce tree that appears in Trafalgar Square in early December. Decorated with lights, it becomes the focus for carol singing versus traffic noise each evening until Christmas Eve.

New Year's Eve

The New Year is welcomed en masse in Trafalgar Square as thousands of inebriated revellers stagger about and slur to *Auld Lang Syne* at midnight. Transport for London runs free public transport all night, sponsored by various public-spirited breweries.

26

FESTIVALS AND EVENTS | Nov–Dec

27

Kids' London

O n first sight London seems a hostile place for children, with its crowds, incessant noise and constant traffic. English attitudes can be discouraging as well, particularly if you've experienced the more indulgent approach of the French or Italians – London's restaurateurs, for example, tend to regard children as if they were one step up the evolutionary scale from rats. Yet, if you pick your destination carefully, even central London can be a delight for the pint-sized, and it needn't overly strain the parental pocket.

Covent Garden's buskers and jugglers provide no-cost entertainment in a car-free setting. Another great area to head for is the **South Bank** and **Southwark**, which are connected by a traffic-free riverside walk that stretches from the **London Eye** to Tower Bridge. And if you don't fancy the walk, there are now plenty of passenger **boats** stopping off at piers along the way.

Right in the centre of the city, you'll find plentiful green spaces, such as **Hyde Park** and **Regent's Park**, providing playgrounds and ample room for general mayhem, as well as a diverting array of city wildlife. If you want something more unusual than ducks and squirrels, head for one of London's several **city farms**, which provide urbanites with a free taste of country life.

Don't underestimate the value of London's **public transport** as a source of fun, either. Children travel free on

London buses, and the #11 double decker from Victoria, for instance, will trundle you past the Houses of Parliament, Trafalgar Square and the Strand on its way to St Paul's Cathedral. The driverless Docklands Light Railway is another guaranteed source of amusement – grab a seat at the front of the train and pretend to be the driver, then take a boat back to the centre of town from Greenwich (see p.155).

Museums and sights

Lots of London's **museums and sights** will appeal to children. Below are those that are primarily geared towards entertaining and/or educating children – some are covered in the main part of our Guide, and are cross-referenced accordingly. Most museums offer child-oriented programmes of workshops, educational story trails, special shows and suchlike during the school holidays. The weekly *Time Out* has listings of kids' events, and also produces the monthly listings magazine *Kids Out*.

Bethnal Green Museum of Childhood
Map 2, J4. Cambridge Heath Rd, E2
℗ 020/8983 5200, ⓦ www.vam.ac.uk
⊖ Bethnal Green. Daily except Fri 10am–5.50pm; free. See p.109. The museum is famous for its collection of historic dolls' houses and toys, and puts on lots of weekend/holiday events and activities – it will be closed for refurbishment until November 2006.

Horniman Museum
Map 2, J7. London Rd, SE23
℗ 020/8699 1872, ⓦ www.horniman.ac.uk Forest Hill train

station, from Victoria or London Bridge. Daily 10.30am–5.30pm; free. See p.153. An ethnographic and musical instrument museum primarily, with lots to interest kids, including a natural history section and lovely grounds with a mini farm.

Kew Bridge Steam Museum
Map 2, D5. Green Dragon Lane, Brentford, TW8
℗ 020/8568 4757, ⓦ www.kbsm.org.uk Kew Bridge train station from Waterloo, or bus #237 or #267 from Gunnersbury. Daily 11am–5pm; adults Mon–Fri £4.25,

Sat & Sun £5.75; children free. See p.164. Best visited at weekends, when the beam engines are in steam and (on Sundays) when the miniature steam railway is in operation. The Water for Life gallery features plenty of grimy details on the capital's water and sewerage network, which should appeal to kids.

London Aquarium
Map 6, A6. County Hall, SE1
℡020/7967 8000, ⍇www.london
aquarium.co.uk⊖ Westminster or
Waterloo. Daily 10am–6pm or later;
adults £8.75–9.75, children 3–14
£5.25–6.25. See p.116. London's
largest aquarium is on the South
Bank, and is very popular with
kids. There are over 350 species from sharks and piranhas
to clown fish and rays. Daily
dives and feeding routines along
with regular talks and interactive
events.

London Zoo
Map 3, E1. Regent's Park, NW1
℡020/7722 3333, ⍇www.london
zoo.co.uk⊖ Camden Town or
Baker Street then bus #274. Daily:
March–Oct 10am–5.30pm; Nov–Feb
10am–4pm; adults £14, children
3–15 £10.75. See p.144. Smaller
kids love the children's enclosure,
where they can actually handle
the animals, and the regular "Animals in Action" live shows. The

invertebrate house, known as BUGS, is also a winner, with lots of creepy-crawlies and hands-on stuff.

Natural History Museum
Map 8, D7. Cromwell Rd, SW7
℡020/7942 5000, ⍇www.nhm
.ac.uk⊖ South Kensington.
Mon–Sat 10am–5.50pm, Sun
11am–5.50pm; free. See p.135.
Dinosaur animatronics and skeletons, stuffed animals, live ants,
an earthquake simulator and lots
of rocks, fossils, crystals and
gems. Older kids might enjoy
going behind the scenes and
meeting the scientists at the Darwin Centre.

Pollock's Toy Museum
Map 4, E2. 1 Scala St, W1
℡020/7636 3452⊖ Goodge Street.
Mon–Sat 10am–5pm; adults £3,
children £1.50. Housed above
a unique toyshop specializing
in toy theatres, the museum's
impressive collection includes
a fine example of the Victorian
paper theatres sold by Benjamin
Pollock.

Science Museum
Map 8, D6. Exhibition Rd, SW7
℡0870/870 4868, ⍇www.science
museum.org.uk⊖ South Kensington. Daily 10am–6pm; free. See
p.134. There's plenty for everyone
here: hands-on fun for the little

ones in the "Garden" or the "Launch Pad" in the basement, and more high-tech gadgetry for older kids in the Wellcome Wing. The daily demonstrations are excellent.

Syon

Map 2, C6. Syon Park, Brentford, Middlesex ☎020/8560 0881, Ⓦ www.syonpark.co.uk Bus #237 or #267 from Gunnersbury. See p.164.

The stately home itself may not tempt the kids, but with the Butterfly House and the Aquatic Experience (see p.165), plus a weekend miniature steam railway in the house's lovely gardens, it's a good place for a day out. One of the most popular attractions is the Snakes and Ladders indoor play area (daily 10am–6pm; adults free, under-5s £3–4, over-5s £4–5).

Parks and city farms

Battersea Park

Map 2, G6. Albert Bridge Rd ☎020/8871 7540 (zoo) or ☎020/8871 7539 (playground), Ⓦ www.wandsworth.gov.uk Battersea Park or Queenstown Road train station, from Victoria. Playground: term time Tues–Fri 3.30–7pm; holidays and weekends 11am–6pm; free. Zoo: daily 10am–5pm; adults £4.95, children 3–12 £3.75. The park has an excellent free adventure playground and activity hut with pool table, a children's zoo with monkeys, reptiles, birds, otters and mongooses, and lots of open space. Recumbent bicycles available for hire. Every August the free "Teddy Bears' Picnic" draws thousands of children and their plush pals.

Coram's Fields

Map 3, I2. 93 Guilford St, WC1 ☎020/7837 6138⊖ Russell Square. Daily 9am–dusk; free. Very useful, centrally located playground with lots of water and sand play plus mini-farm with ducks, sheep, rabbits, goats and chickens. Adults admitted only if accompanied by a child.

Hackney City Farm

Map 2, J4. 1a Goldsmith's Row, E2 ☎020/7729 6381, Ⓦ www .hackneycityfarm.co.uk⊖ Bethnal Green. Tues–Sun 10am–4.30pm. Converted brewery that's now a small city farm, with cows, sheep, pigs, hens, turkeys, rabbits, butterflies and a donkey; also has an organic garden and a great café. Weekend kids' activities.

Hampstead Heath

Map 2, G2. ℡020/7485 4491.
⊖ Hampstead, or Gospel Oak or
Hampstead Heath train stations.
Open daily 24hr. See p.149. Nine
hundred acres of grassland and
woodland, with superb views
of the city. Excellent kite-flying
potential too, and plenty of playgrounds, sports facilities, music
events and fun days throughout
the summer.

Hyde Park/Kensington Gardens

Map 3, D5. ℡020/7298 2100,
🅦www.royalparks.gov.uk⊖ High
Street Kensington or Lancaster Gate.
Daily dawn–dusk. See p.130. Hyde
Park is central London's main
open space and features the
Diana Fountain in which the kids
can dip their feet; in Kensington
Gardens, adjoining its western
side, you can find the George
Frampton's famous Peter Pan
statue and a groovy playground
dedicated to Princess Diana.

Kew Gardens

Map 2, C6. Richmond, Surrey
℡020/8332 5000, 🅦www
.kew.org⊖ Kew Gardens. Daily

9.30am–7.30pm or dusk; adults
£10, children under 16 free. See
p.166. Edifying open spaces,
glasshouses, and a small
aquarium in the basement of
the Palm House.

Mudchute City Farm

Map 2, L5. Pier St, E14 ℡020/7515
5901, 🅦www.mudchute.org.
Mudchute, Crossharbour or Island
Gardens DLR. Daily 9am–4pm; free.
Covering some 35 acres, this is
London's largest city farm, with
farmyard animals, llamas, pets'
corner, study centre and café.
Fantastic location with great
views of Canary Wharf.

Richmond Park

Map 2, D7. Richmond, Surrey
℡020/8948 3209, 🅦www
.royalparks.co.uk⊖ Richmond, or
Richmond train station from Waterloo. Daily: March–Sept 7am–dusk;
Oct–Feb 7.30am–dusk; free. See
p.168. A fabulous stretch of
countryside, with opportunities
for duck-feeding, deer-spotting,
mushroom-hunting and cycling.
Playground situated near Petersham Gate or toddlers play area
near Kingston Gate.

Theatre

Numerous London theatres put on **kids' shows** at the weekend, but there are one or two venues that are almost entirely

child-centred. Ticket prices hover either side of the £5 mark for children and adults alike, unless the show is at a West End theatre, in which case you're looking at more like £15 and upwards.

Little Angel Theatre
Map 2, I3. 14 Dagmar Passage, off Cross St, N1 ℡ 020/7226 1787, Ⓦ www.littleangeltheatre.com ➔ Angel or Highbury & Islington. London's only permanent puppet theatre, with shows usually on Saturdays and Sundays at 11am and 2pm. Extra performances during holidays. No babies are admitted.

Polka Theatre
Map 2, F8. 240 The Broadway, SW19 ℡ 020/8543 4888, Ⓦ www.polka theatre.com ➔ Wimbledon or South Wimbledon. Aimed at kids aged up to around 12, this is a specially designed junior arts centre, with two theatres, a playground,

a café and a toy shop. Storytellers, puppeteers and mimes make regular appearances.

Puppet Theatre Barge
Map 3, B3. Little Venice, Blomfield Rd, W9 ℡ 020/7249 6876 or 07836/202745, Ⓦ www .puppetbarge.com ➔ Warwick Avenue. Wonderfully imaginative marionette shows on a fifty-seater barge moored in Little Venice from November to May, then at various points along the Thames (including Richmond in Sept & Oct). Shows usually start at 2.30pm at weekends and in the school holidays.

Unicorn Theatre
Map 7, J9. Unicorn Passage, SE1 ℡ 0870/535 500, Ⓦ www.unicorn theatre.com ➔ London Bridge. The oldest professional children's theatre in London has moved to new purpose-built premises near City Hall in Southwark. Shows run the gamut from mime and puppetry to traditional plays.

27

KIDS' LONDON | Theatre

Directory

Aids helpline ☎0800/567123, ⓦwww.playingsafely.co.uk
Banks Opening hours for most banks are Mon–Fri 9.30am–4.30pm, with some staying open half an hour later, and some high-street branches opening on Saturday mornings.
Bike rental London Bicycle Tour Company, 1a Gabriel's Wharf SE1 ☎020/7928 6838, ⓦwww.londonbicycle.com◆ Waterloo or Southwark; On Your Bike, 52–54 Tooley St, SE1 ☎020/7378 6669, ⓦwww.onyourbike.net ◆ London Bridge.
Consulates and embassies australia, Australia House, Strand, WC2 ☎020/7379 4334, ⓦwww.australia.org.uk; **Canada**, Canada House, Trafalgar Square, WC2 ☎020/7528 6533 ⓦwww. dfait-maeci.gc.ca; **Ireland**, 17 Grosvenor Place, SW1 ☎020/7235 2171, ⓦwww.irlgov.ie; **New Zealand**, New Zealand

House, 80 Haymarket, SW1 ☎020/7930 8422, ⓦwww.nzembassy.com; **South Africa**, South Africa House, Trafalgar Square, WC2 ☎020/7451 7299, ⓦwww.southafricahouse.com; **USA**, 24 Grosvenor Square, W1 ☎020/7499 9000, ⓦwww.us embassy.org.uk
Cultural institutes Austrian Cultural Forum, 28 Rutland Gate SW7 ☎020/7584 8653, ⓦwww.austria.org.uk; Czech Centre, 13 Harley St, W1 ☎020/7307 5180, ⓦwww.czechcentres.cz/london; French Institute, 17 Queensberry Place, SW7 ☎020/7073 1350, ⓦwww.institut-francais.org.uk; Goethe Institute, 50 Princes Gate, Exhibition Road, SW7 ☎020/7596 4000, ⓦwww.goethe.de; Hungarian Cultural Centre, 10 Maiden Lane, WC2 ☎020/7240 6162, ⓦwww.hungary.org.uk; Instituto Cervantes, 102 Eaton Square SW1

☎020/7235 0353, ⊛londres
.cervantes.es; Italian Cultural
Institute, 39 Belgrave Square,
SW1 ☎020/7235 1461, ⊛www
.italcultur.org.uk

Dentists Emergency treatment:
Guy's Hospital, St Thomas St,
SE1 ☎020/7188 0511; Mon–Fri
9am–5pm; ⊖ London Bridge.

Doctor Walk-in consultation:
Great Chapel Street Medical
Centre, Great Chapel St, W1
☎020/7437 9360; phone for sur-
gery times; ⊖ Tottenham Court
Road.

Electricity Electricity supply in
London conforms to the EU
standard of approximately 230V.

Emergencies For police, fire and
ambulance services, call ☎999.

Hospitals For 24hr accident
and emergency: Charing Cross
Hospital, Fulham Palace Rd,
W6 ☎020/8846 1234; Chelsea
& Westminster Hospital, 369
Fulham Rd, SW10 ☎020/8746
8000; Royal Free Hospital,
Pond St, NW3 ☎020/7794
0500; Royal London Hospital,
Whitechapel Rd, E1 ☎020/7377
7000; St Mary's Hospital, Praed
St, W2 ☎020/7886 6666; Uni-
versity College London Hospital,
Grafton Way, WC1 ☎020/7387
9300; Whittington Hospital, High-
gate Hill, N19 ☎020/7272 3070.

Internet access easyInternetcafe
(⊛www.easy.everything.com) has
24hr branches at 456 Strand,
off Trafalgar Square (⊖ Charing
Cross), 9–16 Tottenham Court Rd
(⊖ Tottenham Court Road) and
9–13 Wilton Rd (⊖ Victoria). Alternatively, there's the more congenial Be the Reds! near Goodge
Street (see p.191).

Laundry Regent Dry Cleaners,
18 Embankment Place WC2
☎020/7839 6775; ⊖ Embank-
ment or Charing Cross.

Left luggage Airports Gatwick:
North Terminal ☎01293/502
013 (daily 5am–9pm), South
Terminal ☎01293/502 014
(24hr); Heathrow: Terminal 1
☎020/8745 5301 (daily 6am–
11pm), Terminal 2 ☎020/8745
4599 (daily 5.30am–11pm),
Terminal 3 ☎020/8759 3344
(daily 5am–11pm), Terminal 4
☎020/8897 6874 (daily 5.30am–
11pm); London City ☎020/7646
0000 (daily 6am–9pm);
Stansted ☎0870/000 0303
(24hr). **Train stations** Charing
Cross ☎020/7402 8444 (daily
7am–11pm); Euston ☎020/7387
1499 (daily 7am–11pm); Victoria ☎020/7963 0957 (daily
7am–midnight); Waterloo International ☎020/7401 8444 (daily
7am–10pm).

Lost property Airports Gatwick
☎01293/503 162 (Mon–Sat
8am–7pm, Sun 8am–4pm);
Heathrow ☎020/8745 7727

(daily 8am–4pm); London City ⓣ020/7646 0000 (Mon–Sat 5.30am–9pm, Sun 10am–9pm); Luton ⓣ01582/395 219 (daily 24hr); Stansted ⓣ0870/000 0303 (daily 6am–midnight). **Buses** ⓣ020/7222 1234, ⓦwww .londontransport.co.uk (24hr); Heathrow Express ⓣ0845/600 1515, ⓦwww.heathrowexpress .co.uk (daily 8am–4pm). **Taxis** (black cabs only) ⓣ020/7833 0966 (Mon–Fri 9am–4pm). **Train stations** ⓦwww.networkrail .co.uk. Euston ⓣ020/7387 8699 (Mon–Fri 9am–5.30pm); King's Cross ⓣ020/7278 3310 (Mon–Sat 9am–5pm); Liverpool Street ⓣ020/7247 4297 (Mon–Fri 9am–5.30pm); Paddington ⓣ020/7313 1514 (Mon–Fri 9am–5.30pm); Victoria ⓣ020/7963 0957 (daily 7am–11pm); Waterloo ⓣ020/7401 8444 (Mon–Fri 7am–11pm).**Tubes** Transport for London ⓣ020/7486 2496, ⓦwww.tfl.gov.uk
Maps Stanfords 12–14 Long Acre, WC2 ⓣ020/7836 1321, ⓦwww.stanfords.co.uk;⊖ Covent Garden or Leicester Square.
Motorbike rental Raceways, 201–203 Lower Rd, SE16 ⓣ020/7237 6494 (⊖ Surrey Quays) and 17 The Vale, Uxbridge Road, W3 ⓣ020/8749 8181 (⊖ Shepherds Bush), ⓦwww.raceways.net. Mon–Sat 9am–5pm.

Police Central police stations include: Charing Cross, Agar St, WC2 ⓣ020/7240 1212; Holborn, 10 Lambs Conduit St, WC1 ⓣ020/7704 1212; Marylebone, 1–9 Seymour St W1 ⓣ020/7486 1212; West End Central, 27 Savile Row, W1 ⓣ020/7437 1212, ⓦwww.met.police.uk; City of London Police, Bishopsgate, EC2 ⓣ020/7601 2222, ⓦwww .cityoflondon.police.uk
Public holidays On the following days you'll find all banks and offices closed while everything else pretty much runs to a Sunday schedule: New Year's Day (Jan 1); Good Friday (late March/ early April); Easter Monday (late March/early April); Spring Bank Holiday (first Mon in May); May Bank Holiday (last Mon in May); August Bank Holiday (last Mon in Aug); Christmas Day (Dec 25); Boxing Day (Dec 26). Note that if January 1, December 25 or December 26 falls on a Saturday or Sunday, the holiday falls on the following weekday.
Rape crisis ⓣ020/8683 3300, ⓦwww.rapecrisis.co.uk; Mon–Fri noon–2.30pm & 7–9.30pm, Sat & Sun 2.30–5pm.
Samaritans Drop-in at 46 Marshall St, W1 (daily 9am–9pm); ⓣ020/7734 2800 (24hr) or ⓣ08457/909090, ⓦwww .samaritans.org.

Telephones A variety of companies have public payphones on the street, the largest one being British Telecom (BT). Most phones take all coins from 10p upwards (minimum call charge is 30p), though some only take phonecards, available from post offices and newsagents, and/or credit cards. International calls can be made from any phonebox, by dialling ☎00, then the country code; to reach the operator, phone ☎100, or for the international operator phone ☎155.

Time Greenwich Mean Time (GMT) is used Oct–March; for the rest of the year the country switches to British Summer Time (BST), one hour ahead of GMT.
Train enquiries For national train enquiries, call ☎08457/484950 or visit Ⓦwww.railtrack.co.uk
Travel agents STA Travel, 33 Bedford St, WC1, ☎020/7240 9821, Ⓦwww.statravel.co.uk; Trailfinders, Lower Ground Floor, Waterstone's, 203–205 Piccadilly, W1 ☎020/7292 1888, Ⓦwww .trailfinders.co.uk

Contexts

Contexts

A brief history of London

Roman Londinium

There is evidence of scattered **Celtic settlements** along the Thames, but no firm proof that central London was permanently settled by the Celts before the arrival of the **Romans** in 43 AD. Although the Romans' principal settlement was at Camulodunum (Colchester) to the northeast, **Londinium (London)** was established as a permanent military camp, and became an important hub of the Roman road system.

In 60 AD, when the Iceni tribe rose up against the invaders under their queen **Boudicca** (or Boadicea), Londinium was burned to the ground, along with Camulodunum. According to the Roman historian Tacitus, the inhabitants were "massacred, hanged, burned and crucified", but the Iceni were eventually defeated and Boudicca committed suicide. In the aftermath, Londinium emerged as the new commercial and administrative (though not military) capital of **Britannia**, and was endowed with an imposing basilica and forum, a governor's palace, temples, bathhouses and an amphitheatre. To protect against further attacks, fortifications were built, three miles long, fifteen feet high and eight feet thick.

Saxon Lundenwic and the Danes

By the fourth century, the Roman Empire was on its last legs, and the Romans officially abandoned the city in 410 AD (when Rome was sacked by the Visigoths), leaving the country – and Londinium – at the mercy of marauding Saxon pirates. The **Saxon** invaders, who controlled most of southern England by the sixth century, appear to have settled, initially at least, to the west of the Roman city.

In 841 and 851 London suffered Danish Viking attacks, and it may have been in response to these raids that the Anglo-Saxons decided to reoccupy the walled Roman city. After numerous sporadic attacks, and the odd extended sojourn, the Danish leader Cnut (or Canute), became King of All England in 1016, and made London the national capital, a position it has held ever since.

Danish rule only lasted 26 years, and with the accession of **Edward the Confessor** (1042–66), the court and church moved upstream to Thorney Island. Here Edward built a splendid new palace so that he could oversee construction of his "West Minster" (later to become Westminster Abbey). Thus it was Edward who was responsible for the geographical separation of power, with royal government based in **Westminster** and commerce centred upstream in the **City of London**.

From 1066 to the Black Death

On his deathbed, the celibate Edward appointed Harold, Earl of Wessex, as his successor. Having crowned himself in the new Abbey – establishing a tradition that continues to this day – Harold was defeated by **William of Normandy** (William the Conqueror) and his invading army at the Battle of Hastings. On Christmas Day, 1066, William crowned himself king in Westminster Abbey. The new king granted the City numerous privileges and, as an insurance policy, also constructed three defensive towers, one of which survives as the nucleus of the Tower of London.

Over the next few centuries, the City waged a continuous struggle with the monarchy for a degree of self-government and independence. In the Magna Carta of 1215, for instance, London was granted the right to elect its own sheriff, or **Lord Mayor**. However, in 1348, the city was hit by the worst natural disaster in its entire history – the arrival of the

Europe-wide bubonic plague outbreak known as the **Black Death**. This disease, carried by black rats, and transmitted to humans by flea bites, wiped out something like half the capital's population in the space of two years.

Tudor London

It was under the **Tudor royal family** that London began to prosper, and the population, which had remained constant at around 50,000 since the Black Death, increased dramatically, trebling in size during the course of the century.

The most crucial development of the sixteenth century was the English **Reformation**, the separation of the English Church from Rome. A far-reaching consequence of this split was Henry VIII's **Dissolution of the Monasteries**, begun in 1536 in order to bump up the royal coffers. The Dissolution changed the entire fabric of the city: previously dominated by its religious institutions, London's property market was suddenly flooded with confiscated estates, which were quickly snapped up and redeveloped by the Tudor nobility.

Henry VIII may have kick-started the English Reformation, but he was a religious conservative, and in the last ten years of his reign he executed as many Protestants as Catholics. Henry's sickly son, **Edward VI** (1547–53), however, pursued an even more staunchly anti-Catholic policy. By the end of his brief reign, London's churches had lost their altars, their paintings, their relics and virtually all their statuary. With the accession of "**Bloody Mary**" (1553–58) the religious pendulum swung the other way. This time, it was Protestants who were martyred with abandon at Tyburn and Smithfield.

Despite all the religious strife, the Tudor economy remained in good health, reaching its height in the reign of **Elizabeth I** (1558–1603). London's commercial success was epitomized by the millionaire merchant Thomas Gresham, who erected the **Royal Exchange** in 1572, establishing London as the premier world trade market. The 45 years of Elizabeth's reign also witnessed the efflorescence of a specifically **English Renaissance**, especially in the field of literature, which reached its apogee in the brilliant careers of **Christopher Marlowe**, **Ben Jonson** and **William Shakespeare**, whose plays were performed in the theatres of Southwark, the city's entertainment district.

Stuart London

In 1603, James VI of Scotland became **James I** of England (1603–25), thereby uniting the two crowns and marking the beginning of the **Stuart dynasty**. His intention of exercising religious tolerance was thwarted by the public outrage that followed the **Gunpowder Plot** of 1605, when Guy Fawkes, in cahoots with a group of Catholic conspirators, was discovered attempting to blow up the king at the State opening of Parliament.

Under James's successor, **Charles I** (1625–49), the animosity between Crown and Parliament culminated in full-blown **Civil War**. London was the key to victory for both sides, and as a Parliamentarian stronghold it came under attack from Royalist forces almost immediately. However, having defeated the Parliamentary forces to the west of London in 1642, Charles hesitated and withdrew to Reading, thus missing his greatest chance of victory. After a series of defeats in 1645, Charles surrendered to the Scots, who handed him over to Parliament. Eventually, in January 1649, the king was tried and executed in Whitehall, and England became a **Commonwealth** under Oliver Cromwell. London found itself in the grip of the Puritans' zealous laws, which closed down all theatres, enforced strict observance of the Sabbath, and banned the celebration of Christmas, which was considered a papist superstition.

In 1660, the city gave an ecstatic reception to **Charles II** (1660–85) when he arrived in the capital to announce the **Restoration** of the monarchy, and the "Merry Monarch" immediately caught the mood of the public by opening up the theatres and concert halls. However, the good times that rolled came to an abrupt end with the onset of the **Great Plague** of 1665, which claimed 100,000 lives. The following year, London had to contend with yet another disaster, the **Great Fire** (see p.94). Some eighty percent of the City was razed to the ground; the death toll didn't even reach double figures, but more than 100,000 were left homeless.

Within five years, 9000 houses had been rebuilt with bricks and mortar (timber was banned), and fifty years later **Christopher Wren** had almost single-handedly rebuilt all the City churches and completed the world's first Protestant cathedral, **St Paul's**. The **Great Rebuilding**, as it was known, was one of London's most remarkable achievements, and extinguished virtually all traces of the medieval city.

Georgian London

With the accession of **George I** (1714–27), the first of the Hanoverian dynasty, London's expansion continued unabated. The shops of the newly developed **West End** stocked the most fashionable goods in the country, the volume of trade more than tripled, and London's growing population – it was by now the world's largest city, with a population approaching one million – created a huge market, as well as fuelling a building boom.

Wealthy though London was, it was also experiencing the worst mortality rates since records began. Disease was rife, but the real killer was **gin**. It's difficult to exaggerate the effects of the gin-drinking orgy that took place among the poor between 1720 and 1751. At its height, gin consumption was averaging two pints a week, and the burial rate exceeded the baptism rate by more than two to one. Eventually, in the face of huge vested interests, the government passed an act that restricted gin retailing and halted the epidemic.

Policing the metropolis was also an increasing preoccupation for the government, who introduced **capital punishment** for the most minor misdemeanours. Nevertheless, crime continued unabated throughout the eighteenth century, the prison population swelled, transportations to the colonies began, and 1200 Londoners were hanged at Tyburn's gallows. Rioting became an ever-more-popular form of protest among the poorer classes in London, the most serious insurrection being the **Gordon Riots** of 1780, when up to 50,000 Londoners went on a five-day rampage through the city.

The nineteenth century

The **nineteenth century** witnessed the emergence of London as the capital of an empire that stretched across the globe. The city's population grew from just over one million in 1801 to nearly seven million by 1901. The world's largest enclosed **dock system** was built in the marshes to the east of the City, and the world's first public transport network was created, with horse-buses, trains, trams and an underground railway. **Industrialization**, however, brought pollution and overcrowding, especially in the slums of the East End; smallpox, measles, scarlet fever and cholera killed thousands of working-class families. It is this era of slum-life, and huge social divides, that Charles Dickens evoked in his novels.

The accession of **Queen Victoria** (1837–1901) coincided with a period in which the country's international standing reached unprecedented heights, and as a result Victoria became as much a national icon as Elizabeth I had been. The spirit of the era was perhaps best embodied by the **Great Exhibition** of 1851, a display of manufacturing achievements from all over the world, which took place in the Crystal Palace erected in Hyde Park.

Local government arrived in 1855 with the establishment of the **Metropolitan Board of Works** (MBW), followed in 1888 by the directly elected **London County Council** (LCC). The achievements of the MBW and the LCC were immense, in particular those of its chief engineer, Joseph

Bazalgette, who helped create an underground sewer system (much of it still in use), and greatly improved transport routes.

While half of London struggled to make ends meet, the other half enjoyed the fruits of the richest nation in the world. Luxury establishments such as the *Ritz* and Harrods belong to this period, personified by the dissolute Prince of Wales, later **Edward VII** (1901–10). For the masses, too, there were new entertainments to be enjoyed: music halls boomed and public houses prospered. The first "Test" cricket match between England and Australia took place in 1880 at the Kennington Oval and, during the following 25 years, nearly all of London's professional football clubs were founded.

From World War I to World War II

During **World War I** (1914–18), London experienced its first aerial attacks, with Zeppelin raids leaving some 650 dead, but these were minor casualties in the context of a war that destroyed millions of lives and eradicated whatever remained of the majority's respect for the ruling classes.

Between the wars, London's population increased further still, reaching close to nine million by 1939. In contrast to the nineteenth century, however, there was a marked shift in population out into the **suburbs**. After the boom of the "Swinging Twenties", the economy collapsed with the crash of the New York Stock Exchange in 1929. The arrival of the Jarrow Hunger March, the most famous protest of the Depression years, shocked London in 1936, the year in which thousands of British fascists tried to march through the predominantly Jewish East End, only to be stopped in the so-called **Battle of Cable Street**.

London was more or less unprepared for the aerial bombardments of **World War II** (1939–45). The bombing campaign, known as the **Blitz** (see p.90), began on September 7, 1940, and continued for 57 consecutive nights. Further carnage was caused towards the end of the war by the pilotless V-1 "doodle-bugs" and V-2 rockets, which caused another 20,000 casualties. In total, 30,000 civilians lost their lives in the bombing of London, with 50,000 injured and some 130,000 houses destroyed.

Postwar London

To lift the country out of its postwar gloom, the **Festival of Britain** was staged in 1951 on derelict land on the south bank of the Thames, a site that was eventually transformed into the **South Bank Arts Centre**. Londoners turned up at this technological funfair in their thousands, but at the same time many were abandoning the city for good, starting a population decline that has continued ever since. The consequent labour shortage was made good by mass **immigration** from the former colonies, in particular the Indian subcontinent and the West Indies. The newcomers, a large percentage of whom settled in London, were given small welcome, and within ten years were subjected to race riots, which broke out in Notting Hill in 1958.

The riots are thought to have been carried out, for the most part, by **Teddy Boys**, working-class lads from London's slum areas and new housing estates, who formed the city's first postwar youth cult. Subsequent cults, and their accompanying music, helped turn London into the epicentre of the so-called **Swinging Sixties**, the Teddy Boys being usurped in the early 1960s by the **Mods**, whose sharp suits came from London's Carnaby Street. Fashion hit London in a big way, and – thanks to the likes of the Beatles, the Rolling Stones and Twiggy – London was proclaimed the hippest city on the planet on the front pages of *Time* magazine.

Thatcherite London

In 1979, **Margaret Thatcher** won the general election for the Conservative Party, and the country and the capital would never be quite the same again. The Conservatives were to remain in power for seventeen years, steering the country into a period of ever-greater social polarization. While taxation policies and easy credit fuelled a consumer boom for the professional classes (the "yuppies" of the 1980s), a calamitous number of people ended up trapped in long-term unemployment. The Brixton riots of 1981 and 1985, and the Tottenham riot of 1985, were reminders of the price of such divisive policies, and of the feeling of social exclusion rife among the city's black youth.

Nationally, the opposition Labour Party went into sharp decline, but in the GLC (successor to the LCC), the party won a narrow victory, led by the radical **Ken Livingstone**, or "Red Ken" as the tabloids dubbed him. Under Livingstone, the GLC poured money into projects among London's ethnic minorities, into the arts, and (most famously) into a subsidized fares policy for public transport. Such schemes endeared Livingstone to the hearts of many Londoners, but it was too much for Thatcher, who abolished the GLC in 1986, leaving London as the only European capital without a citywide elected body.

Abolition exacerbated tensions between the poorer and richer boroughs of the city. For the first time since the Victorian era, **homelessness** returned to London in a big way, with the underside of Waterloo Bridge transformed into a "Cardboard City" sheltering up to 2000 vagrants. At the same time, the so-called "**Big Bang**" took place, abolishing a whole range of restrictive practices on the Stock Exchange and fuelling the building boom in the reclaimed Docklands, the most visible legacy of Thatcherism. Stocks and shares headed into the stratosphere and, shortly after, they inevitably crashed, ushering in a recession that dragged on for the best part of the next ten years.

Twenty-first-century London

On the surface at least, **twenty-first-century London** has come a long way since the bleak Thatcher years. Funded by money from the National Lottery and the Millennium Commission, the face of the city has certainly changed for the better: a new pedestrian bridge now links the City with the stupendous Tate Modern gallery, the British Museum boasts a new covered courtyard, both opera houses have been totally refurbished, Somerset House features a stunning new public fountain and each one of the national museums has totally transformed themselves into state-of-the-art visitor attractions. Less successful were the millennial celebrations focused on the Dome, built and stuffed full of gadgetry for £750 million, but a critical and commercial failure.

The most significant recent political development for London has been the creation of the **Greater London Assembly** (GLA), along with a Mayor of London, both elected by popular mandate. The Labour government, which came to power on a wave of enthusiasm in 1997, did everything they could to prevent the election of the former GLC leader Ken Livingstone, but, despite being forced to leave the Labour Party and run as an independent, he won a resounding victory in the 2000 mayoral elections.

The mayor has continued to grab the headlines, not always for the right reasons, but, once again, the greatest impact he has had is on **transport**. As well as creating more bus routes, introducing bendy buses and backing new tram projects, he managed to push through the introduction of a **congestion charge** for every vehicle entering Central London (see p.22). In a bold move that many thought would finish his political career, he achieved a significant reduction in traffic levels in Central London, and confounded his many critics. The congestion charge hasn't solved all London's problems, but at least it showed that, with a little vision and perseverance, something concrete could be achieved.

The mayor was also instrumental in helping London win the **2012 Olympics** (see p.110). The bid, led by former Olympic athlete (and ex-Tory MP) Sebastian Coe, emphasized its regenerative potential for a deprived, multicultural area of London's East End and, against all the odds, beat Paris in the final head-to-head vote. For a moment, London celebrated wildly. Unfortunately, the euphoria was all too brief. A day after hearing the news about the Olympics, on July 7, 2005, London was hit by four **suicide bombers** who killed themselves and more than fifty commuters in four separate explosions: on tube trains at Aldgate, Edgware Road and King's Cross and one on a bus in Tavistock Square. Two weeks later a similar attack was unsuccessful after the bombers' detonators failed. The public response of Londoners was typically stoical, though in private many have sought alternative means of transport and a familiar air of uncertainty has entered the capital. It remains to be seen, however, whether these are isolated incidents, or the beginning of a concerted campaign.

Books

Given the enormous number of **books** on London, the list below is necessarily a very selective one. The recommendations we've made are all in print; if you want to find the cheapest copy to buy online, try ⊛www.bookbrain.co.uk.

Travel, journals and memoirs

James Boswell *London Journal*. Boswell's diary, written in 1762–63 when he was lodging in Downing Street, is remarkably candid about his frequent dealings with the city's prostitutes, and a fascinating insight into eighteenth-century life.

John Evelyn *The Diary of John Evelyn*. In contrast to his contemporary, Pepys, Evelyn gives away very little of his personal life, but his diaries cover a much greater period of English history and a much wider range of topics.

George Orwell *Down and Out in Paris and London*. Orwell's tramp's-eye view of the 1930s, written from firsthand experience. The London section is particularly harrowing.

🏃 **Samuel Pepys** *The Shorter Pepys*; *The Illustrated Pepys*. Pepys kept a voluminous diary while he was living in London from 1660 until 1669, recording the fall of the Commonwealth, the Restoration, the Great Plague and the Great Fire, as well as describing the daily life of the nation's capital. The unabridged version is published in eleven volumes; *The Shorter Pepys* is abridged, though still massive; *The Ilustrated Pepys* is made up of just the choicest extracts accompanied by contemporary illustrations.

Iain Sinclair *Lights Out for the Territory*; *Liquid City*;

London Orbital. Sinclair is one of the most original London writers of his generation. *Lights Out* is a series of ramblings across London starting in Hackney; *Liquid City* contains beautiful photos and entertaining text about London's hidden rivers and canals; *London Orbital* is an account of his walk round the M25, delving into obscure parts of the city's periphery.

History, society and politics

Peter Ackroyd *London: The Biography*. This massive, densely written, 800-page tome is the culmination of a lifetime's love affair with a living city and its intimate history. Much praised, though it's no easy read.

Angus Calder *The Myth of the Blitz*. A useful antidote to the backs-against-the-wall, "London can take it" tone of most books on this period. Calder dwells instead on the capital's internees – Communists, conscientious objectors and "enemy aliens" – and the myth-making processes of the media of the day.

Ed Glinert *The London Compendium*. Glinert dissects every street, every park, every house and every tube station and produces juicy anecdotes every time. Only let down by its index.

Roy Porter *London: A Social History*. This immensely readable history is one of the best books on London published since the war. It's particularly strong on the continuing saga of London's local government, and includes an impassioned critique of the damage done by Mrs Thatcher's administration.

Ben Weinreb and Christopher Hibbert *The London Encyclopaedia*. More than a thousand pages of concisely presented information on London past and present, accompanied by the odd illustration. The most fascinating book on the capital.

Art, architecture and archeology

Felix Barker and Ralph Hyde *London As It Might Have Been*. A richly illustrated book on the weird and wonderful plans that never quite made it from the drawing board.

Samantha Hardingham *London: A Guide to Recent Architecture*. Wonderful pocket guide to the architecture of the last ten years or so, with a knowledgeable, critical text and plenty of black-and-white photos.

Nikolaus Pevsner and others *The Buildings of England*. Magisterial series, started by Pevsner and to which others have added, inserting newer buildings but generally respecting the founder's personal tone. There are six volumes devoted to London, plus a paperback edition of London Docklands and one on the City Churches.

Richard Trench and Ellis Hillman *London under London*. Fascinating book revealing the secrets of every aspect of the capital's subterranean history, from the lost rivers of the underground to the gas and water systems.

London in fiction

Peter Ackroyd *English Music; Hawksmoor; The House of Doctor Dee; The Great Fire of London; Dan Leno and the Limehouse Golem*. Ackroyd's novels are all based on arcane aspects of London, wrapped into thriller-like narratives, and conjuring up kaleidoscopic visions of various ages of English culture. *Hawksmoor*, about the great church architect, is the most popular and enjoyable.

Monica Ali *Brick Lane*. Acute, involving and slyly humorous debut novel about a young Bengali woman who comes over with her husband to live in London's East End.

Martin Amis *London Fields; Yellow Dog*. With their

short sentences and cartoon characters, Amis's novels tend to provoke extreme reactions in readers. Love 'em or hate 'em, these two are set in London.

Anthony Burgess *A Dead Man in Deptford*. Playwright Christopher Marlowe's unexplained murder in a tavern in Deptford provides the background for this historical novel, which brims over with Elizabethan life.

Angela Carter *The Magic Toyshop*. Carter's most celebrated 1960s' novel, about a provincial woman moving to London.

G.K. Chesterton *The Napoleon of Notting Hill*. Written in 1904 but set eighty years in the future, in a London divided into squabbling independent boroughs – something prophetic there – and ruled by royalty selected on a rotational basis.

Liza Cody *Bucket Nut*; *Monkey Wrench*; *Gimme More*. Feisty, would-be female wrestler of uncertain sexuality, with a big mouth, in thrillers set in lowlife London.

Joseph Conrad *The Secret Agent*. Conrad's wonderful spy story based on the botched anarchist bombing of Greenwich Observatory in 1894, exposing the hypocrisies of both the police and the anarchists.

🏃 **Charles Dickens** *Bleak House*; *A Christmas Tale*; *Little Dorrit*; *Oliver Twist*. The descriptions in Dickens' London-based novels have become the clichés of the Victorian city: the fog, the slums and the stinking river. *Little Dorrit* is set mostly in Borough and contains some of his most trenchant pieces of social analysis, and much of *Bleak House* is set around the Inns of Court that Dickens knew so well.

Arthur Conan Doyle *The Complete Sherlock Holmes*. Deerstalkered sleuth Sherlock Holmes and dependable sidekick Dr Watson penetrate all levels of Victorian London, from Limehouse opium dens to millionaires' pads. *A Study in Scarlet* and *The Sign of Four* are set entirely in the capital.

Graham Greene *The Human Factor*; *It's a*

Battlefield; The Ministry of Fear; The End of the Affair. Greene's London novels are all fairly bleak, ranging from *The Human Factor*, which probes the underworld of the city's spies, to *The Ministry of Fear*, which is set during the Blitz.

Nick Hornby *High Fidelity.* Hornby's extraordinarily successful second book focuses on the loves and life of a thirty-something bloke who lives near the Arsenal … rather like Hornby himself.

Hanif Kureishi *The Buddha of Suburbia; The Black Album; Love in a Blue Time. The Buddha of Suburbia* is a raunchy account of life as an Anglo-Asian in late 1960s suburbia, and on the art scene of the 1970s. *The Black Album* is a thriller set in London in 1989, while *Love in a Blue Time* is a set of short stories set in 1990s London.

Andrea Levy *Small Island.* A warm-hearted novel in which post-war London struggles to adapt to the influx of Jamaicans who in turn find that the land of their dreams is full of prejudice.

Timothy Mo *Sour Sweet.* Very funny and very sad story of a newly arrived Chinese family struggling to understand the English way of life in the 1960s, written with great insight by Mo, who is himself of mixed parentage.

Michael Moorcock *Mother London.* A magnificent, rambling, kaleidoscopic portrait of London from the Blitz to Thatcher by a once-fashionable, but now very much underrated, writer.

Iris Murdoch *Under the Net; The Black Prince; An Accidental Man; Bruno's Dream; The Green Knight. Under the Net* was Murdoch's first, funniest and arguably her best novel, centred on a hack writer living in London. Many of her subsequent novels are set in various parts of middle-class London and span several decades of the second half of the twentieth century. *The Green Knight*, her last novel, is a strange fable mixing medieval and modern London, with lashings of the Bible and attempted fratricide.

George Orwell *Keep the Aspidistra Flying*. Orwell's 1930s critique of Mammon is equally critical of its chief protagonist, whose attempt to rebel against the system only condemns him to poverty, working in a London bookshop and freezing his evenings away in a miserable rented room.

Derek Raymond *Not till the Red Fog Rises*. A book which "reeks with the pervasive stench of excrement" as Iain Sinclair (see p.336) put it, this is a lowlife spectacular set in the seediest sections of the capital.

Iain Sinclair *White Chappell, Scarlet Tracings*; *Downriver, Radon Daughters*. Sinclair's idiosyncratic and richly textured novels are a strange mix of Hogarthian caricature, New Age mysticism and conspiracy-theory rant. Deeply offensive and highly recommended.

Sarah Waters *Affinity; Fingersmith; Tipping the Velvet*. Racy modern novels set in Victorian London. *Affinity* is set in the spiritualist milieu, *Fingersmith* focuses on an orphan girl, while *Tipping the Velvet* is about lesbian love in the music hall.

P.G. Wodehouse *Jeeves Omnibus*. Bertie Wooster and his stalwart butler, Jeeves, were based in Mayfair, and many of their exploits take place with London showgirls and in the Drones gentlemen's club.

Virginia Woolf *Mrs Dalloway*. Woolf's novel relates the thoughts of a London society hostess and a shell-shocked war veteran, with her "stream of consciousness" style in full flow.

Travel
store

VISIT

Apsley House

Meet Heroes of the Battle of Waterloo: The Duke of Wellington and Napoleon Bonaparte

An aristocratic house with a great past and full of English history. See where the Duke of Wellington displayed his remarkable trophies and outstanding art collection including works by Velazquez, Goya, Rubens and Van Dyck.

149 Piccadilly,
Hyde Park Corner,
London W1J 7NT

Tel: 020 7499 5676

Open: Tuesdays – Sundays

More information available from
www.english-heritage.org.uk/apsleyhouse

NOTES

NOTES

NOTES

Small print &
Index

A Rough Guide to Rough Guides

Published in 1982, the first Rough Guide – to Greece – was a student scheme that became a publishing phenomenon. Mark Ellingham, a recent graduate in English from Bristol University, had been travelling in Greece the previous summer and couldn't find the right guidebook. With a small group of friends he wrote his own guide, combining a highly contemporary, journalistic style with a thoroughly practical approach to travellers' needs.

The immediate success of the book spawned a series that rapidly covered dozens of destinations. And, in addition to impecunious backpackers, Rough Guides soon acquired a much broader and older readership that relished the guides' wit and inquisitiveness as much as their enthusiastic, critical approach and value-for-money ethos.

These days, Rough Guides include recommendations from shoestring to luxury and cover more than 200 destinations around the globe, including almost every country in the Americas and Europe, more than half of Africa and most of Asia and Australasia. Our ever-growing team of authors and photographers is spread all over the world, particularly in Europe, the USA and Australia.

SMALL PRINT

In the early 1990s, Rough Guides branched out of travel, with the publication of Rough Guides to World Music, Classical Music and the Internet. All three have become benchmark titles in their fields, spearheading the publication of a wide range of books under the Rough Guide name.

Including the travel series, Rough Guides now number more than 350 titles, covering: phrasebooks, waterproof maps, music guides from Opera to Heavy Metal, reference works as diverse as Conspiracy Theories and Shakespeare, and popular culture books from iPods to Poker. Rough Guides also produce a series of more than 120 World Music CDs in partnership with World Music Network.

Visit www.roughguides.com to see our latest publications.

Rough Guide travel images are available for commercial licensing at www.roughguidespictures.com

Publishing information

This 4th edition published March 2006 by
Rough Guides Ltd, 80 Strand, London WC2R 0RL.
345 Hudson St, 4th Floor, New York, NY 10014, USA.
Distributed by the Penguin Group
Penguin Books Ltd, 80 Strand, London WC2R 0RL
Penguin Group (USA), 375 Hudson Street, NY 10014, USA
14 Local Shopping Centre, Panchsheel Park, New Delhi 110017, India
Penguin Group (Australia), 250 Camberwell Road, Camberwell, Victoria 3124, Australia
Penguin Group (Canada), 10 Alcorn Avenue, Toronto, ON M4V 1E4, Canada
Penguin Group (New Zealand), Cnr Rosedale and Airborne Roads, Albany, Auckland, New Zealand

Typeset in Bembo and Helvetica to an original design by Henry Iles.
Printed and bound in Italy
© Rob Humphreys 2006

364pp includes index
A catalogue record for this book is available from the British Library
ISBN-13: 978-1-84353-584-3
ISBN-10: 1-84353-584-X

The publishers and authors have done their best to ensure the accuracy and currency of all the information in The Mini Rough Guide to London, however, they can accept no responsibility for any loss, injury, or inconvenience sustained by any traveller as a result of information or advice contained in the guide.

1 3 5 7 9 8 6 4 2

Help us update

We've gone to a lot of effort to ensure that the fourth edition of **The Mini Rough Guide to London** is accurate and up to date. However, things change – places get "discovered", opening hours are notoriously fickle, restaurants and rooms raise prices or lower standards. If you feel we've got it wrong or left something out, we'd like to know, and if you can remember the address, the price, the time, the phone number, so much the better.

We'll credit all contributions, and send a copy of the next edition (or any other Rough Guide if you prefer) for the best letters. Everyone who writes to us and isn't already a subscriber will receive a copy of our full-colour thrice-yearly newsletter. Please mark letters: "**Mini Rough Guide London Update**" and send to: Rough Guides, 80 Strand, London WC2R 0RL, or Rough Guides, 4th Floor, 345 Hudson St, New York, NY 10014. Or send an email to **mail@roughguides.com**

Have your questions answered and tell others about your trip at **www.roughguides.atinfopop.com**

Rough Guides credits

Text editor: Sam Cook
Layout: Amit Verma
Cartography: Ashutosh Bharti
Picture editor: Jj Luck

Production: Aimee Hampson
Proofreader: Madhulita Mohapatra
Cover design: Chlöe Roberts
Photographer: Mark Thomas

Acknowledgements

Rob: Thanks to Val for the biblio and Sam for standing at the helm.
Sally: Although it wasn't difficult finding willing volunteers to help test out London's drinking holes, a great big thanks goes to those who ensured that I never got drunk alone, namely: Helena, Katy, Hayden, Freya, James, Jinny, John, Christina, Ed, Cliff, Keith and Ella; and thanks to Tim and Alice for their expert insider info. Most importantly thanks to

Chris and Kate who jointly win the prize for being the best, and most enduring, nightlife voyeurs, as well as great company.
Helena: Thanks to the following for their extraordinary dedication in visiting London's pubs, bars, clubs and restaurants with me: Ed, Clifton, Ruth, Ella, Claire, Gavin, Dan, Matthew, Lisa, Lorna and Markie. Thanks also to co-author Sally.

Readers' letters

Thanks to all the readers who have taken the time to write in with comments and suggestions (and apologies if we've inadvertently omitted or misspelt anyone's name):

Dr Leon Allen, Laura Boggs, Megan Bollman, A. Brodie, Sergio Burns, Charlotte Stewart Clark, John Collins, Russ & Jane Davison, Paul Deneve, John Fisher, Dean Fox, Ron Fry, Angela Greenfield, Chihiro Goddard, Jan Hamilton, Ming Wei Hui, Amy Jackson, Andrew Kleissner, Maria Kleissner, Nathaniel Koschmann, Jim Lyons, Miss C A Mumford, Paul Nicol, Joan Nikelsky, Harley Nott, Christelle Passuello, Candice Pettifer, Debbie Porter, Lorraine Rainbow, Irmgard Rathmacher, H H Saffery, Sasha from E13, Caroline Schubert, Pete Tenerelli, Mr A C Wells, Jim Young, Ellen Zimmerman

SMALL PRINT

Photo credits

ROUGH
GUIDES

SMALL PRINT

Index

Map entries are in colour.

Underwater magic

at the London Aquarium

From sharks, jellyfish and piranhas to clownfish, starfish and seahorses, see over 350 different species, up close, in 14 fantastic zones at the London Aquarium. Visit our website for more information.

WE'RE JUST ALONG FROM THE LONDON EYE – A FEW MINUTES WALK FROM WATERLOO MAINLINE STATION
Tel: 020 7967 8000   www.londonaquarium.co.uk

LONDON
AQUARIUM

1. THE LONDON UNDERGROUND

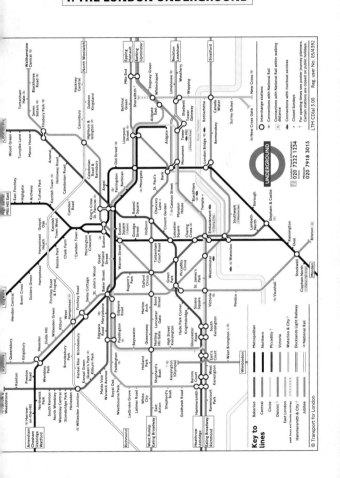

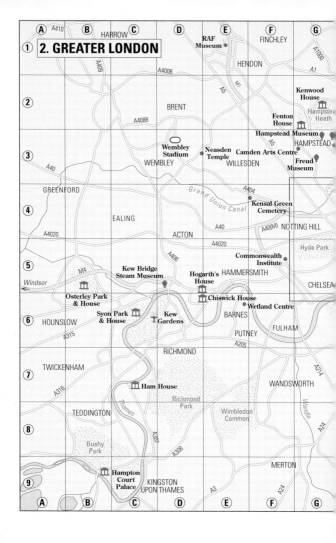

2. GREATER LONDON

RAF Museum
FINCHLEY
HARROW
HENDON
Kenwood House
Hampstead Heath
BRENT
Fenton House
Hampstead Museum
Wembley Stadium
Neasden Temple
Camden Arts Centre
HAMPSTEAD
WEMBLEY
WILLESDEN
Freud Museum
GREENFORD
Grand Union Canal
Kensal Green Cemetery
EALING
NOTTING HILL
ACTON
Hyde Park
Commonwealth Institute
Kew Bridge Steam Museum
Hogarth's House
HAMMERSMITH
CHELSEA
Windsor
Osterley Park & House
Chiswick House
Wetland Centre
Syon Park & House
Kew Gardens
BARNES
HOUNSLOW
PUTNEY
FULHAM
RICHMOND
TWICKENHAM
WANDSWORTH
Ham House
Richmond Park
Wimbledon Common
TEDDINGTON
Thames
Bushy Park
MERTON
Hampton Court Palace
KINGSTON UPON THAMES

A410 A409 A4006 A5 M1 A1000 A1 A4088 A40 A404 A40(M) A40 A4020 A406 A4020 M4 A315 A205 A316 A307 A308 A3 A24 A314 Wandle

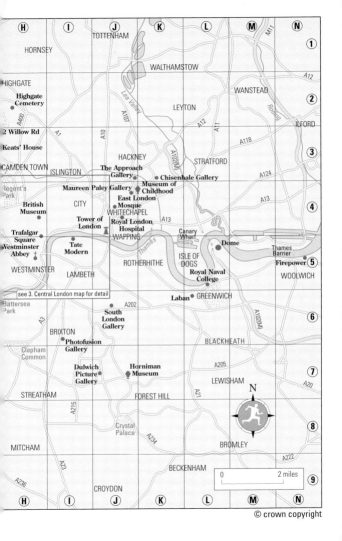

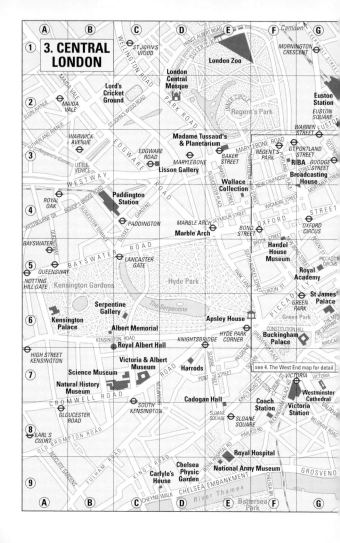

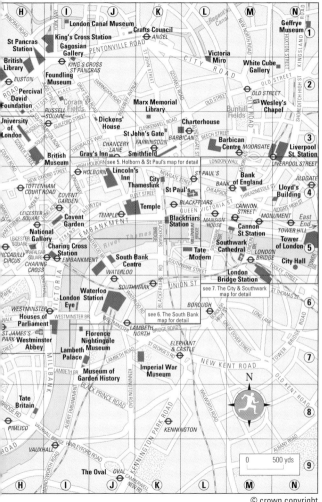

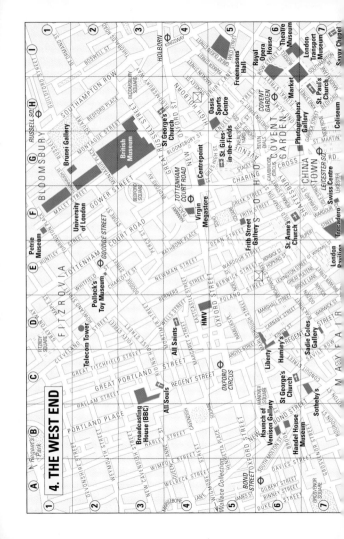

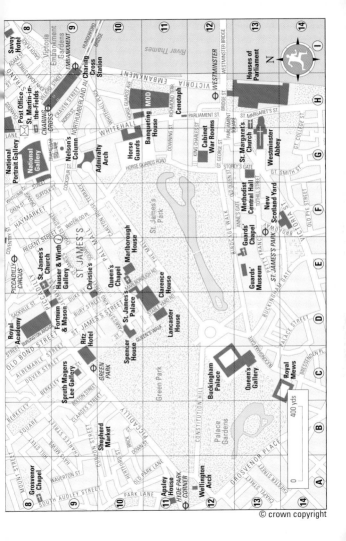

© crown copyright

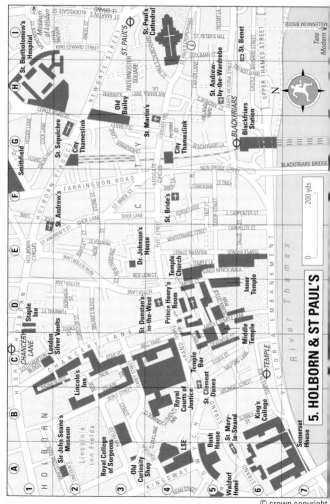

© crown copyright

5. HOLBORN & ST PAUL'S

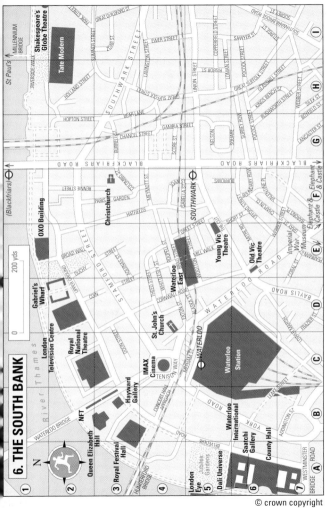

6. THE SOUTH BANK

N

0   200 yds

© crown copyright

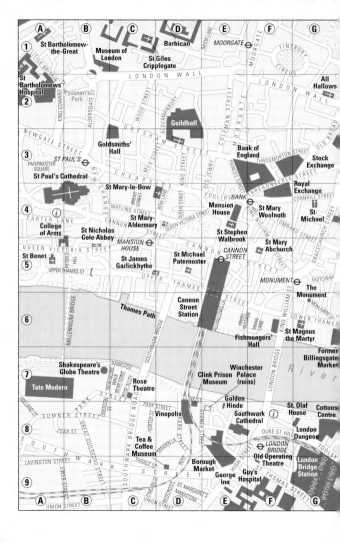

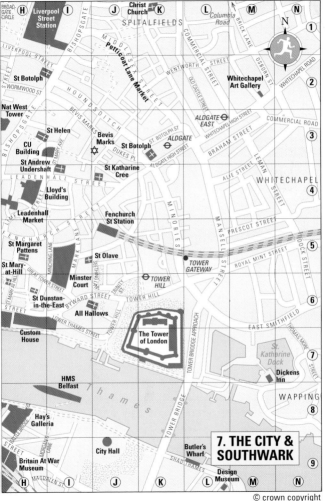

BROAD-
GATE
CIRCLE

LIVERPOOL STREET

St Botolph
S WORMWOOD ST

Nat West
Tower

St Helen

CU
Building

St Andrew
Undershaft

Lloyd's
Building

Leadenhall
Market

St Margaret
Pattens

St Mary-
at-Hill

St Dunstan-
in-the-East

Custom
House

BISHOPSGATE

MIDDLESEX STREET

Petticoat Lane Market

HOUNDSDITCH

BEVIS MARKS

Bevis
Marks

St Mary Axe

DUKES PL

St Katharine
Cree

LEADENHALL STREET

FENCHURCH STREET

LIME STREET

MINCING LANE

GREAT TOWER STREET

ST MARY AT HILL

MARK LANE

SEETHING LANE

St Olave

Minster
Court

St Botolph
ALDGATE

ALDGATE

ALDGATE HIGH STREET

MINORIES

WENTWORTH STREET

COMMERCIAL STREET

OLD CASTLE STREET

ST BOTOLPH ST

ALDGATE
EAST

WHITECHAPEL HIGH STREET

BRAHAM STREET

ALIE STREET

PRESCOT STREET

OSBORN ST

BRICK LANE

Whitechapel
Art Gallery

WHITECHAPEL ROAD

COMMERCIAL ROAD

LEMAN STREET

MANSELL STREET

WHITECHAPEL

ROYAL MINT STREET

DOCK STREET

Fenchurch
St Station

BYWARD STREET

TRINITY SQ

TOWER HILL

All Hallows

TOWER THAMES STREET

TOWER
GATEWAY

TOWER
HILL

The Tower
of London

TOWER BRIDGE APPROACH

EAST SMITHFIELD

THOMAS MORE ST

St
Katharine
Dock

Dickens
Inn

WAPPING

HMS
Belfast

Thames

Hay's
Galleria

Britain At War
Museum

MAGDALEN ST

City Hall

TOWER BRIDGE

Butler's
Wharf

SHAD THAMES

Design
Museum

7. THE CITY &
SOUTHWARK

2
3
4
5
6
7
8
9

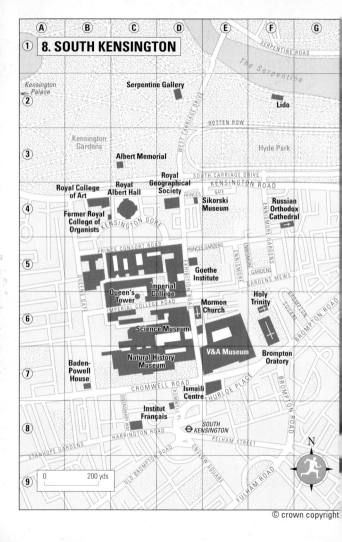

8. SOUTH KENSINGTON

Serpentine Gallery

Lido

SERPENTINE ROAD

The Serpentine

Kensington
Palace →

Kensington
Gardens

ROTTEN ROW

WEST CARRIAGE DRIVE

Hyde Park

Albert Memorial

Royal
Geographical
Society

SOUTH CARRIAGE DRIVE

KENSINGTON ROAD

Royal College
of Art

Royal
Albert Hall

GATE

PRINCES

Sikorski
Museum

Russian
Orthodox
Cathedral

Former Royal
College of
Organists

KENSINGTON GORE

PRINCE CONSORT ROAD

PRINCES GARDENS

Goethe
Institute

EXHIBITION ROAD

ENNISMORE GARDENS

ENNISMORE

ENNISMORE

GARDENS MEWS

Queen's
Tower

Imperial
College

IMPERIAL COLLEGE ROAD

Mormon
Church

Holy
Trinity

BROMPTON SQUARE

BROMPTON ROAD

QUEEN'S GATE

Science Museum

Natural History
Museum

V&A Museum

Brompton
Oratory

BROMPTON ROAD

Baden-
Powell
House

CROMWELL ROAD

CROMWELL

Ismaili
Centre

THURLOE PLACE

Institut
Français

QUEENSBERRY WAY

HARRINGTON ROAD

⊖ SOUTH
KENSINGTON

PELHAM STREET

SOUTH
KENSINGTON

ONSLOW SQUARE

OLD BROMPTON ROAD

STANHOPE GARDENS

FULHAM ROAD

N

0   200 yds

© crown copyright